W9-CGQ-331

The Future of Children

PRINCETON · BROOKINGS

VOLUME 15   NUMBER 1   SPRING 2005

School Readiness: Closing Racial and Ethnic Gaps

3   Preface

5   Introducing the Issue *by Cecilia Rouse, Jeanne Brooks-Gunn, and Sara McLanahan*

15   Assessment Issues in the Testing of Children at School Entry *by Donald A. Rock and A. Jackson Stenner*

35   Can Family Socioeconomic Resources Account for Racial and Ethnic Test Score Gaps? *by Greg J. Duncan and Katherine A. Magnuson*

55   Genetic Differences and School Readiness *by William T. Dickens*

71   Neuroscience Perspectives on Disparities in School Readiness and Cognitive Achievement *by Kimberly G. Noble, Nim Tottenham, and B. J. Casey*

91   Low Birth Weight and School Readiness *by Nancy E. Reichman*

117   Health Disparities and Gaps in School Readiness *by Janet Currie*

139   The Contribution of Parenting to Ethnic and Racial Gaps in School Readiness *by Jeanne Brooks-Gunn and Lisa B. Markman*

169   Early Childhood Care and Education: Effects on Ethnic and Racial Gaps in School Readiness *by Katherine A. Magnuson and Jane Waldfogel*

Preface

Welcome to the new *Future of Children*. In addition to the new look, the journal has a new home—the Woodrow Wilson School at Princeton University in partnership with the Brookings Institution. We are excited about this new venture and are honored to have been given the reins of such a respected journal by the Packard Foundation.

Although the journal has a new publisher, the overall mission remains the same: translating the best social science research into information that is useful to policymakers, practitioners, and the media. We have developed plans to ensure that we get our information into the hands (and heads) of as many people as possible: shorter publications on our website and public events and conferences aimed at policymakers and practitioners. All the information about our outreach efforts can be found on our website, www.futureofchildren.org, and we encourage you to visit and sign up for the e-newsletter so that we can keep you apprised of our efforts.

Probably the biggest change is that we have become primarily a web-based journal. Although some print copies of the journal will continue to be produced, for the most part readers will find us on the web. We made this decision based on the reality of the high costs of producing and mailing large numbers of print volumes for free, coupled with the growing access people have to the internet. We do understand, however, that many readers would like to keep receiving print copies of the journal, so we now offer moderately priced subscriptions as well as single-copy sales.

We hope you like our changes and continue to read and use the journal. We have received a great gift in being able to produce *The Future of Children*, and we will work hard to ensure its quality, integrity, and accessibility.

Sara McLanahan
Editor-in-Chief
The Future of Children

Introducing the Issue

Cecilia Rouse, Jeanne Brooks-Gunn, and Sara McLanahan

Although racial and ethnic gaps in educational achievement have narrowed over the past thirty years, test score disparities among American students remain significant. In the 2002 National Assessment of Educational Progress, 16 percent of black and 22 percent of Hispanic twelfth-grade students displayed "solid academic performance" in reading, as against 42 percent of their white classmates.[1] Similar gaps exist in mathematics, science, and writing. In response to such findings, policymakers have devised high-profile education initiatives to help schools address these disparities. The No Child Left Behind Act of 2002, for example, explicitly aims at closing achievement gaps. And such policies are important. As Christopher Jencks and Meredith Phillips, two highly regarded social scientists, conclude, "reducing the black-white test score gap would probably do more to promote [racial equality] than any other strategy that commands broad political support."[2]

To date, policymakers and practitioners have focused most attention on the gaps in achievement among school-aged children. And yet by many estimates sizable racial and ethnic gaps already exist by the time children enter kindergarten. Indeed, according to one report, about half of the test score gap between black and white high school students is evident when children start school.[3]

Why is so much attention focused on school-aged children? One reason is the lack of data on younger children. Many large and detailed surveys include only older children, and school-based administrative data necessarily exclude preschoolers. A second reason is that federal, state, and local policy focuses on public education, which has traditionally started with kindergarten. Finally, until recently the lives of preschool children were largely viewed as falling under the purview of the family and outside the scope of public policy.

Nevertheless, research findings and common sense both suggest that what happens to children early in life has a profound impact on their later achievement. The behavioral and academic skills that children bring with them

www.future of children.org

Cecilia Rouse is Director of the Education Research Section and Professor of Economics and Public Affairs at Princeton University. Jeanne Brooks-Gunn is Virginia and Leonard Marx Professor of Child Development and Education at Teachers College and the College of Physicians and Surgeons, Columbia University. Sara McLanahan is Director of the Center for Research on Child Wellbeing and Professor of Sociology and Public Affairs at Princeton University. The authors appreciate the assistance of Steve Barnett, William Galston, Amy Wilkins, Christine Connelly, and Wendy Wilbur to school not only determine how schools must spend resources but also potentially affect disparities in outcomes. And some analysts argue that attending to disparities in the early years is likely to be cost effective. As Nobel laureate James Heckman notes, evaluations of social programs targeted at children from disadvantaged families suggest that it is easier to change cognition and behavior in early childhood than in adolescence.[4]

This issue of *The Future of Children* shines the spotlight on school readiness. In its broadest sense, school readiness includes the readiness of elementary school teachers and staff as well as of children and parents. Yet although schools must be ready for the children who arrive at their doors, in this volume we focus on the skills of the children themselves.

Why Gaps in School Readiness Matter

Children who enter school not yet ready to learn, whether because of academic or social and emotional deficits, continue to have difficulties later in life. For example, children who score poorly on tests of cognitive skills during their preschool years are likely to do less well in elementary and high school than their higher-performing preschool peers and are more likely to become teen parents, engage in criminal activities, and suffer from depression. Ultimately, these children attain less education and are more likely to be unemployed in adulthood.[5]

Although most research focuses on academic skills, such as vocabulary size, complexity of spoken language, familiarity with the alphabet and books, basic counting, classification, and what is called "general knowledge," readiness for school also requires social and emotional skills. Children must be able to follow directions, work with a group, engage in

classroom tasks, and exert some impulse control. In a 1997 report, the National Education Goals Panel emphasized that preparedness went beyond academics.[6] And a poll of kindergarten teachers found that they rate knowledge of letters and numbers as less important readiness skills than being physically healthy, able to communicate verbally, curious and enthusiastic, and able to take turns and share.[7]

Like the child whose academic skills are weak, the child who cannot sit still (even for a few minutes), who interferes with his neighbors, who has temper tantrums, or who yells or hits (more than the average kindergartner) is likely to have difficulty in school.[8] Such early problems of self-regulation, as they are sometimes called, are predictive of future problems. For example, preschool children who exhibit highly aggressive and disruptive behaviors are at risk for juvenile delinquency and school drop-out during adolescence.[9] Not surprisingly, children with poor self-regulation not only spend less time "on task" in classrooms, which may lead to academic difficulties, but also elicit more negative reactions from their peers and teachers, further reducing social skills and encouraging disengagement from school.

At the Schoolhouse Door: Ready or Not

How many children arrive at school each year not ready to learn? In a national survey of more than 3,500 kindergarten teachers in the late 1990s, 46 percent of teachers indicated that at least half of the children in their classrooms were having problems following directions, some because of poor academic skills and others because of difficulties working in a group.[10] Problems were more common among black and Hispanic children than among whites. Similarly, teachers in schools with a high proportion of minority children reported substantially more problems than teachers in schools with a low proportion of minorities. In short, kindergarten teachers perceived their black and Hispanic children as lagging behind white children in both the academic and the self-regulatory aspects of school readiness.

We emphasize at the onset that by focusing on school readiness we do not mean to "let schools off the hook." Much work remains to be done to understand and improve education for all children. Rather, by focusing on essential aspects of children's lives before they enter school, we seek to understand how we might ultimately close the racial and ethnic gaps in educational outcomes. Only by having a comprehensive view of all the factors that underlie academic achievement can policymakers and practitioners begin to close those gaps.

In addition, we have chosen to focus on racial and ethnic *differences* in school readiness as opposed to *levels* of readiness. Although we agree that the ultimate goal of public policy should be to improve the readiness of all children, we believe that in a divided society such as the United States, attempting to raise the bar for the most needy students is a worthy goal, consistent with basic American values. We also felt that by focusing on the racial and ethnic gaps in readiness, we would simultaneously highlight policies that were likely to raise the bar for all students.

What the Issue Does

The articles in this issue address several questions. How large are the racial and ethnic gaps in school readiness? How much of the gap is due to differences in children's socioeconomic background or to genetics? How much do disadvantages like poor health,

poor parenting, low-quality preschool child care, and low birth weight contribute to the gaps? What lessons can we learn from new research on brain development? What do we know about what works and what does not work in closing the gaps?

Contributors to this issue were chosen carefully, and each is an expert in his or her field. In our original charge, we encouraged the authors not to discuss every paper written on

---

By focusing on essential aspects of children's lives before they enter school, we seek to understand how we might ultimately close the racial and ethnic gaps in educational outcomes.

---

a particular topic but rather to identify the most important findings and give the reader their "best assessment" of the bottom line. We also asked them to indicate when important information was missing or ambiguous. Thus the issue seeks to clarify what we do and don't know about disparities in school readiness.

We also note that many articles in this issue focus on the black-white test score gap rather than on gaps for other races and ethnicities. The lack of emphasis on Hispanics (and to an even larger degree other races and ethnicities) is largely due to limits in the available data. Newer data sets include more students from a wider range of backgrounds, and we expect to learn much more about other racial and ethnic gaps in the future.

Finally, the articles focus more on the academic than on the social and emotional skills that make up school readiness. As yet, researchers simply know less about racial and ethnic gaps in social and emotional skills and about the conditions (parenting, child care, child and maternal health) that account for these gaps. Whenever such information is available, the authors include it. In the years ahead we expect researchers to place more emphasis on the social and emotional aspects of school readiness.

What We Have Learned

The articles that follow provide the latest information and findings on a wide range of questions, and full summaries are provided at the beginning of each. In this section, we highlight what we see as the most important findings.

Testing for School Readiness

A variety of standardized tests show substantial racial and ethnic disparities at the time children enter school. Estimates of the gap in school readiness range from slightly less than half a standard deviation to slightly more than 1 standard deviation. According to Don Rock and Jack Stenner, estimates of the racial and ethnic gaps in school readiness among preschool children depend on the type of test used to measure readiness. Vocabulary tests typically show gaps of 1 standard deviation or more. Reading and math achievement tests show gaps ranging from four-tenths to six-tenths of a standard deviation. A key question that has yet to be answered by researchers and policymakers is what accounts for the difference in the estimates. The fact that the smallest gap comes from a recent survey conducted by the U.S. Department of Education—the Early Childhood Longitudinal Survey of Kindergarten children (ECLS-K)—makes the question even more crucial. Is the

ECLS-K estimate a more accurate measure (meaning that the gap is overstated in other tests)? Is it smaller because it comes from more recent data (meaning that the gap has narrowed over time)? Or is it smaller because it measures a different aspect of readiness from the other tests? The strongest evidence, although still inconclusive, suggests the difference lies in how the tests measure school readiness.

Socioeconomic Background: Important but Elusive

Greg Duncan and Katherine Magnuson document that 10 percent of white children, as against 37 percent of Hispanic and 42 percent of black children, live in poverty. Further, the better the socioeconomic status of a child's family, the more likely that child is to be "ready" for school. Given the close links between race and ethnicity and family socioeconomic status, on the one hand, and socioeconomic status and school readiness, on the other, it is not surprising that family socioeconomic status appears to explain a substantial portion of the racial and ethnic gaps in readiness.

In some respects, estimates of the role of family socioeconomic status complicate efforts to understand the racial and ethnic gaps. One problem is that family socioeconomic status is a proxy for many of the underlying factors that affect school readiness. For example, parents in families with low socioeconomic status are less likely to talk to, read with, and teach young children than are parents in families with high socioeconomic status. And both socioeconomic conditions and parenting behavior are associated with school readiness.

Another problem is that researchers have not been able to pinpoint what socioeconomic

...pair development of the hip- ...e region of the brain involved in ...memory, and reduce a child's ...ity. Thus the impact of stress on ...ment during childhood may ex- ...portion of the gap in school ...other finding of neuroscience ...t children's brains remain plas- ...le of growth and development ...than previously believed—sug- ...geted educational interventions ...mise of improving both brain ...behavior even among children ...istressing life circumstances.

...proving the health of mothers ...ay also help to close racial and ...school readiness. Janet Currie's ...nvelope calculations suggest ...ferences in health may account ...percent of the racial gap in ...ess, maternal breastfeeding an- ...nt, and maternal depression yet ...rcent. She estimates, then, that ...combined with maternal health and behavior may account for as much as one-fourth of the racial gap in school readiness.

as knowing why it matters and hence how this knowledge can be used to close the gap.

Other Contributors to the Readiness Gap

Other articles in this issue focus on the individual factors that contribute to cognitive development and school readiness and for which socioeconomic status is likely a proxy: environmental stress, health, parenting, early child care experiences, the impact of being born low birth weight, and genetic endowment.

ENVIRONMENTAL STRESS. Although still in its infancy, new research on brain development can potentially shed much light on how to close the gap in school readiness. Kimberly Noble, Nim Tottenham, and B. J. Casey explain that chronic stress or abuse in child-

Nancy Reichman reports that racial and ethnic disparities in low birth weight only explain up to 4 percent of the aggregate gap in school readiness. Although there are substantial black-white differences in rates of low birth weight, and although disabilities arising from very low birth weight can seriously impair cognitive development, Reichman notes that the overall effect on the racial and ethnic gaps is relatively small, because low birth weight affects only a small share of children.

PARENTING. Jeanne Brooks-Gunn and Lisa Markman document substantial racial and ethnic variation in certain parenting behaviors, such as nurturance, discipline, teaching, and language use, that are linked to children's cognitive, social, and emotional skills. Most striking are differences in language use. Black and Hispanic mothers talk less with their young children than do white mothers and are less likely to read to them daily. Black and Hispanic families also have fewer reading materials in their homes. The authors conclude that parenting differences can explain as much as one-half of the racial and ethnic differences in school readiness.

EARLY CHILDHOOD EDUCATION PROGRAMS. Katherine Magnuson and Jane Waldfogel note that children who attend center-based child care or preschool programs enter school more ready to learn. And they find racial and ethnic differences both in the share of children enrolled in preschool programs and in the quality of care they receive. Black children are more likely than white children to be enrolled in preschool, particularly in Head Start, the publicly funded program for children from impoverished families. Hispanic children are much less likely than white children to attend preschool; those who do attend are more likely to attend Head Start. Black children are more likely to attend lower-quality preschool programs than their white peers. According to the authors, equalizing access to center-based care could close up to 26 percent of the gap between Hispanic and white children. Improving the quality of Head Start programs could close between 4 and 10 percent of the black-white gap and between 4 and 8 percent of the Hispanic-white gap. It is not clear, however, how much the racial and ethnic gaps in school readiness would be reduced if all center-based programs, not just Head Start, were to become high quality.

GENETICS. Although cognitive ability is both highly heritable and important for school achievement, William Dickens concludes that genetic endowment does not contribute significantly to black-white gaps in school readiness. He notes, though, that studies of the role of genes and environment in determining school readiness offer some useful lessons in designing interventions to narrow the gaps. For example, he cites the positive effects of preschool interventions designed to increase cognitive ability and suggests ways to counter their often-noted "fadeout effects"—that is, the decline in cognitive gains once the program ends. Such interventions, he says, can induce long-lasting changes by setting off multiplier processes, whereby improved ability leads to more stimulating environments and still further improvements in ability. The best interventions, he argues, would saturate a social group (say, all members of a community or school) and reinforce initial positive effects with new interventions in the elementary school years and perhaps beyond.

Accounting for the Gaps in Readiness: A Caution

As noted, several authors provide estimates of how much different factors contribute to the overall readiness gap. We caution that tempting as it is to try to do so, one cannot simply add up these estimates to determine how much of the overall gap they explain. The difficulty is that these factors are highly correlated with one another, and thus when viewed individually, any one factor is likely to be picking up the effect of others. For example, one set of authors argues that approximately 40–50 percent of the racial and ethnic gap in school readiness may be attributed to parenting behaviors, while another author attributes one-fourth of the gap to differences in child and maternal health and behaviors. Yet it would be a mistake to conclude that taken together parenting and child and maternal health and behaviors explain 65–75 percent of the gap. Why? Because part of the reason why maternal health and behavior matter is that physically and mentally healthy mothers may be better parents. In any case, the effect of child health and maternal health and behaviors on cognitive development is already (at least partly) accounted for by parenting. Adding the two estimates together would overstate what we know about the gap. The same could be said for socioeconomic status and child care.

That said, Roland Fryer and Steven Levitt have examined what explains racial and ethnic gaps in school readiness using the most recent data from the U.S. Department of Education. They found that family socioeconomic status, number of books in the home, low birth weight, and other factors account for 70–80 percent of the gaps in reading and math.[11] In essence, the message of this issue is similar: taken together, family socioeconomic status, parenting, child health, maternal health and behaviors, and preschool attendance likely account for most of the racial and ethnic gaps in school readiness.

Closing the Gaps: What Works and What Doesn't

What does this issue tell us about how to close the racial and ethnic gaps in school readiness? We've learned that some strategies that might seem obvious turn out to be less promising than expected. Although child health, for example, is an important determinant of school readiness and of the racial and ethnic gaps in school readiness, increasing poor children's access to Medicaid and state child health insurance is unlikely to narrow these gaps because poor and near-poor children are already eligible for public insurance. The problem is that not all eligible children are enrolled. And increasing enrollment may not be the answer

either: socioeconomic disparities persist in Canada and the United Kingdom despite universal public health insurance.

Similarly, given the importance of socioeconomic factors, it might appear that the best way to close the gaps in school readiness would be to reduce racial and ethnic disparities in parents' economic resources. Programs such as the earned income tax credit (which supplements the earnings of low-income parents), the minimum wage, and the child tax credit increase low-income families' economic well-being. Making the child tax credit refundable for those who do not earn enough to pay taxes would do even more to raise the family incomes of poor and minority children. To date, however, there is no strong evidence that increasing parental income positively affects the school readiness of children.

Helping parents further their education might also appear to be an effective strategy. Increasing the schooling of all black and Hispanic mothers by one or two years, for example, would significantly narrow the school readiness gap of their children. But to date few interventions have been able to produce such gains in maternal schooling. Although more intensive programs might enjoy more success, they may not be cost effective. In sum, although programs that increase the socioeconomic status of families are likely to reduce economic disparities and make a modest impact on racial gaps, we believe that approaches that directly address the child and parental behaviors that contribute to school readiness will prove more effective.

One such strategy that holds long-term promise comes from the nascent field of neuroscience. Researchers are making great strides in understanding how the brain develops and what aspects of experience help or hinder the process. Educational interventions are already able both to raise children's scores in tests of reading and to increase activity in the brain regions most closely linked with reading. The areas of the brain that are most critical for school readiness may thus prove quite responsive to effective therapeutic interventions—even making it possible to tailor particular interventions for individual

---

We believe that by far the most promising strategy is to increase access to high-quality center-based early childhood education programs for all low-income three- and four-year-olds.

---

children. Although this field is in its infancy, such tailoring may one day make educational interventions quite effective in closing racial and socioeconomic gaps in readiness and achievement.

For the present, however, we believe that by far the most promising strategy is to increase access to high-quality center-based early childhood education programs for all low-income three- and four-year-olds. Such a step would measurably boost the achievement of black and Hispanic children and go far toward narrowing the school readiness gap.

So what should these programs look like? First and foremost, the education component of these programs must be of high quality. This means having small classes with a high teacher-pupil ratio, teachers with bachelor degrees and training in early childhood edu-

cation, and curriculum that is cognitively stimulating. Few of the child care centers and Head Start programs that now serve low-income children meet all of these standards.

Second, the new programs should train teachers to identify children with moderate to severe behavioral problems and to work with these children to improve their emotional and social skills. Although such training is now being provided by some Head Start programs and some preschool programs, it is not available in most center-based child care programs.

Third, the new programs should include a parent-training component that reinforces what teachers are doing in school to enhance children's cognitive and emotional development. Examples of such training would include encouraging parents to read to their children on a daily basis and teaching parents how to deal with behavioral problems. Improving parental skills would have important multiplier effects on what teachers were doing in the classroom.

Fourth, the new programs should provide staff to identify health problems in children and to help parents get ongoing health care for their children. Including an annual home visit as part of this service would allow staff to further screen for serious mental health problems among parents. Although some Head Start programs and child care centers in low-income communities do link parents with health care services for their children, these programs do not include a home visit, nor do they address the health needs of parents.

Finally, the new programs should be well integrated with the kindergarten programs that their children will eventually attend so that the transition from preschool to kindergarten is successful for children, parents, and teachers. Again, to have their greatest impact, high-quality programs must aim at saturating the classroom and the community and changing multiple aspects of the child's environment.

We know that high-quality early childhood programs exist. And the best research confirms that they make great headway in closing racial and ethnic gaps in school readiness. The problem is that these programs reach only a small proportion of low-income children. Decades ago, this country made a commitment to do the unthinkable—to put a man on the moon. Today our aim is both more and less lofty. We know how to help a child begin school ready to learn. We know how to begin to close racial and ethnic gaps in school readiness. We simply must decide to do so.

Endnotes

1. Wendy S. Grigg and others, *The Nation's Report Card: Reading 2002*, NCES 2003-521 (U.S. Department of Education, Institute of Education Sciences, National Center for Education Statistics, 2003).

2. Christopher Jencks and Meredith Phillips, "The Black-White Test Score Gap: An Introduction," in *The Black-White Test Score Gap*, edited by Jencks and Phillips (Brookings, 1998), pp. 3–4.

3. Meredith Phillips, James Crouse, and John Ralph, "Does the Black-White Test Score Gap Widen after Children Enter School?" in *The Black-White Test Score Gap*, edited by Jencks and Phillips (Brookings, 1998).

4. James J. Heckman and Alan B. Krueger, *Inequality in America* (MIT Press, 2004).

5. Nazli Baydar, Jeanne Brooks-Gunn, and Frank F. Furstenberg, "Early Warning Signs of Functional Illiteracy: Predictors in Childhood and Adolescence," *Child Development* 64 (1993): 815–29; Jeanne Brooks-Gunn, "Do You Believe in Magic? What Can We Expect from Early Childhood Intervention Programs?" *Social Policy Report of the Society for Research in Child Development* 17, no. 1 (2003) (www.srcd.org/spr17-1.pdf).

6. National Education Goals Panel, *Special Early Childhood Report* (Government Printing Office, 1997).

7. Sheila Heaviside and Elizabeth Farris, *Public School Kindergarten Teachers' Views of Children's Readiness for School*, NCES 1993-410 (Department of Education, National Center for Education Statistics, 1993).

8. C. Cybele Raver, "Emotions Matter: Making the Case for the Role of Young Children's Emotional Development for Early School Readiness," *Social Policy Report of the Society for Research in Child Development* 16, no. 3 (2002) (www.srcd.org/spr16-3.pdf); Lisa McCabe and others, "Games Children Play: Observing Young Children's Self-Regulation across Laboratory, Home and School Settings," in *Handbook of Infant and Toddler Mental Health Assessment*, edited by Rebecca DelCarmen-Wiggins and Alice Carter (Oxford University Press, 2004), pp. 491–521.

9. B. R. Hamre and Robert C. Pianta, "Early Teacher-Child Relationships and the Trajectory of Children's School Outcomes through Eighth Grade," *Child Development* 72 (2001): 625–88.

10. Sara E. Rimm-Kaufman, Robert C. Pianta, and Martha J. Cox, "Teachers' Judgments of Problems in the Transition to Kindergarten," *Early Childhood Research Quarterly* 15 (2000): 147–66.

11. Roland G. Fryer and Steven D. Levitt, "Understanding the Black-White Test Score Gap in the First Two Years of School," *Review of Economics and Statistics* 86, no. 2 (May 2004): 447–64.

Assessment Issues in the Testing of Children at School Entry

Donald A. Rock and A. Jackson Stenner

Summary

The authors introduce readers to the research documenting racial and ethnic gaps in school readiness. They describe the key tests, including the Peabody Picture Vocabulary Test (PPVT), the Early Childhood Longitudinal Study (ECLS), and several intelligence tests, and describe how they have been administered to several important national samples of children.

Next, the authors review the different estimates of the gaps and discuss how to interpret these differences. In interpreting test results, researchers use the statistical term "standard deviation" to compare scores across the tests. On average, the tests find a gap of about 1 standard deviation. The ECLS-K estimate is the lowest, about half a standard deviation. The PPVT estimate is the highest, sometimes more than 1 standard deviation. When researchers adjust those gaps statistically to take into account different outside factors that might affect children's test scores, such as family income or home environment, the gap narrows but does not disappear.

Why such different estimates of the gap? The authors consider explanations such as differences in the samples, racial or ethnic bias in the tests, and whether the tests reflect different aspects of school "readiness," and conclude that none is likely to explain the varying estimates. Another possible explanation is the Spearman Hypothesis—that all tests are imperfect measures of a general ability construct, g; the more highly a given test correlates with g, the larger the gap will be. But the Spearman Hypothesis, too, leaves questions to be investigated.

A gap of 1 standard deviation may not seem large, but the authors show clearly how it results in striking disparities in the performance of black and white students and why it should be of serious concern to policymakers.

www.future of children.org

Donald A. Rock is with the Educational Testing Service. A. Jackson Stenner is chairman and CEO of Metametrics Inc. The authors thank Timothy Taylor, managing editor of the *Journal of Economic Perspectives*, for extensive contributions to the improvement of this article.

In study after study over the past ten years, researchers from a variety of fields using a variety of testing approaches have consistently found a gap between the readiness of white children and the readiness of black and Hispanic children to enter school. The concept of "readiness," however, has no obvious unit of measurement. Lacking such a tool, researchers have used a range of tests to measure different dimensions of the skills and behaviors—word comprehension, reading, math, the ability to sit still—that make a child "ready" to enter school. If a test is accurate, a child's score can be used to predict his future success or achievement. A student who is measured as more "ready" should have greater success in meeting the demands or challenges of school.

We begin by introducing the main tests that researchers have used to measure the readiness gap for children entering kindergarten. We then review the range of evidence that these studies have produced about the size of the gap. Perhaps not surprisingly, the evidence on the size of the gap differs somewhat from one study to the next, and we discuss how to interpret these differences. The articles that follow in this volume explore possible underlying causes of the readiness gap: family and neighborhood characteristics, genetic differences, neuroscience and early brain development, prenatal experiences, health of young children, and differences in parenting, child care, and early education.

How Can Readiness Be Assessed at Kindergarten Entry?

Many experts in the field suggest that it is difficult if not impossible to assess a child's academic performance accurately before age six.[1] Some studies have argued that scores on preschool or kindergarten readiness tests can predict no more than 25–36 percent of the variance in performance in early grades.[2] Even if these estimates are correct, predicting 25 to 36 percent of the variance in later achievement is not to be sneezed at. But we believe that readiness tests have improved substantially in the past decade or so and that the new tests are likely to provide a better measure of readiness. For example, kindergarten test scores in the Early Childhood Longitudinal Study, which we discuss in more detail later, predict about 60 percent of the variance in performance at third grade. Before reviewing the main tests of kindergartners' readiness to enter school, we will consider some general characteristics of these tests and how they work.

Key Characteristics of Readiness Tests

Readiness tests may be given on a *group* or *individual* basis. Group tests can be less expensive to administer. But for kindergarten students, individual tests are preferred for several reasons. Administrators are more likely to be able to get and hold the attention and cooperation of a beginning kindergartner in a one-on-one setting than in a group.[3] Small children often enjoy the individual attention they get from the test administrator, which helps make the scores more accurate. In a longitudinal study, one scheduled to have multiple retestings over several years, a sizable share of the follow-ups might require one-on-one retestings because the children scatter as time passes. Starting with a group administration and then switching to one-on-one follow-ups could cause variance in the data that would be difficult to quantify. Individualized testing gives children the time they need to finish the assessment and thus gathers relatively complete information on each child. It also allows the test to be adapted to some degree to the abilities of each child.

Indeed, the best readiness tests are *adaptive,* which means that instead of asking every child identical questions, they give children harder questions if they do well on the early questions and easier questions if they do poorly early on. Operationally, a single test form is liable to be too hard for 10–20 percent of the children in the sample and too easy for another 10–20 percent. In this case, a "floor and ceiling" problem will arise: a substantial share of children will answer all or almost all of the questions correctly, while another substantial share will answer all or almost all incorrectly. Floor and ceiling problems are the bane of all readiness tests, because they mean that the distribution of test scores at the top and bottom of the scale will barely spread out at all, thus artificially narrowing the range of student achievement. Floor and ceiling problems also make it difficult to measure whether student scores change over time, because students clustered at the top or the bottom will often remain in this pattern when retested. An adaptive test avoids these problems and allows test scores to reflect the full range of student achievement. The main disadvantage of adaptive testing is cost. It is expensive to develop a large pool of items to cover the appropriate span of abilities and to ensure that a common procedure is followed in deciding when students will receive harder or easier questions. A computer-assisted test format is often helpful in advising the administrator which items are appropriate for each child. Indeed, adaptive tests for older, computer-knowledgeable children can be administered and scored in real time at a computer terminal.

A useful test must be *reliable*, which means that it will produce essentially the same results on different occasions. Reliability can be measured in three ways: retesting, equivalent form, and internal consistency. Retesting, or giving the same test over again to the same students, raises obvious questions about how students react to being given the same test twice. But retesting that produces dramatically different results would certainly raise some flags about reliability. The equivalent form approach uses two equivalent versions of a test, which can then be compared with each other. The internal consistency approach breaks a single test into parts, which

---

Floor and ceiling problems are the bane of all readiness tests, because they mean that the distribution of test scores at the top and bottom of the scale will barely spread out at all, thus artificially narrowing the range of student achievement.

---

are then compared with each other. For example, the results of all even questions might be compared with those of all odd questions (the "split half" test). Or more complex mathematical formulas might be used to split up the test in many different ways and then average those results (to generate a measure known as "coefficient alpha"). Whatever the measure, reliability is assessed along a scale from 0 to 1, where 1 means that a test has perfect reliability and gives exactly the same result each time and 0 means that the results from the test at one time are completely uncorrelated with the results the next time. A reliability score of .90 or above would represent high reliability; in the .80s, medium reliability; and in the .60s or .70s, low but acceptable reliability. A reliability score in the .50s or lower would raise serious questions about the usefulness of the test.

Some have expressed concern that readiness tests may not be reliable for very young children because of their short attention spans. But individualized test assessment typically retains the attention of younger children. And very young children may be less likely than, say, seniors in high school to respond randomly or counterproductively to test questions. Brief descriptions of the major readiness tests used in this volume follow.

Peabody Picture Vocabulary Test—Revised

The Peabody Picture Vocabulary Test—Revised (PPVT-R) is an individually administered test of hearing (or receptive) vocabulary.[4] Each of two forms of the test contains five practice items and a set of 175 test items ordered by difficulty. An easy item might be "cat"; a difficult one, "carrion." All items appear in the same format: four black-and-white illustrations on a single cardboard stock plate. The examiner says a stimulus word aloud, and the examinee selects the image that best illustrates the meaning of the word. The test is adaptive, establishing a floor below which the examinee is assumed to know all word meanings, so that no more words below the floor are asked, and a ceiling above which the examinee is assumed to know no word meanings, so that no more words above the ceiling are asked. Testing typically takes between sixteen and thirty minutes, and the examinee typically responds to thirty-five to forty-five items.

The PPVT-R is a direct measure of vocabulary size. The rank order of item difficulties is highly correlated with the frequency with which the words are used in spoken and writ-

ten discourse.[5] The PPVT-R was normed on a nationally representative sample of 4,200 children and 828 adults.

The PPVT-R is a widely used test, with good reliability. Reviews of its reliability conducted by the ERIC Clearinghouse on Assessment and Evaluation found split-test reliabilities ranging from the .60s to the .80s and test-retest reliabilities ranging from the .70s to the .90s.

For studies of kindergarten readiness, it is useful to test a large sample of children about whose families substantial background data are available. Two large samples of kindergarten children have taken the PPVT-R.

The first is the National Longitudinal Surveys, a set of U.S. government surveys that track people over time. The National Longitudinal Survey of Youth 1979 (NLSY79), began tracking a nationally representative sample of 12,686 young men and women aged fourteen to twenty-two in 1979. They were interviewed each year through 1994 and have been interviewed every other year since. The NLSY79 collected some data on children born to participants in the study, but in 1986 the survey began collecting much more intensive data about all children born to mothers in the NLSY79. The expanded survey administered the PPVT-R to children aged three to five (with some differences, according to the survey year).

A second large data sample of kindergartners is the Infant Health and Development Program (IHDP), a study funded by several private foundations and the U.S. government. It identified a group of 985 infants born with low birth weights in eight different cities in 1985 and tracked their development through 2000 using various tests, including the PPVT-R, which was administered when the children were three and again when they were five.

The PPVT-R finds substantial differences in black-white readiness for kindergarten. For example, the vocabulary of black children in first grade is about half that of white first graders.[6] But two puzzles have arisen about PPVT-R findings. First, the PPVT-R often finds a larger black-white readiness gap than do other readiness tests. Second, studies using the PPVT-R on different samples of children have produced estimates of the black-white readiness gap that vary relatively widely, given that all involve nationally representative samples of children of comparable age using the same vocabulary measure. These issues will be discussed further below.

Wechsler Preschool and Primary Scale of Intelligence—Revised

The Wechsler Preschool and Primary Scale of Intelligence—Revised (WPPSI-R) is an individually administered test of general intellectual functioning for children from ages three to seven years and three months. It does not require reading or writing. The total battery contains many subtests: information, vocabulary, word reasoning, comprehension, similarities, block design, matrix reasoning, picture concepts, picture completion, object assembly, symbol search, coding, receptive vocabulary, and picture naming. Each subtest may include questions of several types. In the vocabulary subtest, for example, the child is asked to name an object (like a hammer) when she sees its picture and is asked to define a word when she hears it spoken. The test is not adaptive.

The components of the Wechsler test can be analyzed for individual patterns of learning, but readiness studies typically use an overall score based on all test components. Raw scores are converted into IQ scores with an average of 100. The IQ scores are scaled according to age groups, based on a nationally representative sample of 1,700 children in the relevant years. Reliability estimates for scores on the Wechsler test are high, typically ranging from the high .80s into the mid-.90s, depending on the kind of reliability that is reported.

The Wechsler test is often administered to learning-disabled or gifted children, but because such children are not randomly selected, their tests are of little use in researching the readiness gap. The WPPSI-R was, however, given to the children in the Infant Health and Development Program when they were five years old, thus providing a broad sample for analysis.

Stanford Binet

The Stanford-Binet Intelligence Scale, fourth edition (SB-IV), is a measure of "cognitive abilities that provides an analysis of pattern, as well as the overall level of an individual's cognitive development," according to the examiner's handbook.[7] The SB-IV is individually administered. It uses results from the vocabulary test to determine starting items for fourteen other tests, and thus is somewhat adaptive. Items in each of the fifteen tests are ordered as to difficulty. Raw scores are then converted to standard age scores for four cognitive areas: verbal reasoning, abstract/visual reasoning, quantitative reasoning, and short-term memory. The scores for each of these cognitive areas plus a composite standard age score (CSAS) are set to average 100 for each age group.

Reliability scores for the composite Stanford-Binet score as calculated by the internal consistency method (that is, dividing the test into parts and comparing the parts with each other) range from .95 to .99. The reliability of the four cognitive area scores ranges from .80 to .97. These high correlations between the four area scores and the composite scores suggest that the cognitive area profiles are unlikely to provide reliable diagnostic information beyond that provided by the total score.

Like the Wechsler Preschool and Primary Scale of Intelligence, the Stanford-Binet test was also given as part of the Infant Health and Development Program (IHDP), in this case when the children were three years old, thus providing a substantial sample for analysis.

Woodcock–Johnson Psycho-Educational Battery—Revised

The Woodcock-Johnson—Revised (WJ-R) is an extensive battery of cognitive and academic achievement tests intended for people as young as two and as old as ninety-five. All tests are individually and adaptively administered. Seven abilities are tested and separately reported: fluid reasoning; comprehension/knowledge; visual processing; auditory processing; processing speed; long-term retrieval; and short-term memory. The standard battery then reports on four achievement clusters: broad reading, broad mathematics, broad written language, and broad knowledge. Two forms are available for the achievement tests. Raw scores are converted into grade and age equivalents.

The test manual reports high reliability. Internal consistency reliabilities for the cognitive and achievement clusters are all in the .90s. The shorter cognitive subtests that contribute to the seven ability scores have internal consistency reliabilities in the mid .70s to low .90s. The reliabilities of the achievement subtests that contribute to the broad achievement clusters are all in the high .80s and low .90s. Although alternate forms are available

for the achievement clusters, these reliabilities are not reported in the manual.

Measures of Behavioral Readiness

The tests discussed so far have focused on academic achievement—that is, skills involving words, patterns, and the like. But another important dimension of readiness for kindergarten involves behavior, such as the ability to manage one's own emotions and to work well with others.

The Achenbach System of Empirically Based Assessment offers a range of diagnostic tests for behavior. The Child Behavior Checklist (CBCL), once called the Revised Child Behavior Questionnaire, asks mothers 120 questions about how frequently they have observed various behaviors in their children over the past six months. The checklist was given to the mothers of the children in the IHDP dataset when the children were aged three and five, thus providing a broad basis for analysis. The Achenbach checklist can be used to diagnose many behavioral issues, but it commonly focuses on two broad concerns: "internalizing" behavior, such as being too fearful, anxious, unhappy, sad, or depressed; and "externalizing" behavior, such as destroying objects or having temper tantrums.

The Behavioral Problems Index (BPI), derived from the Achenbach test and other tests of child behavior, asks mothers twenty-eight questions about the frequency of behaviors they have observed in their children over the past three months.[8] Results can be used to produce internalizing and externalizing scores. The test also produces an overall composite score, which is expected to average 100. The BPI was given to the women who entered the NLSY data set in 1979 after they had become mothers, when their children were at least four years old.

Yet another approach to assessing a child's behavioral readiness is direct observation. Often a parent and child are asked to play with some toys or to solve a puzzle together. The session is videotaped. Coders who have had extensive training watch the videotapes and rate behaviors like enthusiasm, persistence, frustration, and engagement.[9]

Early Childhood Longitudinal Study— Kindergarten Battery

Until the late 1990s, the study of school readiness rested on the few tests already described (all of which were originally developed for broader or different purposes than assessing school readiness) and on the two main sources of systematic data already mentioned, the NLSY and the IHDP. Without in any way disparaging the work done with these data, researchers felt that addressing a new source of nationally representative data with up-to-date instruments for evaluation might prove extremely helpful. The result was the Early Childhood Longitudinal Study, Kindergarten Class of 1998–99 (ECLS-K), administered by the National Center for Education Statistics. The new data set began with a base year fall assessment of 21,260 kindergartners who were then reassessed in the spring of their kindergarten year and in the spring of their first and third grade years.[10] Retests are also scheduled for the spring of fifth grade.

In an effort to move away from one-dimensional cognitive assessments toward multidimensional approaches, the ECLS-K evaluates kindergartners along several dimensions in tests that are individually administered and adaptive in design.[11] The direct cognitive assessments focus on three areas: reading, mathematics, and "general knowledge" (knowledge of the social and physical world). In addition, kindergarten teachers assess both cognitive progress and social or behavioral skills, and parents assess social competence and skills. Finally, children receive a physical assessment, including measures of fine and gross motor skills. So far, the parental questions and the tests of fine and gross motor skills have not proven reliable. With the former, the main concern is that parents often have little basis for determining whether behavior is age appropriate. With the latter, the main concern is that the scores may be measuring a child's ability to comprehend the instructions as much as his motor skills. As a result, we will not discuss the parents' assessments or motor skills tests.

Cognitive tests of kindergarten readiness tend to concentrate on reading and to a lesser extent on mathematics because reading and math abilities are believed to be more modifiable by preschool programs, parental behavior, and formal schooling than some other aspects of readiness. In the ECLS-K the adaptive tests in reading and mathematics begin with a first-stage test of fifteen to eighteen test items covering the full range of difficulty. A computer calculates a score and then advises the test administrator which second-stage form is appropriate for that child. The direct cognitive assessment takes from fifty to seventy minutes.[12]

Because most entering kindergartners cannot read, the "reading" test at the kindergarten level emphasizes the child's performance on the sequential learning steps based on the phonics approach to reading development, including tasks having to do with familiarity with print, identifying upper- and lower-case letters by name, associating letters with sounds at the beginning of words, associating sounds with letters at the end of words, and recognizing common words by sight. As the ECLS-K moves through later grades, the emphasis in the item pool shifts toward reading comprehension skills, such as showing a more complete understanding of what is read, connecting knowledge from the text with the child's personal knowledge, and showing some ability to take a critical stance toward the text.

The ECLS-K mathematics test assesses knowledge in the following areas (in order of difficulty): identifying one-digit numerals, recognizing geometric shapes, and one-to-one counting up to ten objects; reading all one-digit numerals, counting beyond ten, and

---

Good rating scales attempt to anchor subjective assessments by including specific descriptions of grade-appropriate performance or behaviors that are then rated on a five-point scale.

---

using nonstandard units of length to compare objects; reading two-digit numbers, recognizing the next number in a sequence, ordinality of objects; solving simple addition and subtraction problems; and solving simple multiplication and division problems. Again, the kindergarten test emphasizes the easier skills, and the tests in later grades shift toward the more advanced skills.

The direct cognitive measures of reading and mathematics have reliability in the low .90s—equal to or better than scores typically found in cognitive achievement tests given to older children. Moreover, it was frequently reported that the children did not want to end

their assessment, largely because they enjoyed the individual attention from the test administrator. The test administrators received considerable training, including practice sessions, and the materials in the test were colorful and "game-like."

Kindergarten teachers also evaluated their students along both cognitive and behavioral dimensions. Good rating scales attempt to anchor subjective assessments by including specific descriptions of grade-appropriate performance or behaviors that are then rated on a five-point scale, with the highest number indicating that the child is proficient at the specified skill. In testing cognitive skills, the teacher evaluations follow the same general categories of reading, math, and general knowledge. The teacher social skills rating scale (TSRS) rates the kindergarten children on five socioemotional skills. "Approaches to learning" rates a child's attentiveness, task persistence, eagerness to learn, learning independence, flexibility, and organization. "Self-control" measures the child's ability to control behavior by respecting the property rights of others, controlling temper, accepting peer ideas for group activities, and responding appropriately to peer pressure. "Interpersonal skills" rates the child's behavior in forming and maintaining friendships; getting along with people who are different; helping and comforting other children; expressing feelings, ideas, and opinions in positive ways; and being sensitive to the feelings of others. "Externalizing problem behaviors" measures the likelihood that a child argues, fights, gets angry, acts impulsively, and disrupts ongoing activities. "Internalizing problem behaviors" measures anxiety, loneliness, low self-esteem, and sadness.

Although these teacher ratings may seem subjective, they proved almost as reliable as the direct cognitive scores. The teacher's rating of the child's reading development was a very respectable .87, while the teacher's rating of a child's mathematical development was .92. Similarly the teacher social ratings all had reliability close to .90, except for the measure of self-control, which had an acceptable reliability of .79.

How well are the direct cognitive ratings correlated with the teacher evaluations? Such correlations help evaluate what researchers call "construct validity," the extent to which a test measures what it is intended to measure. A measure has construct validity if it correlates well with other tests that theory suggests are measuring similar things ("convergent validity") and if it correlates relatively poorly with other tests that theory suggests are measuring different things ("discriminant validity").[13] In this case, the difficulty is that the teacher evaluations of reading and math achievement are quite highly correlated, at .83. The correlation between teacher evaluations of reading and cognitive evaluation of reading, at .60, is exactly the same as for math. Similarly, the teacher evaluation of math has only a very slightly higher correlation with the cognitive measure of math, at .54, than it does with the cognitive measure of reading, at .51.

In addition, some of the nonacademic teacher ratings of social skills, notably self-control and interpersonal skills, are more highly correlated with the academic ratings than are the corresponding test scores, which suggests a possible "halo" effect among the teacher ratings. However, the high correlation of the self-control scale and the interpersonal skills scale with the teachers' ratings of academic performance, and to a lesser extent with the tested academic performance, is also consistent with Andrew Pellegrini's theory

that social skill development predicts literacy performance.[14]

The Size of the Readiness Gap

Various studies have used the tests and data sources described here to measure the readiness gap for kindergartners. Table 1 lists some selected studies that have measured academic readiness; table 2 presents studies that have measured social or behavioral readiness. The first column of each table lists the authors and the date of the study. The second column identifies the test used. The third column comments on the data used. The final columns list what are called "raw gaps" and "adjusted gaps," measured in "standard deviation units." These terms require further explanation.

Using Standard Deviation as a Common Yardstick

The human sciences in general—and psychology and education in particular—lack common, shared interchangeable metrics for expressing differences on many important constructs, like reading achievement, health risk, or depression. There are more than 200 nonexchangeable metrics for assessing how well students read.[15] Each reading test reports in a scale specific to that test—like the PPVT or the ECLS-K reading scale—but no tables exist for converting the score on one reading scale into the metric of another. How can researchers compare the results of studies done with different instruments?

To visualize the problem, consider figure 1, which shows a common pattern that arises in studies of readiness among black and white children. The darker line shows the distribution of scores for black children, the lighter line that for white children, in a study using the PPVT as the test and the NLSY79 data. The test scores have been coded so that the

Table 1. Selected Estimates of the Academic School Readiness Gap

Study	Test	Sample	White-black		White-Hispanic	
			Raw	Adjusted	Raw	Adjusted
Fryer and Levitt (2004)	ECLS-K Math test	20,000 kindergartners (ECLS-K)	0.64	0.09[a]	0.72	0.20[a]
	ECLS-K Reading test		0.40	0.12[a]	0.43	0.06[a]
	ECLS-K Math teacher assessment		0.28	0.10[b]	0.24	0.10[b]
	ECLS-K Reading teacher assessment		0.27	0.07[b]	0.35	0.18[b]
Brooks-Gunn, Klebanov, Smith, Duncan, and Lee (2003)	PPVT-R Vocabulary	315 five-year-olds (IHDP)	1.63	0.86[c]		
	WPPSI IQ	315 five-year-olds (IHDP)	1.21	0.38[c]		
	PPVT-R Vocabulary	1,354 five- to six-year-olds (NLSY child data)	1.15	0.73[c]		
Phillips, Brooks-Gunn, Duncan, Klebanov, and Crane (1998)	PPVT-R Vocabulary/IQ	Five- and six-year-olds (NLSY)	1.14	0.95[d]		
	PPVT-R Vocabulary/IQ	Five-year-olds (IHDP)	1.71	0.69[d]		
	WPPSI IQ	Five-year-olds (IHDP)	1.28	0.26[d]		

Sources: Roland G. Fryer and Steven D. Levitt, "Understanding the Black-White Test Score Gap in the First Two Years of School," *Review of Economics and Statistics,* vol. 86, no. 2 (May 2004): 447–64; Jeanne Brooks-Gunn, Pamela K. Klebanov, Judith Smith, Greg J. Duncan, and Kyunghee Lee, "The Black-White Test Score Gap in Young Children: Contributions of Test and Family," *Applied Developmental Science* 7, no. 4 (2003): 239–52; Meredith Phillips, Jeanne Brooks-Gunn, Greg J. Duncan, Pamela Klebanov, and Jonathan Crane, "Family Background, Parenting Practices, and the Black-White Test Score Gap," in *The Black-White Test Score Gap*, edited by Christopher Jencks and Meredith Phillips (Brookings, 1998), pp. 103–45.

Notes: To standardize the score differentials, we used 16 as the standard deviation on the Stanford-Binet and 15 as the standard deviation on the PPVT-R and the WPPSI, unless the author gave the actual standard deviation for the entire sample. ECLS-K is the Early Childhood Longitudinal Study-Kindergarten Cohort; IHDP is the Infant Health and Development Program; EHS is the Early Head Start Research and Evaluation Program; NLSY is the National Longitudinal Survey of Youth Child Supplement.

a. Controls for composite measure of socioeconomic status, a quadratic in the number of children's books, sex, age attending kindergarten, birth weight, mother's age at birth, and WIC participation.

b. Same as note a with the addition of teacher fixed effects.

c. Controls for family income, female headship, mother's education, mother's age at birth, and home environment.

d. Controls for family income, female headship, mother's educational attainment, neighborhood socioeconomic status, home learning environment, and home warmth.

average score for white and black children combined is 50. The median score for blacks (that is, the score that half the children are above and half below) is 40; the median score for whites is 52. Most children, however, are not exactly at the middle, but are rather above or below it, and so graphs of scores on readiness tests typically take on a hill, or bell, shape, with relatively few children at the extremes and more clustered near the middle of the distribution. The gap between the me-

dian white and black scores is 12 points—but who knows what that means compared with any other vocabulary or readiness scale?

Statisticians have a tool called the standard deviation for measuring the spread of a bell-shaped distribution.[16] A standard deviation tells how far a distribution is spread out around the average score—the numerical scale used to measure the scores doesn't matter. To put it another way, imagine that in fig-

Table 2. Selected Estimates of the Behavioral School Readiness Gap

Authors	Test	Sample	White-black		White-Hispanic	
			Raw	Adjusted	Raw	Adjusted
Magnuson (2004)	Approaches to learning	20,000 kindergartners, teacher reports	.36		.21	
	Self-control	(ECLS-K)	.38		.13	
	Externalizing behavior		−.31		.01	
	Internalizing behavior		−.06		−.05	
Chase-Lansdale, Gordon, Brooks-Gunn, and Klebanov (1997)	Internalizing behavior (Achenbach CBCL)	642 five-year-olds, maternal reports (IHDP)		−.30[a]		
	Externalizing behavior (Achenbach CBCL)			−.20[a]		
	Internalizing behavior (BPI)	699 five- to six-year-olds, maternal reports (NLSY-CS)		−.01[a]		
	Externalizing behavior (BPI)			−.22[a]		

Sources: Katherine Magnuson, analyses prepared for this article from the Early Childhood Longitudinal Study-Kindergarten Cohort, School of Social Work, University of Wisconsin (2004); P. Lindsay Chase-Lansdale, Rachel A. Gordon, Jeanne Brooks-Gunn, and Pamela K. Klebanov, "Neighborhood and Family Influences on the Intellectual and Behavioral Competence of Preschool and Early School-Age Children," in *Neighborhood Poverty*, vol. 1, *Context and Consequences for Children*, edited by Jeanne Brooks-Gunn, Greg L. Duncan, and J. Lawrence Aber (New York: Russell Sage, 1997), pp. 79–118.
Notes: ECLS-K is the Early Childhood Longitudinal Study-Kindergarten Cohort; IHDP is the Infant Health and Development Program; NLSY-CS is the National Longitudinal Survey of Youth—Child Supplement.
a. Controls for gender, family income, female headship, mother's age at birth, mother's employment, age, and school status.

ure 1, all the scores on the horizontal axis were multiplied by a factor of 10, or 20, or any number you choose. The scores themselves would change, and the measure of the gap between the peaks of the white and black distributions would change, but the number of standard deviations between the two peaks would be exactly the same. Thus, instead of expressing the readiness gap in terms of scores on a particular test, which cannot readily be compared with scores on other tests, researchers can express the readiness gap in terms of standard deviations. In figure 1, the standard deviation is 10 points, so a gap of 12 points means 1.2 standard deviations.

Using standard deviations to compare distributions is based on the underlying assumption that the hill shapes of the distributions are the same. This assumption is not literally true. But it remains useful for researchers,

because it creates a "scale free" measure of effects that allows comparisons across studies with different numerical scales.[17]

Now look back at table 1 and the column showing the white-black "raw" gap, the gap between the averages for white and for black children before scores are adjusted to take into account such factors as the age or education of a child's mother, family income, or whether the child was born at low birth weight. By this measure, the studies listed in table 1 typically find a white-black gap of more than 1 standard deviation, with many of the estimates roughly similar to the gap illustrated in figure 1. But the estimates of the white-black raw gap at entrance to kindergarten using the ECLS-K data are substantially lower, often hovering at about 0.5 standard deviation. Finally, the highest estimates of the raw gap in the table are generated

Figure 1. Vocabulary Scores for Three- and Four-Year-Olds, by Race

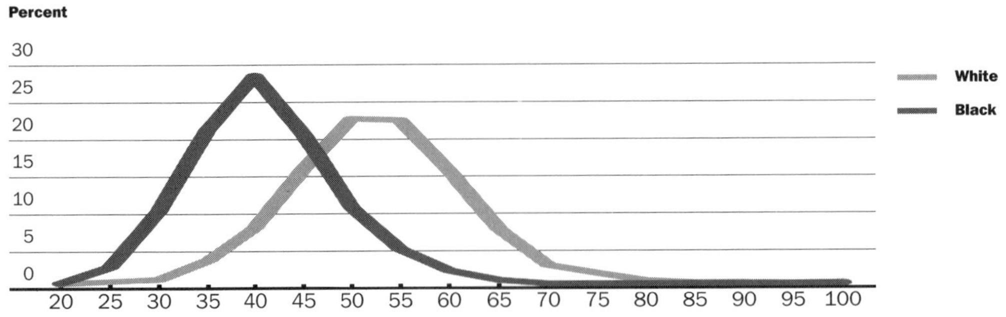

Source: Christopher Jencks and Meredith Phillips, eds., *The Black-White Test Score Gap* (Brookings, 1998).
Notes: The data are from National Longitudinal Survey of Youth Child study, 1986–94. For blacks, N = 1,134; for whites, N = 2,071. The figure is based on black and white three- and four-year-olds who took the Peabody Picture Vocabulary Test-Revised. The test is the standardized residual, coded to a mean of 50 and a standard deviation of 10, from a weighted regression of children's raw scores on their age in months, age in months squared, and year-of-testing dummies.

using the PPVT, some of which are substantially greater than 1 standard deviation. The studies listed in table 2 find a much smaller gap in behavioral readiness, with the raw gap often in the range of 0.0 to 0.3 standard deviation. Some measures even find a negative gap in behavioral readiness, meaning that black or Hispanic children were more behaviorally ready for kindergarten on this dimension than white children.

How Much Does 1 Standard Deviation Matter?

Should a gap of, say, 1 standard deviation in reading ability be considered a big difference? To what extent should policymakers take note of a white-black achievement gap that averages 1 standard deviation?

Statisticians often work with what they call a "normal" distribution, the bell-shaped distribution produced by many random observations, such as flipping 100 coins and seeing how many times heads comes up or rolling two dice and seeing how often each total comes up. A rule of thumb for normal distributions is that 68 percent of all scores will be within 1 standard deviation above or below

the mean score, while 95 percent of all scores will be within 2 standard deviations of the mean. In that spirit, consider the situation in which the gap between the peak of the hill-shaped distributions of scores for white and black children is 1 standard deviation. Under the assumptions that the two distributions have the same standard deviation and that both distributions are "normal," the following six statements about the degree of overlap between the two distributions will all hold true.[18]

First, randomly selecting one black child and one white child and comparing their scores will show the white child exceeding the black child 76 percent of the time and the black child exceeding the white child 24 percent of the time. Second, 84 percent of white children will perform better than the average black child, while 16 percent of black children will perform better than the average white child. Third, if a class that is evenly divided by race is divided into two equal-sized groups based on ability, then black students will compose roughly 70 percent, and whites 30 percent, of the students in the lower performing group. Fourth, if a school district chooses only the top-scoring 5 percent of students for "gifted" courses, such classes will have thirteen times more whites than blacks. Fifth, assume that a school district's student body mimics the national racial distribution (17 percent black, 83 percent white and other). The district chooses the lowest-scoring 5 percent of all students for a special needs program. Although 17 percent of the district's children are black, 72 percent of the special needs students will be black. Finally, assume that a reading textbook is written so that the average white student will read it at a 75 percent comprehension rate. The implied comprehension rate for the average black student will be 53 percent, virtually guaranteeing that such a reader will not engage with the text.[19]

These statements strongly suggest that a gap of 1 standard deviation is quite important in terms of student performance and should be of serious concern to policymakers. Indeed, even a gap of 0.5 standard deviation will result in striking differences between races, especially in matters like how many students are assigned to gifted or to remedial classes.

Raw Gap versus Adjusted Gap

Two columns in table 1 are labeled "raw gap," one referring to the gap between whites and blacks and the other to that between whites and Hispanics. As noted, the raw gap is calculated by looking at the distributions for white students and for either black or Hispanic students and calculating the difference between the mean scores, measured in terms of standard deviations, without making any further adjustments.

Two other columns are labeled "adjusted gap." The adjusted gap is the raw gap adjusted statistically to take into account different factors that might affect scores. For ex-

ample, the 2003 study by Jeanne Brooks-Gunn and others listed in table 1 accounts for family income, whether a woman is the head of the family, the mother's level of education, the mother's age at the child's birth, and aspects of the home environment. The adjusted gap calculates how much one would expect a white and black (or Hispanic) student to differ even if both had the same family income, the same type of head of household, mothers of the same education and age, and the same home environment. Different studies use different data on the child and family, so one study's adjusted score will account for different factors than another's. The specific factors taken into account in the adjusted scores are listed in the notes to tables 1 and 2.

The adjusted gap often substantially reduces the raw gap, although how much it does so varies across test instruments and studies. This pattern suggests that influences outside school, such as family background, health, and neighborhood, can have important effects on a child's academic readiness for school. In some of the calculations using the ECLS-K data in table 1, these other factors can almost completely account for the raw gap in white-black academic scores. In most, however, some gap in academic scores remains even after adjustment. In table 2, the adjusted scores are often near zero or even negative, suggesting that outside factors can more than explain any behavioral readiness gap.

Can the Differing Estimates of Readiness Be Reconciled?

No one would reasonably expect the gaps in school readiness between white, black, and Hispanic students to be the same in every study, regardless of the particular test and the data used. What factors might help explain and interpret some of the differences across tests? In particular, why does the most recent and seemingly up-to-date study, the ECLS-K, produce a substantially lower measure of the readiness gap than do other tests and data?

Sample Characteristics

When two studies differ, a first obvious question is whether they are based on different data. But the data from both the NLSY and the ECLS-K are chosen to be nationally representative, so they should show no systematic difference. And the IHDP data set, although it was not chosen to be nationally representative, is a large enough group and has been studied for long enough that it is unlikely to have a buried flaw that would call results into question. Many of the studies of kindergarten readiness discussed here struggle with such issues as how to make good comparative measurements with children who do not speak English as a first language, or are blind, or perhaps have a condition like cerebral palsy that makes it difficult to finish the test, and to address these issues they make various adjustments. But although differences in the samples certainly explain some of the variation around the edges, they seem unlikely to account for substantial variation.

Racial or Ethnic Bias in the Tests?

A common concern is that the readiness gap measured between white and minority children may be caused by systematic bias in the test; for example, perhaps certain vocabulary words are more commonly used in white families than in black or Hispanic ones. There are many ways to check for racial or ethnic bias.

One straightforward approach is to look at groups of white and minority children who have the same overall scores on the test. These children should also have essentially the same breakdown of right and wrong answers on each question on the test. Otherwise, "differential item functioning" exists, and an item on the test may be sorting by race or ethnicity rather than ability.

A related concept is construct bias; that is, whether a test measures what it purports to measure. A test is construct biased if items tend to be more familiar to one group than another, so that the characteristics of the test question help to explain why whites, blacks, or Hispanics find the questions hard or easy to answer. More than thirty years of intense examination of the possibility of construct bias, with particular focus on white-black differences, has failed to demonstrate that they are due to construct bias in achievement tests.[20]

Prediction bias might arise if a school district used a "school readiness battery" administered in kindergarten to predict third grade reading proficiency and found that the ability of the test to predict later proficiency differed for blacks, Hispanics, and whites. In general, though, achievement test items like reading, vocabulary, mathematics, social studies, and science function the same for blacks and whites. That is, test scores on achievement tests predict similarly for blacks and whites—and indeed, at the high school level, they have a slight tendency to overpredict black outcomes in college grades and workplace performance (rather than underpredict, as would be expected if there were prediction bias).[21] Thus, claims of prediction bias for achievement tests are, for the most part, not sustainable.

Another possibility is that even if the test instruments themselves are not racially or ethnically biased, the broader social context in which these tests and their uses are embedded may lead to racial or ethnic gaps in outcomes. Claude Steele and Joshua Aronson have conducted studies that show that calling a test "a diagnostic measure of ability" produces in black students a "stereotype threat," resulting in poorer test performance. The black-white gap is markedly reduced when the test does not bear the label "intellectual ability." Steele and Aronson caution against generalizing these findings beyond high achievers at a prestigious university and call for further study of the central hypothesis and its many implications.[22] In particular, it is not clear whether this issue would affect kindergartners.

Are the Tests Different Ways of Measuring a Common Underlying Readiness?

There is little evidence that distinctions such as verbal versus nonverbal, group administered versus individually administered, spatial versus numerical, or paper-and-pencil versus performance test explain the pattern of gap size estimates. Differences in the readiness gap across the tests can to some extent, however, be explained by the Spearman Hypothesis. This hypothesis states that all tests are imperfect measures of a general ability construct, commonly known as g. The more highly a given test correlates with g, the larger will be the black-white readiness gap.[23]

Highly specific school-related tasks, like those involving handwriting or auditory memory span, have lower correlations with general ability (g). But tests that involve reasoning with figures or vocabulary tests like the PPVT-R correlate highly with g. When a test combines multiple task types into a composite, as do all the tests reviewed above (other than the PPVT-R), the composite score correlates more highly with g than do the specific subtests—in keeping with the

Spearman Hypothesis. In effect, composite scores average out the specific contributions of particular task types, leaving what is common among them—that is, general ability, g. Researchers have tested the Spearman Hypothesis repeatedly over the past twenty years by looking at the common factors across the intelligence tests, and the hypothesis has successfully predicted the pattern of black-white differences in thirteen studies using a broad array of cognitive tests.[24]

But the "vocabulary" construct measured by the PPVT-R seems to pose a challenge to the Spearman Hypothesis. Even though one would expect vocabulary to be highly correlated with general ability (g), it is only one measure and thus should presumably produce a smaller black-white readiness gap than do composite scores. But as noted, the PPVT-R produces some of the highest estimates of the readiness gap. Further, theories of vocabulary acquisition emphasize that words with high frequency in written and oral discourse are learned first, and words with low frequency are learned later; that is, children learn words primarily because they are exposed to them.[25] And the order of vocabulary acquisition is highly invariant for advantaged and disadvantaged populations. Perhaps the greater exposure to words in some way exaggerates differences in underlying general ability, but the reasons why vocabulary tests often produce a larger readiness gap than composite achievement tests remain to be investigated.

What about the ECLS-K?

The readiness gap as measured by the ECLS Kindergarten sample is consistently smaller than that detected by the other methods, whether using raw or adjusted scores. Why might this be so? The ECLS test was designed more recently, with many useful updates in its methodology and administration, and it has a larger and more recent database. These factors might contribute to a smaller measure of the readiness gap.

Another possibility that fits with the Spearman Hypothesis, however, is that the version of the ECLS-K test given to kindergarten students is less correlated with general abil-

---

Student scores on the ECLS kindergarten test are very highly correlated with their scores on the test in third grade, suggesting that the two tests are not measuring different constructs.

---

ity, *g*, than is the version given later to, say, third graders. Remember that the ECLS-K test evolves and looks different for different age levels. In kindergarten the ECLS-K reading test involves basic phonics and decoding tasks; by third grade, the emphasis of the reading test has shifted toward comprehension, with a heavy word-meaning component. As the ECLS-K assessment moves on from basic skill processes in kindergarten to product outcomes in third grade it finds a larger black-white readiness gap. Indeed, the ECLS-K readiness gap as of third grade is much closer to that found by other test instruments. It is possible that the lower ECLS readiness gap at the kindergarten level may reflect the specific way it tests kindergartners.[26] At the same time, student scores on the ECLS kindergarten test are very highly correlated with their scores on the test in third grade, suggesting that the two tests are

not in fact measuring different constructs. Clearly, the reasons why the ECLS-K test generates smaller estimates of the racial and ethnic gaps in school readiness are not well understood and are worthy of serious future study, because of the important implications for education policy.

Future Directions for Research on the Readiness Gaps

Future research on the school readiness gaps among black, white, and Hispanic children will depend to a large extent on the availability of new data and the uses of new methods. Data from the ECLS Kindergarten 1998–99 cohort have invigorated research in this area. And ECLS is also now tracking a sample of 10,600 children born in 2001 whom it plans to follow through first grade. The new study seems certain to provide further evidence about the size and underlying causes of the racial and ethnic readiness gaps. Researchers should also be on the lookout for situations in which a large group of kindergarten-age children, such as the IHDP group, might usefully be administered an achievement test.

Another approach is to use different methods. A relatively new line of thought emphasizes a kind of cognitive measurement that is highly correlated with general ability, *g*. "Choice reaction time" is the time it takes the subject to react to a light stimulus by moving her index finger from a home base to one or more of eight lights arranged in a semicircle. Total reaction time is decomposed into the milliseconds it takes the examinee to remove her index finger from the home base after the stimulus light is activated and the time it takes *after* removing the index finger to touch the stimulus switch. The two times are experimentally independent. The procedure is simple, can be used for all ages, requires no memory component, and is highly reliable.

And the time it takes a subject to remove a finger from the home base is remarkably highly correlated with cognitive test composites.[27] Some tantalizing links also exist between reaction time and vocabulary development.

Most data sets described in this paper are longitudinal—that is, they track groups of children over time. Such an approach is obviously useful for investigating the determinants and effects of school readiness. But it is not the only possible approach. For example, if assessors are interested in a snapshot of the status of the children at a specific time, a single cross-sectional study can be less costly and less complex than a longitudinal study.

Yet another approach is to conduct an experiment by assigning children to different government intervention programs and having each intervention test the children's school readiness. For example, the federal government has supported the Early Head Start Research and Evaluation Project (EHS), which has studied seventeen Head Start programs around the United States since the late 1990s using a methodology in which 3,000 children were randomly assigned either to Early Head Start or to a control group. The first phase of the study focused on children from birth to age three, but a second phase from 2001 to 2004 is tracking children from the time they leave Early Head Start until they enter kindergarten. The project is evaluating prekindergarten children using many of the tools already discussed: the PPVT, the Woodcock Johnson Psycho-Educational Test Battery, the Achenbach Child Behavior Checklist, analysis of videotaped problem-solving and play sessions, and others. These data will surely generate a wave of studies of kindergarten readiness, often with policy implications, in the next few years. Of course, experimental evidence of this sort need not be collected nationwide; such experiments can also be carried out at the state or metropolitan levels.

Future research on the readiness gap at kindergarten will prove useful, but it seems highly unlikely to overturn the conclusion that the raw readiness gaps, between white and black children in particular but also between white and Hispanic children, are real and large. The remainder of this issue is devoted to exploring possible explanations for this very serious problem, along with their policy implications.

Endnotes

1. Lori Shepherd, Sharon Lynn Kagan, and Emily Wurtz, eds., *Principles and Recommendations for Early Childhood Assessments* (Washington: National Education Goals Panel, February 1998).

2. Samuel J. Meisels, "Can Head Start Pass the Test?" *Education Week* 22, no. 27 (March 19, 2003): 44; Anthony D. Pellegrini and Carl D. Glickman, "Measuring Kindergarteners' Social Competence," *Young Children* (May 1990): 40–44.

3. Sally Atkins-Burnett, Brian Rowan, and Richard Correnti, "Administering Standardized Achievement Tests to Young Children: How Mode of Administration Affects the Reliability of Standardized Measures of Student Achievement in Kindergarten and First Grade," paper presented at the annual meeting of the American Educational Research Association, April 2001 (available at www.sii.soe.umich.edu/papers.html).

4. Although the studies reviewed in this issue use the PPVT-R, the test has recently been revised, and studies now in the field use the PPVT-III. For discussion, see Jeanne Brooks-Gunn, Pamela K. Klebanov, Judith Smith, Greg J. Duncan, and Kyunghee Lee, "The Black-White Test Score Gap in Young Children: Contributions of Test and Family," *Applied Developmental Science* 7, no. 4 (2003): 239–52.

5. A. Jackson Stenner, Malbert Smith, and Donald S. Burdick, "Toward a Theory of Construct Definition," *Journal of Educational Measurement* 20, no. 4 (1983): 304–15.

6. George A. Miller and Patricia M. Gildea, "How Children Learn Words," *Scientific American* 257, no. 3 (1987): 94–99.

7. Elizabeth P. Hagen, Elizabeth A. Delaney, and Thomas F. Hopkins, *Stanford-Binet Intelligence Scale—Examiner's Handbook: An Expanded Guide for Fourth Edition Users* (Chicago: Riverside Publishing Company, 1987).

8. For the genesis of the Behavioral Problems Index, see James L. Peterson and Nicholas Zill, "Marital Disruption, Parent-Child Relationships, and Behavioral Problems in Children," *Journal of Marriage and the Family* 48, no. 2 (May 1986). For a discussion of how the BPI is used in the NLS, see Center for Human Resource Research, *NLSY79 Child and Young Adult Data Users Guide* (Ohio State University, December 2002), especially pp. 91–94.

9. The article by Jeanne Brooks-Gunn and Lisa Markman in this issue describes in more detail how this approach was used in one study of 2,000 three-year-olds, with data from the Early Head Start Research and Evaluation Project (EHS). These data are also discussed further at the end of the present article.

10. National Center for Education Statistics, *U.S. Dept. of Education, ECLS-K Base Year Data Files and Electronic Codebook* (2001).

11. Susan M. Benner, *Assessing Young Children with Special Needs: An Ecological Perspective* (New York: Longman, 1992); Everett Waters and Alan L. Sroufe, "Social Competence as a Developmental Construct," *Developmental Review* 3 (1983): 79–97; Anthony Pellegrini, Lee Galda, and Donald L. Rubin, "Context in Text: The Development of Oral and Written Language in Two Genres," *Child Development* 55 (1984): 1549–55.

12. Frederick M. Lord and Melvin R. Novick, *Statistical Theories of Mental Test Scores, with Contributions by Alan Birnbaum* (Reading, Mass.: Addison-Wesley, 1968); Frederick M. Lord, *Applications of Item Re-*

sponse Theory to Practical Testing Problems (Hillsdale, N.J.: Lawrence Erlbaum Associates, 1980). See also Benner, *Assessing Young Children* (see note 11).

13. Donald T. Campbell and Donald W. Fiske, "Convergent and Discriminant Validation by the Multi-Trait Multi-Method Matrix," *Psychological Bulletin* 56 (1959): 81–105.

14. Pellegrini, Galda, and Rubin, "Context in Text" (see note 11).

15. A. Jackson Stenner and Benjamin D. Wright, "Readability, Reading Ability, and Comprehension" (paper presented at the Association of Test Publishers Hall of Fame induction for Benjamin D. Wright, San Diego, 2002), in *Making Measures,* edited by Benjamin D. Wright and Mark H. Stone (Chicago: Phaneron Press, 2004).

16. The mathematical formula for calculating standard deviation works like this: (1) calculate the average of the scores; (2) calculate the difference between each individual score and the average; (3) square these differences from the average, and then add them up; (4) take the square root of the total. This calculation will give the number of points that are equal to 1 standard deviation for this group of scores.

17. Space does not permit a full treatment of the soundness of all assumptions underlying the standard deviation as a common unit of effect. However, we did compare the standard deviations for five well-known reading tests that were linked to a common scale and found they ranged from a low of .94 to a high of 1.13. This modest variability across grades and tests provides a context for evaluating the variability in estimates of the black-white achievement gap across various studies and instruments reported in this volume.

18. For purposes of this discussion we made the usual simplifying assumptions of bivariate normality, homogeneity of variance, and equal sample sizes in the two groups. Furthermore, we assume that the 1 standard deviation difference is in construct measures, not test score performances, which are uncorrected for measurement error.

19. Using data from the NCES-NAEP website, we estimate that 1.0 standard deviation on NAEP is equivalent to 220L (220 Lexiles). A back check on this number is to average four norm-referenced achievement test (NRT) standard deviations. The RMSA standard deviation for the four NRTs is 229L. Comprehension rate is modeled as the difference between reader ability and text readability. A difference of 225L between a targeted reader (75 percent comprehension rate) at fourth grade and the average black fourth grader implies a 53 percent comprehension rate for a "book bag" of fourth grade textbooks. See Lexile.com, the Lexile Calculator.

20. For background on construct validity, see Stenner, Smith, and Burdick, "Toward a Theory of Construct Definition" (see note 5). For discussion of the evidence, see Richard E. Nisbett, "Race, Genetics, and IQ," in *The Black-White Test Score Gap*, edited by Christopher Jencks and Meredith Phillips (Brookings, 1998). The psychometric literature has largely given up on the term "bias" in favor of the less emotionally charged terms "differential item functioning" and "differential instrument functioning."

21. See Thomas J. Kane, "Racial and Ethnic Preferences in College Admissions," Frederick E. Vars and William G. Bowen, "Scholastic Aptitude Test Scores, Race, and Academic Performance in Selective Colleges and Universities," and William R. Johnson and Derek Neal, "Basic Skills and the Black-White Earning Gap," in *The Black-White Test Score Gap*, edited by Jencks and Phillips (see note 20).

22. Claude M. Steele, "Race and the Schooling of Black America," *Atlantic Monthly* (April 1992): 68–78; Claude M. Steele, "A Threat in the Air: How Stereotypes Shape the Intellectual Identities and Performance of Women and African Americans," *American Psychologist* (June 1997): 613–29; Claude M. Steele and Joshua Aronson, "Stereotype Threat and the Intellectual Test Performance of African Americans," *Journal of Personality and Social Psychology* 69, no. 5 (1995): 797–811.

23. Arthur R. Jensen, *Bias in Mental Testing* (New York: Free Press, 1980), especially p. 146-147; Arthur R. Jensen, "Spearman's Hypothesis Tested with Chronometric Information-Processing Tasks," *Intelligence* 17 (1993): 47–77.

24. Arthur R. Jensen, "Psychometric g and Achievement," in *Policy and Perspectives on Educational Testing,* edited by Bernard R. Gifford (Boston: Kluwer Academic, 1993), pp. 117–227.

25. Betty Hart and Todd R. Risley, *The Social World of Children Learning to Talk* (Baltimore: Brooks, 1999). See Stenner, Smith, and Burdick, "Toward a Theory of Construct Definition" (see note 5), and Miller and Gildea, "How Children Learn Words" (see note 6), for introductions to exposure theory. See Jensen, *Bias in Mental Testing* (see note 23) for an introduction to education theory.

26. Meredith Phillips, James Crouse, and John Ralph, "Does the Black-White Test Score Gap Widen after Children Enter School?" in Jencks and Phillips, *The Black-White Test Score Gap* (see note 20), pp. 229–71.

27. Jensen, *Bias in Mental Testing* (see note 23). See also William Hick, "On the Rate of Information," *Quarterly Journal of Experimental Psychology* 4 (1952): 11–26.

Can Family Socioeconomic Resources Account for Racial and Ethnic Test Score Gaps?

Greg J. Duncan and Katherine A. Magnuson

Summary

This article considers whether the disparate socioeconomic circumstances of families in which white, black, and Hispanic children grow up account for the racial and ethnic gaps in school readiness among American preschoolers. It first reviews why family socioeconomic resources might matter for children's school readiness. The authors concentrate on four key components of parent socioeconomic status that are particularly relevant for children's well-being—income, education, family structure, and neighborhood conditions. They survey a range of relevant policies and programs that might help to close socioeconomic gaps, for example, by increasing family incomes or maternal educational attainment, strengthening families, and improving poor neighborhoods.

Their survey of links between socioeconomic resources and test score gaps indicates that resource differences account for about half of the standard deviation—about 8 points on a test with a standard deviation of 15—of the differences. Yet, the policy implications of this are far from clear. They note that although policies are designed to improve aspects of "socioeconomic status" (for example, income, education, family structure), no policy improves "socioeconomic status" directly. Second, they caution that good policy is based on an understanding of causal relationships between family background and children outcomes, as well as cost-effectiveness.

They conclude that boosting the family incomes of preschool children may be a promising intervention to reduce racial and ethnic school readiness gaps. However, given the lack of successful large-scale interventions, the authors suggest giving only a modest role to programs that address parents' socioeconomic resources. They suggest that policies that directly target children may be the most efficient way to narrow school readiness gaps.

www.future of children.org

Greg J. Duncan is the Edwina S. Tarry Professor of Human Development and Social Policy at Northwestern University. Katherine Magnuson is an assistant professor of social work at the University of Wisconsin at Madison. The authors are grateful to the Family and Child Well-Being Research Network of the National Institute of Child Health and Human Development for research support; to Amy Claessens and Mimi Engel for research assistance; and to the volume editors, Susan Mayer, and Meredith Phillips, for helpful comments.

Greg J. Duncan and Katherine A. Magnuson

National tests regularly show sizable gaps in school readiness between young white children and young black and Hispanic children in the United States. In the nation's most comprehensive assessment of school readiness among kindergartners, the 1998 Early Childhood Longitudinal Study (ECLS-K), both black and Hispanic children scored about two-thirds of a standard deviation below whites in math (the equivalent of roughly 10 points on a test with a mean of 100 and a standard deviation of 15) and just under half a standard deviation (7–8 points) below whites in reading (see figure 1).[1]

What might be causing such gaps? One prominent possibility is that the historical racial and ethnic inequalities in the United States have created disparate socioeconomic circumstances for the families in which white, black, and Hispanic children are reared. As graphed in figure 1, the racial gaps in family socioeconomic status (SES) of the children in the ECLS-K closely matched the gaps in test scores.[2] The average socioeconomic level of black kindergartners was more than two-thirds of a standard deviation below that of whites. Hispanic children had even lower socioeconomic standing relative to whites.

With such similar racial and ethnic gaps in test scores and SES, it is tempting to conclude that equalizing the social and economic circumstances of white, black, and Hispanic preschoolers would eliminate most if not all of the achievement gap. Whether this is likely is the subject of this article. We begin by considering theories about why family socioeconomic resources might matter for children's school readiness and reviewing studies of interventions designed to boost those resources

in various ways. We then summarize results from studies that attempt to account for the racial and ethnic achievement gaps by examining differences in family socioeconomic status.

Material Hardship and Family Socioeconomic Status

Life is very different for a family with a single parent struggling to make ends meet by working at two minimum-wage jobs and a family with one highly paid wage earner and a second parent at home caring for their children. One family faces a vast range of material and psychological hardships, while the other is largely spared such stressors.[3] The first family, for example, may have a lower-quality home environment that exposes children to pollutants and toxins, such as lead, and provides fewer learning opportunities in the home or lower-quality child care outside it. Greater stress may increase the mother's irritability and reduce her warmth and responsiveness to her children. Across racial and ethnic groups in the United States, such differences in family resources, particularly financial resources, are systematic and often large, prompting researchers to investigate whether family resource differences may account for the racial and ethnic differences in school readiness.

Material Hardship and Household Resources

The ECLS-K data in figure 2 reveal striking differences both in a broad range of indicators of family hardships and in the accumulation of those disadvantages between poor and nonpoor children. (Some of the indicators do not, strictly speaking, point to socioeconomic status but relate to conditions, such as low birth weight and depressive symptoms, and behaviors, like harsh parenting, that are discussed in other articles in this volume.) The

Figure 1. Racial and Ethnic Gaps in Selected Test Scores and in Family Socioeconomic Status for Kindergartners

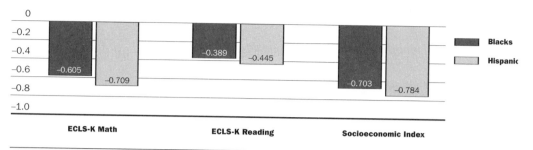

Standard deviation difference from whites

Source: Authors' calculations based on data taken from the ECLS-K.

first four items in figure 2 (mother a high school dropout, single-parent family, mother with no job or a job with low prestige, and unsafe neighborhood) are relatively common indicators of inadequate family economic and social resources. The next seven items are resource-related disadvantages often faced by poor families with children: large family size (three or more siblings), residential instability (child moved four or more times before starting school), harsh discipline (child spanked two or more times in the past week), few learning materials (fewer than ten children's books in the house), low birth weight (infant less than 5.5 pounds at birth), young parents (child born to a teen mother), and high levels of maternal depressive symptoms.

The contrasts between poor and other children could hardly be more stark. In almost every case, more than twice as many poor as nonpoor children suffer the given hardship, and for several hardships (high school dropout mother, bad job, and few children's books) the rate is more than three times as high.

The distribution of hardships differs not only by poverty status, but also by race and ethnicity (see table 1). With the exception of residential instability, black and Hispanic children are much more likely to experience hardships than are white children. The prevalence of single-parent families, low birth weight, harsh parenting, and maternal depressive symptoms is highest among black children. Hispanic children are most likely to have mothers who did not complete high school and to have few children's books in their homes.

Racial and ethnic differences are also apparent in the total number of hardships that children face. The vast majority of black and Hispanic children suffer at least one hardship, compared with just over half of white children. Experiencing four or more hardships is very rare for white children, but much more common among Hispanic, and especially black, children.

Socioeconomic Status or Socioeconomic Resources?

Some social scientists gather a variety of indicators of financial and social resources under the umbrella term of "socioeconomic status" (SES). For them, socioeconomic status refers to one's social position as well as the privileges and prestige that derive from access to economic and social resources. Because it may be difficult to measure directly a family's access to resources or its position in a social hierar-

Figure 2. Percent of Poor and Nonpoor Children Experiencing Hardships

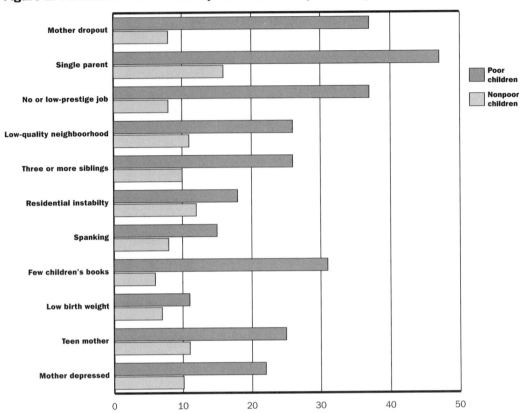

Source: Same as figure 1.

chy, analysts often use one indicator (typically occupation) or combine several indicators (for example, parental education and occupation) into scales that indicate families' relative positions in a social hierarchy.[4] The differences in socioeconomic status shown in figure 1 exemplify this single-indicator approach. Using a summary index to measure SES emphasizes social stratification as an organizing force in individuals' lives and presumes that one's social standing is a more important determinant of life chances than any of the economic and social resources that determine it.[5]

A different approach to measuring SES is based on the premise that distinct types of socioeconomic resources contribute to social inequality and stratification along differing economic and social dimensions.[6] For example, although parents' educational attainments, incomes, and occupations are related, each may affect children in different ways.[7] Rather than using a summary measure, proponents of this approach consider each component separately, as seen in figure 2. This method requires a complicated sorting out of the separate effects of correlated social and economic disadvantages, which if done incorrectly may understate the importance of either the constellation or the accumulation of household resources. We take this multidimensional approach throughout this article by concentrating on four key dimensions of parental socioeconomic resources—income, education, family structure, and neighborhood conditions.[8]

Table 1. Percent of Children Experiencing Poverty and Hardships, by Race and Ethnicity

Characteristic	White	Black	Hispanic
Experiencing poverty	10	42	37
Experiencing Hardships			
Mother high school dropout	7	18	35
Single parent	15	50	24
No or low-prestige job	8	18	21
Low-quality neighborhood	5	23	21
Three or more siblings	11	21	18
Residential instability	13	12	13
Spanking	7	17	10
Few children's books	2	20	29
Low birth weight	6	15	8
Teen mother	10	22	19
Mother depressed	11	20	13
One or more hardships	52	87	81
Four or more hardships	4	29	18

Source: Based on data from the ECLS-K study.

Are Socioeconomic Resources Really the Issue?

Before taking a more detailed look at these resources, we raise a fundamental question: does SES really determine achievement? Causation is notoriously difficult to prove in the social sciences, and just because middle-class children's academic achievement exceeds that of poor children, one should not necessarily infer that eliminating the income gap would eliminate the achievement gap.

Maybe what really matters for children's achievement is the psychological dispositions of their parents, including, for example, depression. As noted, depression is more prevalent among low- than higher-income parents, as discussed by Janet Currie in her article in this volume. Perhaps income and child achievement are linked because both are higher in the case of better-adjusted parents. Or maybe the asso-ciation between socioeconomic status and achievement stems from the poorer health and greater developmental problems of the children, which can both lower a child's academic achievement and reduce a family's resources by limiting parents' employment. Moreover, as pointed out by William Dickens in his article in this volume, many behavioral geneticists, concluding that socioeconomic conditions are relatively unimportant, put forth a different logic. They argue that genetic endowments of ability are key determinants of test scores, and children reared in more affluent families score higher on achievement tests in part because of genetic endowments passed on from one generation to the next.

If parental mental health, child health, or genetic endowments are what really matter for children's achievement, then increasing parents' income or education without also addressing these other causes would not boost achievement. Our discussion of the relationships between achievement and the four most important components of SES—income, education, family structure, and neighborhood—is mindful of the difficulties of establishing causal effects.

The best evidence on the effects of socioeconomic resources on children's development comes from experimental studies in which participants are randomly assigned to a treatment or a control group. But such studies are rare in the social sciences. Second-best strategies involve following large samples of children for many years and using a host of statistical strategies to rule out alternative explanations for the presumed effects.

Household Income

It is easy to see how higher family incomes might give children a big edge in academic achievement. Financial resources can enable parents to secure access to good prenatal health care and nutrition; rich learning environments, both in the home and through child care settings and other opportunities outside the home; a safe and stimulating neighborhood; and, for older children, good schools and a college education.[9]

But despite abundant evidence of correlations between income and achievement, the issue of whether family income is causally linked to children's achievement and behavior remains controversial. A study by Judith Smith and colleagues compared the achievement of children in families whose average income fell below the poverty line between their birth and age five with that of children in families whose average income remained above the poverty line during this period of their childhood.[10] They used statistical techniques to ensure that any differences in achievement between poor and nonpoor children were not due to differences in their mothers' education, children's low birth weight, or family structure. Poverty, they found, accounted for about 0.30 standard deviation of the gap in achievement between poor and nonpoor children (the equivalent of about 4–5 points on a test with a mean of 100 and a standard deviation of 15)—enough to explain a substantial share of the racial gap in achievement. The achievement gap between middle-income and higher-income families was not nearly as large, suggesting that boosting household income during early childhood would help poor children more than children from wealthier families. Children whose families faced deep and persistent poverty fared the worst and registered the largest achievement gap, which again suggests that these children would gain the most from added income.[11]

Smith's study, as well as several others, concludes that the key advantage bestowed by

higher income is a stimulating learning environment. The number of books and newspapers in the home and the access of children to learning experiences routinely explain about a third of the poverty "effect," as discussed in the article by Jeanne Brooks-Gunn and Lisa Markman in this issue.[12]

Although suggestive of a causal link between poverty and achievement, this evidence should not be taken as the final word. A subsequent study, based on the same data used by Smith and her coauthors but ruling out a longer list of alternative explanations for the achievement gap, estimated a considerably smaller difference between low- and high-income children.[13]

A series of experimental welfare reform evaluation studies during the 1990s made it possible to observe how increases in family income affect children's development. Although all the experimental programs increased parental employment, only certain programs increased family income. Only when income was increased did preschool and elementary school children's academic achievement improve.[14] For young children, family income gains of roughly $1,000 a year translated into achievement gains of about 0.07 standard deviation, about 1 point on our reference test. Sustained over time, even such small gains may be economically profitable, leading to sizable increases in lifetime earnings.[15]

Income, it appears, does matter for children's achievement, although perhaps not as much as some early studies suggested. Estimated at more than $30,000, the gaps in family income between white children and black and Hispanic children are huge. What policies might begin to close these gaps?

One strategy, embodied in several of the welfare reform programs described above, is to promote low-income parents' participation in the labor market and reduce their reliance on welfare. But even the most generous welfare reform programs boosted average family incomes by only $1,000 or $2,000 a year. Other work-oriented interventions, such as low-cost job search programs, have produced relatively small absolute income gains for women—a few hundred dollars over the course of a year or two.[16] More intensive, training-based programs have netted women proportionately bigger earnings gains—a few thousand dollars over several years—but none created the kind of long-term income increases that would begin to narrow the income gap between white families and ethnic and racial minority families. Employment interventions for disadvantaged adult men have had even less encouraging results. Only about a third of such interventions increased either employment or earnings, and none emerged as a panacea.

Another approach is to supplement the incomes of poor working families through the earned income tax credit.[17] A refundable federal tax credit for low-income working families with children, the EITC was expanded during the 1990s and is now the nation's largest cash transfer program for low-income families. In 2003 the maximum benefit for a family with two children was about $4,200, and nearly 19 million families received the credit.[18] In 1997 the program lifted about 2.2 million children out of poverty.[19] By providing income support for low-wage work, the tax credit also encourages work in single-parent families. Increases to the EITC in the 1990s raised the annual employment of poorly educated single mothers by almost 9 percent.[20]

Parental Human Capital
Human capital includes parental skills, acquired both formally and informally, that are valuable in the labor market and at home.[21] Formal schooling is the most familiar and most studied form of human capital, and research confirms that more schooling leads to better employment and earnings.[22] More schooling may thus indirectly benefit children by increasing family income, but other parental skills may also directly enhance child well-being, for example, by improving parenting and the ability to accomplish parenting goals.[23]

Parents' completed schooling varies widely by race and ethnicity and is particularly low among Hispanics, reflecting their immigration history. Among the ECLS-K sample of kindergartners, 35 percent of Hispanic mothers had not completed high school, compared with only 7 percent of white mothers and 18 percent of black mothers (table 1). At the other end of the scale, 28 percent of white mothers had completed a four-year college program, whereas only 9 percent of black and 8 percent of Hispanic mothers had done so.[24]

Children with highly educated parents routinely score higher on cognitive and academic achievement tests than do children of parents with less education. Remarkably, the link between children's cognitive development and parental education is evident as early in a child's life as three months of age.[25] Yet research has not clearly isolated parental education as the cause of high child achievement.[26] Few studies are able to disentangle parents' schooling from other sources of advantage, such as cognitive endowments, that may have increased achievement among both parents and children. The few U.S. studies that have tried to isolate the effects of parental education per se typically find positive but modest effects of maternal and paternal education on children's achievement, with an additional year of schooling linked to an increase in children's test scores of about 0.15 standard deviation, or about 2 points on our reference test.[27]

It may be that increasing schooling for mothers who are high school dropouts raises their children's achievement more than increasing education for college-trained mothers.[28] According to a recent study, welfare recipients'

Income, it appears, does matter for children's achievement, although perhaps not as much as some early studies suggested.

---

participation in mandated education or training improved their young children's school readiness by as much as a quarter of a standard deviation, or almost 4 points on our reference test.[29]

With large gaps in parental education among racial and ethnic groups, interventions that increase rates of high school completion may have a large payoff for future generations. But few academic programs developed to increase high school graduation rates among at-risk adolescents have been effective so far. A recent review of sixteen random-assignment evaluations of dropout-prevention programs found only one to be successful.[30] Rigorous evaluations of a few intensive teen mentoring programs have found more promising results, but nevertheless success is not guaranteed, particularly when these programs are implemented on a large scale.[31]

Studies of low-income populations routinely report that without any programmatic inter-

vention, close to 50 percent of disadvantaged mothers return to school.[32] Yet even with high rates of continued schooling, educational attainment among economically disadvantaged parents remains much lower than among advantaged families. Thus another intervention approach is to promote educational activities among parents. For example, programs targeting teen mothers may provide support and incentives to stay in school after the birth of a child, or welfare programs may make cash benefits contingent on mothers' participation in education and training. But evaluations suggest that to date these types of interventions have not been successful in boosting mothers' educational activity above the relatively high level of participation of control group mothers.[33]

The high enrollment in further education of disadvantaged mothers suggests that mothers might be benefiting from current efforts to offset the costs of education, particularly higher education, and to increase access to educational opportunities. Indeed, expansions in public spending on higher education, including more generous financial aid and an increase in community college funding, have consistently been linked to higher levels of college attainment and enrollment. However, the extent to which educational expenditures have specifically benefited low-income students appears to vary, depending on the specifics of the spending.[34] Still another approach is to raise the age at which students may leave school or begin to work. Such policy changes over the past century have modestly increased youths' years of schooling.[35]

Family Structure

Today about one-third of all children are born outside marriage, and more than half of all children will live in a single-parent family at some point in their childhood. This causes concern because resources can be scarce in single-parent families.[36] Young children living with single mothers face poverty at five times the rate of preschoolers in intact families (50 percent versus 10 percent), and the declines in income for households with children after a divorce are dramatic and lasting.[37] Financial and time constraints may limit a single parent's ability to supervise and discipline children and to provide a supportive and stimulating home environment.[38] Furthermore, because fathers are often absent from single-parent families, children in these households tend to have fewer male role models, which may not bode well for their social development.[39]

As with education and income, family structure differences across racial groups are large. Rates of single-parenthood in the ECLS-K sample averaged 15 percent for white children, 24 percent for Hispanic children, and 50 percent for black children (table 1).[40] Black children are more likely to be born outside marriage; white children, to experience divorce.

On average, children raised by single parents have lower social and academic well-being than the children of intact marriages.[41] Most research on single-parent families has lumped all varieties of such families together or focused only on the effects of divorce.[42] The few studies that have tried to draw distinctions find little difference between children of divorced and never-married parents; both groups are at greater risk of poor achievement and behavioral problems than children from intact families.[43]

Rates of teenage childbearing have been steadily falling, dropping 22 percent between 1991 and 2000, from 62.1 births to 48.1 births per 1,000 fifteen- to nineteen-year-olds.[44] Nevertheless, U.S. rates of teen parenthood continue to exceed those of European countries. And U.S. teen birth rates differ substantially by race. As table 1 shows, about one in five black or Hispanic children was born to a mother younger than twenty, nearly twice the rate for white children. Typically, children of teen mothers face a constellation of socioeconomic hardships, including single parenthood, poverty, and lower maternal educational attainment.[45]

Although most children from broken families fare worse than those in intact families, and children born to teen mothers fare worse than those born to older mothers, in both cases it appears that differences in parental characteristics, such as educational attainment, rather than family structure or maternal age per se, account for a portion of the gaps. Once these differences in family background are taken into account, growing up with a single or remarried parent has persistent, but much more modest negative effects on children's achievement.[46] For example, a recent adoption study suggests that differences in the parental backgrounds of single- and two-parent families account for a substantial proportion of children's achievement problems after a divorce.[47] Similarly, the extent to which children would benefit from their mothers' postponing childbearing for a few years is uncertain, although likely modest.[48]

Economic insecurity explains part of the poor outcomes of children reared in single-parent or blended families and by young parents. And parental conflict and strain in divorcing families may impair children's development, particularly with respect to their behavior.[49] Finally, children in young and single-parent families may face many transitions in family life, including subsequent cohabitations, remarriages, separations, and divorces. Such instability may pose additional risks to child well-being.[50]

We know little about whether interventions can promote marriage and prevent divorce among disadvantaged populations.[51] Yet even if the current round of federal marriage-promotion programs succeeds, it is unlikely to make much of a dent in the huge differences of family structure between blacks and whites. Furthermore, it appears that for marriage to promote children's achievement substantially, it must go hand in hand with increases in family resources, such as income. Whether higher rates of marriage will improve other aspects of socioeconomic circumstances is unclear.[52] Evaluations of new marriage programs should shed light on the feasibility of increasing marriage rates, as well as on how doing so will promote children's well-being.

Programmatic interventions to prevent teen childbearing by reducing sexual activity and promoting contraceptive use among adolescents have not been very successful. More often than not, programs designed to postpone sexual behavior fail to delay its onset or reduce its frequency.[53] Of twenty-eight carefully evaluated programs focused on abstinence, sexual education, and HIV prevention, only ten delayed the age of sexual initiation. Of the nineteen that measured the frequency of youths' sexual activity, thirteen had no significant effect. Nor did the programs substantially increase contraceptive use. Only four of the eleven program evaluations that measured teenagers' use of contraception found positive effects. A handful of more intensive interventions that provided mentoring and constructive after-school activities had more positive results.[54] But

whether these intensive programs can be replicated on a larger scale is uncertain. As with dropout-prevention programs, concentrated intervention is a necessary but not sufficient condition for success.[55]

Neighborhoods

Neighborhoods shape children's development in many ways, although kindergartners are probably less susceptible to neighborhood influences than are adolescents.[56] The risks posed by low-quality neighborhoods are most striking in high-poverty urban communities plagued by violence, gangs, drug activity, old housing stock, and vacant buildings, where watchful parents may not allow children to walk to school alone or play outside.[57] Such neighborhoods may influence children through increased stress, perhaps stemming from community violence; social disorganization, including a lack of positive role models and shared values, which may lead to problem behavior; a lack of institutional resources, such as strong schools and police protection; and negative peer influences, which may spread problem behavior.[58] Nevertheless, studies suggest that neighborhood characteristics can explain no more than 5 percent of the variation in children's achievement and 10 percent of the variation in their behavior.[59]

A recent experiment that offered families the opportunity to move from high-poverty to low-poverty neighborhoods provides a compelling test of the extent to which neighborhood matters for children's development. The results are striking. The Moving to Opportunity (MTO) experiment gave housing-project residents in five of the nation's largest cities a chance to move to low-poverty neighborhoods. But data collected four to seven years after the families moved revealed no differences between program and control group children, even among those who were preschoolers when the program began.[60] Despite dramatic improvements in neighborhood conditions, children made no gains on test scores, school success or engagement, or behaviors. Why not?

One possible explanation is that although the neighborhoods improved a great deal, the schools attended by the children did not.[61] And although MTO-related neighborhood advantages appeared to improve the mental health of mothers, they did not translate into other kinds of household resources or advantages that might have promoted children's well-being.[62] After moving, MTO adults still resembled their control-group counterparts in their employment, welfare dependence, family income, parenting practices, and connections to their children's schools and to the parents of their children's friends.

Residential mobility programs, then, will not by themselves remedy the achievement problems of children in public housing and in high-poverty neighborhoods. Interventions focused exclusively on neighborhoods rather than on influences directly related to the child, family, and school cannot solve the myriad problems of children growing up in high-poverty urban neighborhoods.

Can Family SES Account for the Gaps?

Both theory and evidence suggest that the family socioeconomic environments in which children are reared may account for at least some differences in school-entry achievement. Here we review so-called accounting studies, which estimate the extent to which socioeconomic differences across groups are linked to racial and ethnic achievement gaps.[63] We reiterate our warning regarding causation: accounting studies assume that

SES differences *cause* achievement differences. To the extent that this does not hold true, estimates of the effect of socioeconomic differences on achievement gaps will likely overstate the potential of policies to eliminate differences.

Accounting for the Gaps

Figure 3 shows representative results from four recent studies of black-white differences in test scores as children enter school. Math and reading results (in the left half of the figure) are taken from the study conducted by Ronald Fryer and Steven Levitt using data from the ECLS-K.[64] The first bars show the simple, unadjusted mean racial and ethnic differences. As noted, black children score two-thirds of a standard deviation lower than whites in math and close to half a standard deviation lower in reading.

To what extent are these gaps due to differences in socioeconomic resources? A handful of family and child SES-related measures explain nearly all of the racial math gap and the entire racial reading gap. These differences in family and child background include SES composite, number of children's books in the home, age of entry into kindergarten, birth weight, age of mother at time of birth, and whether the mother received the Special Supplemental Nutrition Program for Women, Infants, and Children (WIC). The same characteristics also explain racial and ethnic gaps in each of the five components of the math test (for example, counting, relative size) and the reading test (letter recognition, beginning sounds) and the gaps for sample subgroups defined by child gender as well as the location and racial composition of the child's school.[65] Figure 4, also using data drawn from the Fryer and Levitt study, shows that the same set of SES-related family characteristics accounts for nearly all of the math

Figure 3. Accounting for Black-White Test Score Gaps with SES

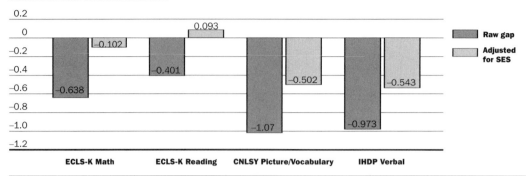

Sources: ECLS-K data are taken from Fryer and Levitt, "Understanding the Black-White Test Score Gap in the First Two Years of School," *Review of Economics and Statistics* 86 (2004): 447–64; NLSY data are taken from Meredith Phillips, Jeanne Brooks-Gunn, Greg J. Duncan, Pamela Klebanov, and Jonathan Crane, "Family Background, Parenting Practices, and the Black-White Test Score Gap," in *The Black-White Test Score Gap*, edited by Christopher Jencks and Meredith Phillips (Brookings, 1998), pp. 103–45; IHDP data are taken from Jeanne Brooks-Gunn, Pamela K. Klebanov, Judith Smith, Greg J. Duncan, and Kyunghee Lee, "The Black-White Test Score Gap in Young Children: Contributions of Test and Family," *Applied Developmental Science* 7, no. 4 (2003): 239–52.
Note: Effect sizes calculated by authors using the standard deviation for the sample of white students as the denominator. Variables used to adjust for SES gap in Fryer and Levitt include an SES composite, number of children's books in the home, age of entry into kindergarten, birth weight, age of mother at time of birth, and whether the mother received the Special Supplemental Nutrition Program for Women, Infants, and Children (WIC). Variables used to adjust for SES in Phillips and others include grandparents' education; grandparents' occupation; Southern roots; mother's number of siblings; mother's number of older siblings; no one in mother's family subscribed to magazines, newspapers, or had a library card; percent of white students in mother's high school; student-teacher ratio in mother's high school; percent teacher turnover in mother's high school; mother's educational expectations; mother's self esteem index; two indicators for mother's sense of control or mastery; interviewer's assessment of mother's attitude toward interview; mother's education; father's education; child birth weight; child birth order; family structure; mother's age at child's birth; household size; set of dummy variables for average income; mother's AFQT score; mother's class rank in high school; and interviewer's assessment of mother's understanding of interview. For the Brooks-Gunn and others analyses the SES variables include measures of the income-to-needs ratio averaged over three years, maternal education, family structure, maternal age at birth, and maternal verbal ability.

and reading gaps between Hispanic and white children.

It is unusual for researchers to find that SES differences explain all the racial and ethnic test score gaps. For example, the third set of bars in figure 3 summarizes results from a study of gaps in the picture-vocabulary scores

of black and white five- and six-year-olds from the Children of the National Longitudinal Study of Youth (CNLSY).[66] Not only is the unadjusted gap much larger in the CNLSY than in the ECLS-K data—more than 1 standard deviation, or about 16 points on our reference test—but a similar collection of family background measures accounts

Figure 4. Accounting for White-Hispanic Test Score Gaps with SES

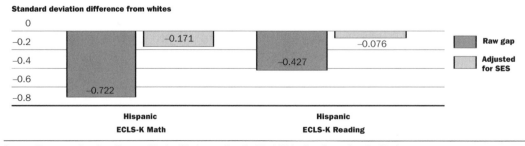

Source: Data are taken from Fryer and Levitt, "Understanding the Black-White Test Score Gap," table 2.

for only about half of the racial gap, or about 7–8 points.

Figure 3 also presents data on five-year-olds in the Infant Health and Development Program (IHDP) study.[67] As with the CNLSY, the IHDP verbal test score gap amounts to about a full standard deviation (about 15 points), and about half the gap (8 points) appears to be the result of SES differences between white and black children. Although these findings may appear to be contradictory, an interesting consistency is that SES explains roughly the same absolute amount of the gap. In all studies, a collection of SES-related measures seems to account for a difference of about half a standard deviation in white-black test scores (7–8 points), regardless of the assessments used or the populations studied.

Summary

On average, when black and Hispanic children begin school, their academic skills lag behind those of whites. Accounting studies find that differences in socioeconomic status explain about half a standard deviation of the initial achievement gaps. But because none of the accounting studies is able to adjust for a full set of genetic and other confounding causes of achievement, we regard them as providing upper-bound estimates of the role of family socioeconomic status.

If, indeed, differences in the socioeconomic backgrounds of young white, black, and Hispanic children play a causal role in creating achievement gaps, what are the implications for policy? The answer is far from clear. First, no policies address "socioeconomic status" directly. They address only its components—income, parental schooling, family structure, and the like. Moreover, wise policy decisions require an understanding of both causal

mechanisms *and* cost-effective interventions that can produce desired changes.

To illustrate, suppose that increasing maternal schooling by one year raises children's kindergarten achievement scores by one quarter of a standard deviation, or roughly 4 points on our reference test. With the achievement gaps between whites and both blacks and Hispanics at one-half to three-quarters of a standard deviation (7 to 11 points), a policy that could increase maternal schooling for all black and Hispanic mothers by an average of one or two years would significantly narrow the achievement gap. But few programmatic interventions can deliver such gains, and whether further expansions in educational funding will increase Hispanic or black mothers' educational attainment will depend on the specifics of how the money is spent.

In the case of household income, it appears that reducing the racial and ethnic differences in family income by several thousand dollars would reduce achievement gaps. Political support for work-based approaches to boosting income, such as the earned income tax credit, has increased considerably over the past decade. Moreover, because income appears to matter more for preschoolers than for older children—and much more for poor children than for others—it seems that an effective policy would be to adopt child-focused redistributive efforts using, say, European-style child allowances or increases in the EITC with benefits restricted to families with preschool children. Such programs may prove politically feasible, because it would be considerably cheaper to cover only a fraction of children than to cover all children.[68]

All in all, given the dearth of successful large-scale interventions, it may be wise to assign only a modest role to programs that aim to increase parents' socioeconomic resources. In the end, policies that directly target children's aptitude or mental and physical health, discussed in other articles in this issue, may be the most efficient way to address the gap.

Endnotes

1. See the article in this issue by Donald A. Rock and A. Jackson Stenner for a discussion of the different tests and estimates of the gap.

2. The ECLS-K asked children's parents about their own schooling, occupations, and household incomes and then combined these elements into a single socioeconomic status index.

3. Robert Haveman and Barbara Wolfe, *Succeeding Generations: On the Effect of Investments in Children* (New York: Russell Sage Foundation, 1994); Gary Evans, "The Environment of Childhood Poverty," *American Psychologist* 59 (2004): 77–92.

4. Charles Mueller and Toby L. Parcel, "Measures of Socioeconomic Status: Alternatives and Recommendations," *Child Development* 52 (1981): 13–30.

5. For a discussion of differing approaches to measuring socioeconomic status, see Kenneth A. Bollen, Jennifer L. Glanville, and Guy Stecklov, "Socioeconomic Status and Class in Studies of Fertility and Health in Developing Countries," *Annual Review of Sociology* 27 (2001): 153–85; Robert Hauser and John Robert Warren, "Socioeconomic Indexes for Occupations: A Review, Update, and Critique," *Sociological Methodology* 27: 177–298.

6. Bollen, Glanville, and Stecklov, "Socioeconomic Status and Class" (see note 5).

7. Greg Duncan and Katherine A. Magnuson, "Off with Hollingshead: Socioeconomic Resources, Parenting, and Child Development," in *Socioeconomic Status, Parenting, and Child Development,* edited by Marc Bornstein and Robert Bradley (Mahwah, N.J.: Lawrence Erlbaum Associates, 2001), pp. 83–106.

8. We do not review the literature on the effects of occupation on young children primarily because the research is sparse and there are no clear interventions that directly target occupation.

9. Greg Duncan and Jeanne Brooks-Gunn, eds., *Consequences of Growing Up Poor* (New York: Russell Sage, 1997); Evans, "The Environment of Childhood Poverty" (see note 3); Katherine A. Magnuson and Greg Duncan, "Parents in Poverty," in *Handbook of Parenting,* edited by Marc Bornstein (Mahwah, N.J.: Lawrence Erlbaum Associates, 2002), pp. 95–121. Vonnie McLoyd, "Socioeconomic Disadvantage and Child Development," *American Psychologist* 53 (1998): 185–204.

10. Judith Smith, Jeanne Brooks-Gunn, and Pamela Klebanov, "The Consequences of Living in Poverty on Young Children's Cognitive Development," in *Consequences of Growing Up Poor,* edited by Greg Duncan and Jeanne Brooks-Gunn (New York: Russell Sage, 1997), pp. 132–89.

11. Duncan and Brooks Gunn, *Consequences of Growing Up Poor* (see note 9); Smith, Brooks-Gunn, and Klebanov, "The Consequences of Living in Poverty" (see note 10). See also Eric Dearing, Kathleen McCartney, and Beck A. Taylor, "Change in Family Income-to-Needs Matters More for Children with Less," *Child Development* 72 (2001): 1779–93; Greg Duncan and others, "How Much Does Childhood Poverty Affect the Life Chances of Children?" *American Sociological Review* 63 (1998): 406–23.

12. Smith, Brooks-Gunn, and Klebanov, "The Consequences of Living in Poverty" (see note 10).

13. Meredith Phillips and others, "Family Background, Parenting Practices, and the Black-White Test Score Gap," in *The Black-White Test Score Gap,* edited by Christopher Jencks and Meredith Phillips (Brookings, 1998).

14. Pamela A. Morris and others, *How Welfare and Work Policies Affect Children: A Synthesis of Research* (New York: Manpower Demonstration Research Corporation, 2001).

15. Krueger and Whitmore estimate that the one-fifth standard deviation increase in test scores from the Tennessee STAR class-size experiment could increase future earnings between $5,000 and $50,000, depending on assumed discount and future earnings growth rates. The .07 effect size, if permanent, would increase earnings by one-third of these amounts. See Alan Krueger and Diane Whitmore, "The Effect of Attending a Small Class in the Early Grades on College Test Taking and Middle School Test Results: Evidence from Project STAR," *Economic Journal* 11 (2001): 1–28.

16. James Heckman, Robert LaLonde, and Jeffrey Smith, "The Economics and Econometrics of Active Labor Market Programs," in *Handbook of Labor Economics*, edited by Orley Ashenfelter and David Card (New York: Elsevier, 1999), pp. 1865–2097.

17. Marcia K. Meyers and others, "Inequality in Early Childhood Education and Care: What Do We Know?" in *Social Inequality,* edited by Kathryn Neckerman (New York: Russell Sage Foundation, forthcoming).

18. U.S. House of Representatives, Committee on Ways and Means, *2004 Green Book* (http://waysandmeans. house.gov/Documents.asp?section=813 [April 26, 2004]).

19. Council of Economic Advisers, *Good News for Low Income Families: Expansions in the Earned Income Tax Credit and the Minimum Wage* (Washington, 1998).

20. Bruce Meyer and Dan T. Rosenbaum, "Welfare, the Earned Income Tax Credit and the Labor Supply of Single Mothers," *Quarterly Journal of Economics* 116 (2001): 1063–114.

21. Gary Becker, *A Treatise on the Family* (Harvard University Press, 1981).

22. David Card, "The Causal Effect of Education on Earnings," in *Handbook of Labor Economics*, vol. 3A, edited by Orley Ashenfelter and David Card (New York: Elsevier, 1999), pp. 1801–63.

23. Erika Hoff, "The Specificity of Environmental Influence: Socioeconomic Status Affects Early Vocabulary Development via Maternal Speech," *Child Development* 74 (2003): 1368–78; Luis Laosa, "Maternal Teaching Strategies in Chicano and Anglo-American Families: The Influence of Culture and Education on Maternal Behavior," *Child Development* 51 (1980): 759–65; Robert T. Michael, *The Effect of Education on Efficiency in Consumption* (Columbia University Press, 1972).

24. Four-year college degree attainment is from authors' calculations from the ECLS–K data. For more detailed information on maternal schooling, see http://nces.ed.gov/programs/coe/2003/section1/tables/t02_1a.asp [April 13, 2004].

25. Kiki Roe and Robin Bronstein, "Maternal Education and Cognitive Processing at Three Months as Shown by Infants' Vocal Response to Mother vs. Stranger," *International Journal of Behavioral Development* 11 (1988): 389–95.

26. Pamela Davis-Kean and Katherine Magnuson, "The Influence of Parental Education on Child Development," mimeo, University of Michigan, 2004; James A. Mercy and Lulu Steelman, "Familial Influence on Intellectual Attainment of Children," *American Sociological Review* 42 (1982): 532–42.

27. See Michelle Neiss and David C. Rowe, "Parental Education and Child's Verbal IQ in Adoptive and Biological Families in the National Longitudinal Study of Adolescent Health," *Behavior Genetics* 30 (2000):

487–95; Mark R. Rosenzweig and Kenneth I. Wolpin, "Are There Increasing Returns to Intergenerational Production of Human Capital? Maternal Schooling and Child Intellectual Development," *Journal of Human Resources* 29 (1994): 670–93. Studies using European data have been less conclusive; see Sandra E. Black, Paul J. Devereux, and Kjell G. Salvanes, "Why the Apple Doesn't Fall Far from the Tree," Working Paper 10066 (Cambridge, Mass.: National Bureau of Economic Research, 2004); Eric Plug, "Estimating the Effects of Mothers' Schooling on Children's Schooling Using a Sample of Adoptees," *American Economic Review* 94 (2003): 358–68. Many studies attempt to adjust for parent cognitive ability.

28. Robert Haveman and Barbara Wolfe, "The Determinants of Children's Attainments: A Review of Methods and Findings," *Journal of Economic Literature* 23 (1995): 1829–78; Katherine Magnuson, "The Effect of Increases in Maternal Education on Children's Academic Trajectories: Evidence from the NLSY," mimeo, Columbia University, 2004.

29. The National Evaluation of Welfare-to-Work Strategies Child Outcome Study (NEWWS COS). See Katherine Magnuson, "The Effect of Increases in Welfare Mothers' Education on Their Young Children's Academic and Behavioral Outcomes: Evidence from the National Evaluation of Welfare-to-Work Strategies Child Outcomes Study," Institute for Research on Poverty Discussion Paper (University of Wisconsin, 2003), pp. 1274–303.

30. Mark Dynarski, "Making Do with Less: Interpreting the Evidence from Recent Federal Evaluations of Dropout Prevention Programs," paper presented at the conference Dropouts: Implications and Findings, held at Harvard University, 2001.

31. Jodie Roth and Jeanne Brooks-Gunn, "Promoting Healthy Adolescents: Synthesis of Youth Development Program Evaluations," *Journal of Research on Adolescence* 8 (1998): 423–59; David L. Dubois and others, "Effectiveness of Mentoring Programs for Youth: A Meta-Analytic Review," *Journal of Community Psychology* 30 (2002): 157–97.

32. Frank F. Furstenberg, Jeanne Brooks-Gunn, and S. Philip Morgan, *Adolescent Mothers in Later Life* (Cambridge University Press, 1987); John M. Love and others, *Making a Difference in the Lives of Infants and Toddlers and Their Families: The Impacts of Early Head Start*, vol. 1, *Final Technical Report* (Princeton: Mathematica Policy Research, 2002).

33. Sharon M. McGroder and others, *National Evaluation of Welfare-to-work Strategies: Impacts on Young Children and Their Families Two Years after Enrollment: Findings from the Child Outcomes Study* (U.S. Department of Health and Human Services, Office of the Assistant Secretary for Planning and Evaluation, Administration for Children and Families, 2000); Janet C. Quint, Johannes M. Bos, and Denise F. Polit, *New Chance: Final Report on a Comprehensive Program for Young Mothers in Poverty and Their Children* (New York: Manpower Research Demonstration Corporation, 1997).

34. Susan Dynarski, "The Consequences of Lowering the Cost of College," *American Economic Review* 92 (2002): 279–85; Neil Sefter and Sarah Turner, "Back to School: Federal Student Aid Policy and Adult College Enrollment," *Journal of Human Resources* 37 (2002): 336–52; Sarah Turner and John Bound, "Closing the Gap or Widening the Divide? The Effects of the G.I. Bill and World War II on the Educational Outcomes of Black Americans," *Journal of Economic History* 63 (2003): 145–77.

35. Daron Acemoglu and Joshua Angrist, "How Large Are the Social Returns to Compulsory Schooling Effects? Evidence from Compulsory Schooling Laws," Working Paper 7444 (Cambridge, Mass.: National Bu-

reau of Economic Research, 1999); Philip Oreopoulus, Marianne Page, and Anne H. Stevens, "Does Human Capital Transfer from Parent to Child? The Intergenerational Effects of Compulsory Schooling," Working Paper 10164 (Cambridge, Mass.: National Bureau of Economic Research, 2003).

36. Sara McLanahan and Gary Sandefur, *Growing Up with a Single Parent: What Hurts, What Helps* (Harvard University Press, 1994).

37. U. S. Census Bureau. http://ferret.bls.census.gov/macro/032003/pov/new03_100_01.htm accessed April 26, 2004.

38. Paul R. Amato, "Children's Adjustment to Divorce: Theories, Hypotheses and Empirical Support," *Journal of Marriage and the Family* 55 (1993): 23–38; K. Alison Clarke-Stewart and others, "Effects of Parental Separation and Divorce on Very Young Children," *Journal of Family Psychology* 14 (2000): 304–26; Rebecca L. Coley, "Children's Socialization Experiences and Functioning in Single Mother Households: The Importance of Fathers and Other Men," *Child Development* 69 (1998): 219–30; Jane E. Miller and Diane Davis, "Poverty History, Marital History, and Quality of Children's Home Environments," *Journal of Marriage and the Family* 59 (1997): 996–1007.

39. Maureen Black, Howard Dubowitz, and Raymond H. Starr, "African American Fathers in Low Income, Urban Families: Development, Behavior, and Home Environment of Three-Year-Old Children," *Child Development* 70 (1999): 967–78; Coley, "Children's Socialization Experiences" (see note 38).

40. For data on all children, see www.childtrendsdatabank.org/tables/59_Table_1.htm [March 24, 2004].

41. McLanahan and Sandefur, *Growing Up with a Single Parent* (see note 36).

42. Sara McLanahan, "Parent Absence or Poverty: Which Matters More?" in *Consequences of Growing Up Poor,* edited by Greg Duncan and Jeanne Brooks-Gunn (New York: Russell Sage Foundation, 1997), pp. 35–48.

43. Marcia J. Carlson and Mary E. Corcoran, "Family Structure and Children's Behavioral and Cognitive Outcomes," *Journal of Marriage and the Family* 63 (2001): 779–92; Elizabeth Cooksey, "Consequences of Young Mothers' Marital Histories for Children's Cognitive Development," *Journal of Marriage and the Family* 59 (1997): 245–61; McLanahan, "Parent Absence or Poverty" (see note 42); Thomas DeLeire and Ariel Kalil, "Good Things Come in 3's: Multigenerational Coresidence and Adolescent Adjustment," *Demography* 39 (2002): 393–413.

44. Stephanie J. Ventura, T. J. Mathews, and Brady E. Hamilton, "Teenage Births in the United States: State Trends, 1991–2000, an Update," *National Vital Statistics Reports* 50 (2002): 1–2.

45. Rebecca L. Coley and P. Lindsay Chase-Lansdale, "Adolescent Pregnancy and Parenthood: Recent Evidence and Future Directions," *American Psychologist* 53 (1998): 152–66.

46. Carlson and Corcoran, "Family Structure and Children's Behavioral and Cognitive Outcomes" (see note 43); Clarke-Stewart and others, "Effects of Parental Separation and Divorce" (see note 38).

47. Thomas G. O'Connor and others, "Are Associations between Parental Divorce and Children's Adjustment Genetically Mediated? An Adoption Study," *Developmental Psychology* 36 (2000): 429–37.

48. Sara Jaffee and others, "Why Are Children Born to Teen Mothers at Risk for Adverse Outcomes in Young Adulthood? Results from a 20-Year Longitudinal Study," *Development and Psychopathology* 13 (2001):

377–97; Judith A. Levine, Harold Pollack, and Maureen Comfort, "Academic and Behavioral Outcomes among Children of Young Mothers," *Journal of Marriage and the Family* 63 (2001): 355–69; Ruth N. L. Turley, "Are Children of Young Mothers Disadvantaged Because of Their Mother's Age or Family Background?" *Child Development* 74 (2003): 465–74.

49. O'Connor and others, "Are Associations between Parental Divorce and Children's Adjustment Genetically Mediated?" (see note 47).

50. Jaffee and others, "Why Are Children Born to Teen Mothers at Risk" (see note 48); Wendy Sigle-Rushton and Sara McLanahan, "For Richer or Poorer: Marriage as an Anti-Poverty Strategy in the United States," Working Paper 01–17–FF (Princeton University, Center for Research on Child Wellbeing, 2003).

51. M. Robin Dion and others, "Helping Unwed Parents Build Strong and Healthy Marriages: A Conceptual Framework for Interventions" (Princeton: Mathematica Policy Research, 2002).

52. Sigle-Rushton and McLanahan, "For Richer or Poorer" (see note 50).

53. Douglas Kirby, *Emerging Answers: Research Findings on Programs to Reduce Teen Pregnancy* (Washington: National Campaign to Prevent Teen Pregnancy, 2001).

54. Coley and Chase-Lansdale, "Adolescent Pregnancy and Parenthood" (see note 45); Andrea Kane and Isabel V. Sawhill, "Preventing Teen Childbearing" in *One Percent for the Kids,* edited by Sawhill (Brookings, 2003), pp. 56–75.

55. Coley and Chase-Lansdale, "Adolescent Pregnancy and Parenthood" (see note 45).

56. Jeanne Brooks-Gunn, Greg J. Duncan, and J. Lawrence Aber, *Neighborhood Poverty: Context and Consequences for Children,* vols. 1 and 2 (New York: Russell Sage, 1997).

57. Robin Jarrett, "African American Family and Parenting Strategies in Impoverished Neighborhoods," *Qualitative Sociology* 20 (1997): 275–88.

58. Christopher Jencks and Susan Mayer, "The Social Consequences of Growing Up in a Poor Neighborhood," in *Inner-City Poverty in the United States,* edited by Laurence E. Lynn and Michael G. H. McGeary (Washington: National Academy Press., 1990), pp. 111–86; Robert J. Sampson, Jeffrey D. Morenoff, and Thomas Ganon-Rowley, "Assessing Neighborhood Effects: Social Processes and New Directions in Research," *Annual Review of Sociology* 94 (2002): 774–80.

59. Tama Leventhal and Jeanne Brooks-Gunn, "The Neighborhoods They Live In: The Effects of Neighborhood Residence on Child and Adolescent Outcomes," *Psychological Bulletin* 126 (2000): 309–37.

60. Larry Orr and others, *Moving to Opportunity Interim Impacts Evaluation* (U.S. Department of Housing and Urban Development, Office of Policy Development and Research, 2003), pp. 1–178; Lisa Sanbonmatsu and others, "Neighborhoods and Academic Achievement: Results from the Moving to Opportunity Experiment," Industrial Relations Section Working Paper (Princeton University, 2004).

61. Sanbonmatsu and others, "Neighborhoods and Academic Achievement" (see note 60).

62. Orr and others, *Moving to Opportunity* (see note 60); Jeffrey Kling and others, "Moving to Opportunity and Tranquility: Neighborhood Effects on Adult Economic Self-Sufficiency and Health from a Randomized Housing Voucher Experiment," Industrial Relations Section Working Paper (Princeton University, 2004).

63. Whereas all of the accounting studies do a good job of measuring family components of SES, few measure neighborhood conditions very well. An exception is Phillips and others, "Family Background, Parenting Practices, and the Black-White Test Score Gap" (see note 13), whose look at racial gaps at age five includes an assessment of the role of conditions in the neighborhoods in which the children are raised. While they find considerable racial differences in neighborhood conditions, these appear inconsequential for the racial gap. This is not surprising, given that a general finding from the neighborhood effects literature is that neighborhood conditions add little to the explanation of child outcomes once family conditions are taken into account; see Brooks-Gunn, Duncan, and Aber, *Neighborhood Poverty* (see note 56). In the accounting exercises, this translates into the finding that racial differences in neighborhood conditions account for little of the gap, once racial differences in family conditions are taken into account.

64. Ronald Fryer and Steven D. Levitt, "Understanding the Black-White Test Score Gap in the First Two Years of School," *Review of Economics and Statistics* 86 (2004): 447–64.

65. Using the same data, other scholars have reached similar conclusions. See Valerie Lee and David Burkam, *Inequality at the Starting Gate: Social Background Differences in Achievement as Children Begin School* (Washington: Economic Policy Institute, 2002).

66. Phillips and others, "Family Background, Parenting Practices, and the Black-White Test Score Gap" (see note 13).

67. Jeanne Brooks-Gunn and others, "The Black-White Test Score Gap in Young Children: Contributions of Test and Family Characteristics," *Applied Developmental Science* 7 (2003): 239–52.

68. Greg Duncan and Katherine Magnuson, "Promoting the Healthy Development of Young Children," in *One Percent for the Kids*, edited by Isabel Sawhill (Brookings, 2003), pp. 16–39.

Genetic Differences and School Readiness

William T. Dickens

The author considers whether differences in genetic endowment may account for racial and ethnic differences in school readiness. While acknowledging an important role for genes in explaining differences *within* races, he nevertheless argues that environment explains most of the gap *between* blacks and whites, leaving little role for genetics.

Based on a wide range of direct and indirect evidence, particularly work by Klaus Eyferth and James Flynn, the author concludes that the black-white gap is not substantially genetic in orgin. In studies in 1959 and 1961, Eyferth first pointed to the near-disappearance of the black-white gap among children of black and white servicemen raised by German mothers after World War II. In the author's view, Flynn's exhaustive 1980 analysis of Eyferth's work provides close to definitive evidence that the black disadvantage is not genetic to any important degree.

But even studies showing an important role for genes in explaining within-group differences, he says, do not rule out the possibility of improving the school performance of disadvantaged children through interventions aimed at improving their school readiness. Such interventions, he argues, should stand or fall on their own costs and benefits. And behavioral genetics offers some lessons in designing and evaluating interventions. Because normal differences in preschool resources or parenting practices in working- and middle-class families have only limited effects on school readiness, interventions can have large effects only if they significantly change the allocation of resources or the nature of parenting practices.

The effects of most interventions on cognitive ability resemble the effect of exercise on physical conditioning: they are profound but short-lived. But if interventions make even small permanent changes in behavior that support improved cognitive ability, they can set off multiplier processes, with improved ability leading to more stimulating environments and still further improvements in ability. The best interventions, argues the author, would saturate a social group and reinforce individual multiplier effects by social multipliers and feedback effects. The aim of preschool programs, for example, should be to get students to continue to seek out the cognitive stimulation the program provides even after it ends.

www.future of children.org

William T. Dickens is a senior fellow in the Brookings Economic Studies program. He acknowledges the excellent research assistance of Rebecca Vichniac and Jennifer Doleac.

In national tests of school readiness, black preschoolers in the United States are not doing as well as white preschoolers. Researchers find black-white gaps not only in achievement and cognitive tests, but also in measures of readiness-related behaviors such as impulse control and ability to pay attention. Could some of these differences in school readiness be the consequence of differences in genetic endowment? In what follows I will review research evidence on this question.[1]

Evidence on the Role of Genetic Differences

To evaluate the research findings on the role of genetic differences in cognitive ability, I begin by drawing a clear distinction between evidence that genetic endowment explains a large fraction of differences *within* races and evidence that it explains differences *between* races and ethnic groups. There can be little doubt that genetic differences are an important determinant of differences in academic achievement within racial and ethnic groups, though the size of that effect is not known precisely. Depending on the measure of achievement used, the sample studied, and the age of the subjects, estimates of the share of variance explained by genetic differences within racial and ethnic groups range from as low as 20 percent to upward of 75 percent. However, most estimates, particularly those for younger children, seem to cluster in the range of 30 to 40 percent. The fraction of variance explained by genetic differences in a population is termed the *heritability* of the trait for that population.[2]

But the heritability of academic achievement *within* racial or ethnic groups says little about whether genes play a role in explaining differences between racial groups. Suppose one scatters a handful of genetically diverse seed

corn in a field in Iowa and another in the Mojave Desert. Nearly all the variance in size within each group of seedlings could be due to genetic differences between the plants, but the difference between the average for those growing in the Mojave and those growing in Iowa would be almost entirely due to their different environments.

If researchers were able to identify all the genes that cause individual differences in school readiness, understand the mechanism by which they affect readiness and the magnitude of those effects, and assess the relative frequency of those genes in the black and white populations, they would know precisely the extent to which genetic differences explain the black-white gap. But only a few genes that influence cognitive ability or other behaviors relevant to school readiness have been tentatively identified, and nothing is known about their frequency in different populations. Nor are such discoveries imminent. Although genetic effects on several different learning and school-related behavior disorders have been identified and many aspects of personality are known to have a genetic component, genes have their primary effect on school readiness through their effect on cognitive ability.[3] Experts believe that a hundred or more genes are responsible for individual differences in cognitive ability. Many of these genes are likely to have weak and indirect effects that will be difficult to detect. It could be decades before enough genes are identified, and their frequencies estimated, to make it possible to determine what role, if any, they play in explaining group differences.

So it is necessary to turn to less direct ways of answering the question. Much has been written on this topic in the past fifty years. James Flynn's *Race, IQ, and Jensen*, published in 1980, remains the most thoughtful and thor-

Clearing Up a Confusion

It is difficult to discuss genetic causation of the black-white test score gap. The reason, I believe, is that people confuse genetic causation with intractability. Suppose that the entire black-white gap in school readiness were genetic in origin, but that a shot could be given to black babies at birth to offset completely the effects of the genetic difference. Would anyone care about the genetic component of the racial gap? If it is possible to remedy or ameliorate the black-white difference, the only question is how much it would cost and whether society is willing to pay the price. As this article explains, genetic causation is nearly irrelevant to the question of how malleable a trait is.

Some argue that a genetic cause for black-white differences would lessen the moral imperative for removing them, but as the example of the shot illustrates, this is not the case. It would be hard to argue that the fact that the differences were genetic rather than environmental in origin would make it any less of an imperative for society to be sure that every black child got the shot. Some would say that the fact that the cause is beyond the child's control would make it more important. Jessica L. Cohen and I have made this argument in more detail in "Instinct and Choice: A Framework for Analysis," in *Nature and Nurture: The Complex Interplay of Genetic and Environmental Influences on Human Behavior and Development*, edited by Cynthia Garcia Coll, Elaine L. Bearer, and Richard Lerner (Hillsdale, N.J.: Lawrence Erlbaum and Associates, 2003), pp. 145–70.

ough treatment available.[4] More recently Richard Nisbett wrote a shorter review of this literature.[5] Both Flynn and Nisbett take the view, as do I, that genetic differences probably do not play an important role in explaining differences between the races, but the point remains controversial, and Arthur Jensen provides a recent discussion from a hereditarian perspective.[6] Here I will review the major types of evidence and explain why I think they suggest that environmental differences likely explain most, if not all, of the black-white gap in school readiness. I will concentrate entirely on the evidence on cognitive ability, as it is the most studied trait that influences school readiness, and genetically induced differences in cognitive ability account for the vast majority of genetically induced differences in school readiness within ethnic groups. Almost no studies have been done of racial differences in other traits

that might influence school readiness. And I choose to focus on the black-white gap rather than to consider the role of genetic differences in determining the academic readiness of disadvantaged groups more generally, again, because it is a topic that has been more thoroughly studied.

Direct Evidence on the Role of Genes: European Ancestry and Cognitive Ability

Blacks in the United States have widely varying degrees of African and European ancestry. If their genetic endowment from their African ancestors is, on average, inferior to that from their European ancestors, then their cognitive ability would be expected to vary directly in proportion to the extent of their European ancestry. Some early attempts to assess this hypothesis linked skin color with test scores and found that lighter-skinned blacks typically had higher scores. But skin color is not strongly related to degree of European ancestry, while socioeconomic status clearly is. Thus the differences might reflect environmental rather than genetic causes. Nearly all commentators agree that these early studies are not probative.

More recent studies have looked at measures of European ancestry, such as blood groups or reported ancestry, that are not visible. Such studies have found little or no correlation between the measure of ancestry and cognitive ability, though all are subject to methodological criticisms that could explain their failure to find such a link. Thus although these studies do not provide evidence for a role for genes in explaining black-white differences, they do not provide strong evidence against it.

Direct Evidence on the Role of Environment: Adoption and Cross-Fostering

If there is no direct evidence of a role for genes in explaining the black-white gap, perhaps there is direct evidence that environment can or cannot account for the whole difference between blacks and whites. Several studies have shown that environmental differences between blacks and whites can, in a statistical sense, "explain" nearly all of the difference in cognitive ability between black and white children.[7] But because the studies do not completely control for the genetic endowment of either the child or the parents and because many of the variables used to explain the difference are themselves subject to genetic influence, the effect being attributed to environment may in reality be due to genetic differences.

What is needed is a way to see the effect of environment without confusing it with the ef-

fect of genetic endowment. For example, randomly choosing white and black children at birth and assigning them to be fostered in either black or white families would ensure that the children's environments were not correlated with their genetic potential and would show how much difference environment makes. No existing study replicates the conditions of this experiment exactly, but some come close. The strongest evidence for both the environmentalist and hereditarian perspectives is of this sort.

After the end of World War II both black and white soldiers in the occupying armies in Germany fathered children with white German women. Klaus Eyferth gathered data on a large number of these children, of mainly working-class mothers, and gave the children intelligence tests.[8] He found almost no difference between the children of white fathers and those of black fathers. The finding is remarkable given that the black children faced a somewhat more hostile environment than the white children. Hereditarians have challenged these findings by appealing to the possibility that the black soldiers who fathered these children might have been a particularly elite group. Flynn has researched the plausibility of this explanation and concludes that such selection did not play more than a small role.[9] Thus Eyferth's study suggests that the black-white gap is largely, and possibly entirely, environmental.

A study similar to Eyferth's found the cognitive ability of black children raised in an orphanage in England to be slightly higher than that of white children raised there.[10] Again, critics have raised the possibility that the black children were genetically advantaged relative to other blacks, and the whites disadvantaged relative to other whites. And again, Flynn finds it unlikely that this contention explains much of the disappearance of the black-white gap.[11] This study, too, suggests that the black-white gap is mainly environmental.

If the black-white gap is mainly genetic in origin, children's cognitive ability should not depend on the race of their primary caregiver, comparing those of the same race. Yet two studies comparing the experience of black children raised by black or white mothers suggest that it does.[12] Here too, because the children were not randomly assigned to their caregivers, it is possible that the children raised by black mothers were of lower genetic potential, but it would be hard to make such a selection story explain more than a small fraction of the apparent environmental effect.

Another transracial adoption study provides mixed evidence, but some of the strongest that genes play a role in explaining the black-white gap.[13] A group of children, some with two black parents and some with one white and one black parent, were raised in white middle-class families. When the children's cognitive ability was tested at age seven, the children with two black parents scored 95, higher than the average black child in the state (89) and only slightly below the national average for whites, while the mixed-race children scored 110, which was considerably above it.[14] On the one hand, this finding suggests a huge effect of environment on the cognitive ability of the adopted black and mixed-race children. On the other hand, the higher scores of the mixed-race children suggest that parents' genes may account for some of the difference from the black children, and that the mixed-race children may have had a better inheritance by virtue of having one white parent. Both black and mixed-race children scored worse than the biological children of their adoptive parents

(who scored 116), an expected finding because the adopting parents were an elite group and likely passed on above-average genetic potential to their children. But they also scored considerably below the average of 118 for comparison white children adopted into similar homes.

When the same children were retested ten years later, the results were different.[15] The

The disappearance of the salutary effect of the adoptive home, however, does not mean that genes determine black-white differences.

scores of the children with two black parents had dropped to about the average for blacks in the state where they lived before they were adopted (89). The scores of the mixed-race children had dropped too (99), but remained intermediate between those of the children with two black parents and those of the adoptive parents' biological children, which had also declined, to 109. The scores of the white children raised in adoptive homes had dropped the most, falling to 106.

The disappearance of the salutary effect of the adoptive home, however, does not mean that genes determine black-white differences. We can assume that as the children aged and moved out into the world, the effect of the home environment diminished, and both whites and blacks tended to the average for their own population because of either genetic or environmental effects. By showing how the effect of a child's home environment disappears by adolescence, this study suggests that environmental disadvantages experienced by blacks as children cannot explain the deficit in their cognitive ability as adolescents and adults. But environmental disadvantages facing black adolescents and adults could still explain those deficits. The transience of environmental effects on cognitive ability is a theme to which I shall return. The persistence of the advantage of the mixed-race children over the children with two black parents is suggestive of a role for genes. It is not, though, definitive: several other explanations have been offered, including the late adoption of the children with two black parents and parental selection effects unrelated to race.[16]

Indirect Evidence on the Role of Genetic Differences

Although the direct evidence on the role of environment is not definitive, it mostly suggests that genetic differences are not necessary to explain racial differences. Advocates of the hereditarian position have therefore turned to indirect evidence.[17]

Several authors have argued that estimates of the heritability of cognitive ability put limits on the plausible role of environment.[18] The argument is normally made in a mathematical form, but it boils down to this. First, it is now widely accepted that differences in genetic endowment explain at least 60 percent of the variance in cognitive ability among adults in the white population in the United States.[19] If all the environmental variation among U.S. whites can explain only 40 percent of the variance among whites, how could environmental differences explain the huge gap between blacks and whites? The mathematical argument implies that the average black environment would have to be worse than at least 95 percent of white environments, but observable characteristics of blacks and whites are

not that different. For example, black deficits in education or in socioeconomic status place the average black below only about 60 to 70 percent of whites.[20]

The heritability of cognitive ability is also crucial to a second type of indirect evidence for a role of genetic differences in explaining the black-white gap. Arthur Jensen has advanced what he calls "Spearman's Hypothesis," after the late intelligence researcher Charles Spearman, who observed that people who had large vocabularies were good at solving mazes and logic problems and were also more likely to have command of a wide range of facts. Spearman posited that a single, largely genetic, mental ability that he called g (for general mental ability) explained the correlation of people's performance across a wide range of tests of mental ability. Researchers now know that a single underlying ability cannot explain all the tendency of people who do well on one type of test to do well on another.[21] But it is possible to interpret the evidence as indicating that there is a single ability that differs among people, that is subject to genetic influence, and that explains much of the correlation across tests. Other interpretations are also possible, but this one cannot be discounted. In a series of studies Jensen and Rushton have argued that different types of tests tap this general ability to different degrees; that the more a test taps g, the more it is subject to genetic influence; and that black-white differences are largest on the tests most reflective of the underlying general ability, g.[22]

Using several restrictive assumptions about the nature of genetic and environmental influence on genetic ability, researchers can use this information to estimate the fraction of the black-white gap that is due to differences in genetic endowment. The more the pattern of black-white differences across different tests resembles the pattern of genetic influence on different tests, the more the statistical procedure will attribute the black-white differences to genetic differences. Using this method, David Rowe and Jensen have independently estimated that from one-half to two-thirds of the black-white gap is genetic in origin.[23]

A Problem for the Indirect Arguments: Gains in Cognitive Ability over Time

Over the past century, dozens of countries around the world have seen increases in measured cognitive ability over time as large as or even larger than the black-white gap.[24] The phenomenon has been christened the "Flynn Effect," after James Flynn, who did the most to investigate and popularize this worldwide trend. The score gains have been documented even between a large group of fathers and sons taking the same test only decades apart, making it impossible that the gains are due to changes in genes. Clearly environmental changes can cause huge leaps in measured cognitive ability. Although it might not seem plausible that the average black environment today is below the 5th percentile of the white distribution of environments, it is certainly plausible that the average black environment in the United States today is as deprived as the average white environment of thirty to fifty years ago—the time it took for cognitive ability to rise by an amount equal to the black-white gap in many countries. These gains in measured cognitive ability over time point to a problem in the argument that high heritability estimates for cognitive ability preclude large environmental effects.

Gains in cognitive ability over time also challenge the logic of Jensen's genetic explanation for the pattern of black-white differ-

ences across different types of tests. All studies show that gains on different tests are positively correlated with measures of test score heritability, and most studies show that gains are positively correlated with the extent to which a test taps the hypothesized general cognitive ability.[25] There is little doubt that applying the same method as Rowe and Jensen used to data on gains in cognitive ability over time would show them to be partially genetic in origin, something we know cannot be true.

So, what is it that is wrong with the logic of these two arguments, that the high heritability of cognitive ability limits the possible effect of the environment and that the pattern of black-white differences across different tests shows those differences to be genetic in origin? And in particular, where is the problem in the first?

It is important to detect the flaw, because if the logic of the argument were sound, the case for environmental causes of black-white differences would be difficult to make, and the possibility of remedying those differences would be remote. But before I explain, I want to cite two other pieces of evidence marshaled by advocates of the hereditarian position that suggest the limited power of the environment to change cognitive ability (and therefore to explain the entire black-white gap). The first is that the heritability of cognitive ability rises with age. It does so at the expense of the effect of family environment, which disappears nearly completely in most studies of late adolescents and adults.[26] The disappearance of the effect on black children of being raised in white families, which I have already noted, is just one case of a general finding from several different types of studies. A second piece of evidence is the fade-out of the effect of preschool programs on cognitive ability. Although such programs have been shown to have profound effects on the measured ability of children, the effects fade once the programs end, leaving little evidence of any effect by adolescence.[27] Is it possible to reconcile the high heritability of cognitive ability with large, but transient, environmental effects?

The Interplay of Genes and the Environment

To explain this puzzle, James Flynn and I have proposed a formal model in which genes and environment work together, rather than independently, in developing a person's cognitive ability.[28] The solution involves three aspects of the process by which individual ability is molded that are overlooked by the logic that implies small environmental effects. We illustrate our argument with a basketball analogy.

How can genes and environment both be powerful in shaping ability? Consider a young man with a small genetic predisposition toward greater height and faster reflexes. When he is young, he is likely to be slightly better than his playmates at basketball. His reflexes will make him generally better at sports, and his height will be a particular advantage when it comes to passing, catching, and rebounding. These advantages by themselves confer only a small edge, but they may be enough to make the game more rewarding for him than for the average person and get him to play more than his friends and to improve his play more over time. After a while, he will be considerably better than the average player his age, making it likely that he will be picked first for teams and perhaps receive more attention from gym teachers. Eventually, he joins a school team where he gets exhaustive practice and professional coaching. His basketball ability is now far su-

perior to that of his old playmates. Through a series of feedback loops, his initial minor physical advantage has been multiplied into a huge overall advantage. In contrast, a child who started life with a predisposition to be pudgy, slow, and small would be very unlikely to enjoy playing basketball, get much practice, or receive coaching. He would therefore be unlikely to improve his skills. Assuming children with a range of experience between these two extremes, scientists would find that a large fraction of the variance of basketball playing ability would be explained by differences in genetic endowment—that basketball ability was highly heritable. And they would be right to do so. But that most certainly would not mean that short kids without lightning reflexes could not improve their basketball skills enormously with practice and coaching.

The basketball analogy so far illustrates two of the considerations that Flynn and I believe are important for understanding the implications of behavioral genetic studies of cognitive ability. First, genes tend to get *matched* to complimentary environments. When that happens, some of the power of environment is attributed to genes. Only effects of environment shared by all children in the same family and effects of environment uncorrelated with genes get counted as environmental. Second, the effect of genetic differences gets *multiplied* by positive feedback loops. Small initial differences are multiplied by processes where people's initially varying abilities are matched to complimentary environments that cause their abilities to diverge further.

In theory this same multiplier process could be driven by small environmental differences. But to drive the multiplier to its maximum, the environmental advantage would have to be as constant over time as the genetic difference, because in the absence of the initial advantage there will be a tendency for the whole process to unwind. For example, suppose that midway through high school the basketball enthusiast injures a leg, which makes him less steady and offsets his initial advantage in height and reflexes. Because of all his practice and learning, he will still be a superior player. But his small decrement in performance could mean discouragement, more bench time, or not making the cut for the varsity team. This could lead to a further deterioration of his skills and further discouragement, until he gives up playing on the team entirely. Although each individual's experience will differ, the theory that Flynn and I lay out would have people with average physical potential reverting to average ability over time, on average.

The transitory nature of most environmental effects not driven by genetic differences helps explain why environmental differences do not typically drive large multipliers and produce the same large effects as genetic differences. That same transience helps explain why environment can be potent but still cause a relatively small share of the variance of cognitive ability in adults.[29]

Social Multipliers and the Effect of Averaging

If most external environmental influences are transitory and transitory environmental effects are unable to drive multipliers, what explains the large gains in cognitive ability over the past century? That question has two answers. One is the social multiplier process. The other is that many random transient environmental effects that lean in one direction when *averaged* together can substitute for a single persistent environmental cause. This is the third point missed by the argument that

claims that high heritability implies small environmental effects.

Another basketball analogy will help explain social multipliers. During the 1950s television entered many U.S. homes. Professional basketball, with its small arena, could not reach as wide an audience as baseball, but basketball translated much better to the small screen. Thus public interest in basketball began to grow. The increased interest made it easier for enthusiasts to find others to play with, thus increasing the opportunities to improve skills. As skills improved, standards of play rose, with players learning moves and skills from each other. As more people played and watched the game, interest increased still further. More resources were devoted to coaching basketball and developing basketball programs, providing yet more opportunities for players to improve their skills. In the end, the small impetus provided by the introduction of television had a huge impact on basketball skills.

A similar process may well be at work for cognitive ability. An outpouring of studies in recent years suggests that social effects have an important influence on school performance.[30] One study of an experimental reduction in school class size resulting in major achievement score gains suggests that a very large fraction of the gains came through the children's extended association with their peers, who shared the experience of small class sizes.[31] In this case an arguably minor intervention had large and long-lasting effects largely owing to a social multiplier effect.

But improvements in cognitive ability could have many triggers, rather than a single one. Many such triggers over the past half-century averaged together could be acting to raise cognitive ability. Increasing cognitive demands from more professional, technical, and managerial jobs; increased leisure time; changing cognitive demands of personal interactions; or changing attitudes toward intellectual activity could all be playing a role. And small initial changes along any of these dimensions would be magnified by individual and social multipliers.

Genes *and* Environment and the Black-White Gap

The black-white gap in measured cognitive ability may come about in a similar way, but it could have even more triggers. Segregation and discrimination have caused many aspects of blacks' environment to be inferior to that of whites. Averaged together, the total impact can be large, even if each individual effect is small. Suppose, for example, that environment relevant to the formation of cognitive ability consists of 100 factors, each with an equal effect. If for each of these 100 factors the average black were worse off than 65 percent of whites, he would be worse off than 90 percent of whites when the effects of all the environmental factors were considered together. (The disparity is the necessary result of accumulating a large number of effects when two groups have slightly different means for all the effects.)[32] Taking the total effect of environment in this way, considering the underestimate of the total effect of environment because some of its power is attributed to genes, and considering individual and social multipliers, a purely environmental explanation for black-white differences becomes plausible despite high estimates for the heritability of cognitive ability.

Moreover, our model also has explanations for the correlation of the heritability of scores on different tests with the size of the black-white gap on those tests and the anomalous correlation of the size of gains in cognitive ability over time on different tests with the heritability of those test scores. Those cognitive abilities for which multiplier processes are most important will be the ones that show the largest heritability, because of the environmental augmentation of the genetic differences. But they will also be the ones on which a persistent change in environment will have the biggest influence. Thus we might expect that persistent environmental differences between blacks and whites, as well as between generations, could cause a positive correlation between test score heritabilities and test differences.[33] Rushton and Jensen's indirect evidence of a genetic role in black-white differences is, therefore, not probative.

Implications and Conclusions

The indirect evidence on the role of genes in explaining the black-white gap does not tell us how much of the gap genes explain and may be of no value at all in deciding whether genes do play a role. Because the direct evidence on ancestry, adoption, and cross-fostering is most consistent with little or no role for genes, it is unlikely that the black-white gap has a large genetic component.

But what if it does? What would be the implications for the school readiness of children? Much of the variance in human behavior, including cognitive ability and achievement test scores, can be traced to differences in individuals' genetic endowments. But as indisputable as is the role of genes in shaping differences in outcomes within races, so is the role of environment. Studies of young children show that environmental differences explain more variation than do genetic differences. And even studies showing an important role for genes in no way rule out the possibility of improving the school performance of disadvantaged children through interventions aimed at enhancing their school readiness. Interventions should stand or fall on their own costs and benefits and not be prejudged on the basis of genetic pessimism.

In fact, studies of the role of genes and environment in determining school readiness offer some useful lessons in designing and evaluating interventions. These studies show that normally occurring differences in preschool resources or parenting practices in working- and middle-class families have only limited effects on school readiness once the correlation due to parents' and children's genes is taken out of play.[34] Thus small interventions that make only modest changes in the allocation of resources or the nature of parenting practices will have limited to modest effects at best. Effects will likely be somewhat larger if interventions target very disadvantaged families, probably because the room for improvement is greater.[35]

Achieving permanent effects on cognitive ability is harder than achieving large effects. Most environmental effects on cognitive ability seem to be like the effect of exercise on physical conditioning: profound but short-lived. But even short-lived improvements in cognitive ability can be valuable if they mediate longer-term changes in achievement—for example, if improved cognitive ability for some period of time allows students to learn to read more quickly, putting them on a permanently higher achievement path. And evidence suggests that programs aimed at improving cognitive ability do have long-term effects on achievement even if they have no significant long-term effects on cognitive ability. However, if interventions make even

small permanent changes in behavior that support improved cognitive ability, they can set off multiplier processes, with improved ability leading to better environments and still further improvements in ability. If we knew what aspects of preschool programs help elevate cognitive ability, and if we could get children to continue to seek out such stimulation after they leave preschool programs, their increased ability could lead them to associate with more able peers, to have the confidence to take on more demanding academic challenges, and to get the further advantage of yet more positive stimulation from these activities. This, in turn, could further develop their cognitive ability. Long-lived effects are more likely to be large effects.

Effects are particularly likely to be large if an intervention saturates a social group and allows the individual multiplier effects to be reinforced by social multipliers or feedback effects. If students find themselves among others with greater ability, individual interactions and group activities are more likely to give rise to further improvements in cognitive ability. In this same vein, evaluations that do not take into account the social effects of the intervention on children who did not directly take part may be missing an important aspect of the effects of an intervention.

Although much of normal environmentally induced variance in cognitive ability seems to be transient, if interventions could induce even small long-lasting changes in behavior, they might produce very large effects through the multiplier process. Taking advantage of such processes may make it possible to overcome the black-white gap and put black and white children on an even footing.

Endnotes

1. The review necessarily highlights only the most important studies; a complete review of all the arguments on both sides of this debate would require hundreds of pages and be beyond the scope of this article.

2. Heritability is estimated by examining the similarity of people with different degrees of genetic similarity raised in similar sorts of environments, and there is some reason to believe that most estimates are somewhat overstated by existing methods. Robert Plomin and others, *Behavioral Genetics*, 4th ed. (New York: Worth Publishers, 2001), in chapter 5 and the appendix, provide a thorough discussion of the methods used to estimate heritability. Mike Stoolmiller, "Implications of the Restricted Range of Family Environments for Estimates of Heritability and Nonshared Environment in Behavior-Genetic Adoption Studies," *Psychological Bulletin* 125 (1999): 392–409, shows that adoption studies probably overstate the degree of heritability and speculates on reasons why some other methods may as well.

3. Robert Plomin and others, *Behavioral Genetics* (see note 2), examine learning disorders on pp. 145–49, ADHD on pp. 227–29, and personality in chapter 12. For the effects of genes on cognitive ability, see Marcie L. Chambers and others, "Variation in Academic Achievement and IQ in Twin Pairs," *Intelligence* (forthcoming); Lee Anne Thompson and others, "Associations between Cognitive Abilities and Scholastic Achievement: Genetic Overlap but Environmental Differences," *Psychological Science* 2 (1991): 158–65; and Sally J. Wadsworth, "School Achievement," in *Nature and Nurture during Middle Childhood*, edited by John C. DeFries, Robert Plomin, and David W. Fulker (Oxford: Blackwell, 1994), pp. 86–101.

4. James R. Flynn, *Race, IQ, and Jensen* (London: Routledge, 1980).

5. Richard Nisbett, "Race, Genetics, and IQ," in *The Black-White Test Score Gap*, edited by Christopher Jencks and Meredith Phillips (Brookings, 1998), pp. 86–102.

6. Arthur Jensen, *The g Factor* (Westport, Conn.: Praeger, 1998), pp 350–531.

7. Jane R. Mercer, "What Is a Racially and Culturally Nondiscriminatory Test? A Sociological and Pluralistic Perspective," in *Perspectives on "Bias in Mental Testing,"* edited by Cecil R. Reynolds and Robert T. Brown (New York: Plenum Press, 1984); Jonathan Crane, "Race and Children's Cognitive Test Scores: Empirical Evidence That Environment Explains the Entire Gap," mimeo, University of Illinois at Chicago, 1994; and Jeanne Brooks-Gunn and others, "Ethnic Differences in Children's Intelligence Test Scores: Role of Economic Deprivation, Home Environment, and Maternal Characteristics," *Child Development* 67, no. 2 (1996): 396–408.

8. This is based on the account by James R. Flynn (*Race, IQ, and Jensen*, pp. 84–87; see note 4) of Klaus Eyferth, "Leistungen verschiedener Gruppen von Besatzungskindern in Hamburg-Wechsler Intelligenztest fur Kinder (HAWIK)," *Archiv fur die gesamte Psychologie* 113 (1961): 222–41.

9. Flynn, *Race, IQ, and Jensen*, pp. 84–102 (see note 4).

10. Barbara Tizard, "IQ and Race," *Nature* 247, no. 5439 (February 1, 1974).

11. Flynn, *Race, IQ, and Jensen*, pp. 108–11 (see note 4).

12. Elsie G. J. Moore, "Family Socialization and the IQ Test Performance of Traditionally and Transracially Adopted Black Children," *Developmental Psychology* 22 (1986): 317–26; and Lee Willerman and others, "Intellectual Development of Children from Interracial Matings: Performance in Infancy and at 4 Years," *Behavioral Genetics* 4 (1974): 84–88.

13. Sandra Scarr and Richard A. Weinberg, "IQ Test Performance of Black Children Adopted by White Families," *American Psychologist* 31 (1976): 726–39; and Sandra Scarr and Richard A. Weinberg, "The Minnesota Adoption Studies: Genetic Differences and Malleability," *Child Development* 54 (1983): 260–67.

14. These are IQ scores, which have a mean of 100 and a standard deviation of 15 in the U.S. population.

15. Sandra Scarr and others, "The Minnesota Transracial Adoption Study: A Follow-Up of IQ Test Performance at Adolescence," *Intelligence* 16 (1992): 117–35.

16. But see Arthur Jensen, *The g Factor*, pp. 477–78 (see note 6), on whether late adoption can explain the difference.

17. One body of evidence is difficult to judge. See J. Philippe Rushton, *Race, Evolution, and Behavior: A Life History Perspective*, 3rd ed. (Port Huron, Mich.: Charles Darwin Research Institute, 2000). Rushton has proposed a theoretical framework that would explain a genetic gap in cognitive ability between blacks and whites and has marshaled evidence for it. But because much of the evidence was known before the theory was proposed, some view the theory as nothing more than post hoc rationalization for hereditarian views on the black-white gap. At most it suggests that some of the black-white gap may be genetic, but it does not suggest how much.

18. Arthur Jensen, *Educability and Group Differences* (New York: Harper and Row, 1973), pp. 135–39, 161–73, 186–90; Arthur Jensen, *Educational Differences* (London: Methuen, 1973), pp. 408–12; Jensen, *The g Factor*, pp. 445–58 (see note 6); and Richard Herrnstein and Charles Murray, *The Bell Curve: Intelligence and Class Structure in American Life* (New York: Simon and Schuster, 1994), pp. 298–99.

19. Plomin and others, *Behavioral Genetics*, p. 177 (see note 2); and Ulric Neisser and others, "Intelligence: Knowns and Unknowns," *American Psychologist* 51, no. 2(1996): 85.

20. Author's calculations from the 1979 National Longitudinal Survey of Youth.

21. John B. Carol, *Human Cognitive Abilities: A Survey of Factor-Analytic Studies* (Cambridge University Press, 1993), is the most comprehensive survey of what is known about the correlation of scores on different types of mental tests.

22. See J. Philippe Rushton and Arthur Jensen, "Thirty Years of Research on Race Differences in Cognitive Ability," *Psychology, Public Policy, and Law* (forthcoming), for a review of this evidence and citations to the original studies.

23. David Rowe, Alexander Vazsonyi, and Daniel Flannery, "Ethnic and Racial Similarity in Developmental Process: A Study of Academic Achievement," *Psychological Review* 101, no. 3 (1994): 396–413; Jensen, *The g Factor*, pp. 464–67 (see note 6).

24. James R. Flynn, "Massive Gains in 14 Nations: What IQ Tests Really Measure," *Psychological Bulletin* 101 (1987): 171–91; James R. Flynn, "IQ Gains over Time," in *Encyclopedia of Human Intelligence*, edited by Robert J. Sternberg (New York: Macmillan, 1994), pp. 617–23; James R. Flynn, "IQ Gains over Time: Toward Finding the Causes," in *The Rising Curve: Long-Term Gains in IQ and Related Measures*, edited by Ulric Neisser (Washington: American Psychological Association, 1998), pp. 551–53.

25. Existing evidence suggests that IQ gains across subtests are probably positively correlated with g loading. See Roberto Colom, Manuel Juan-Espinosa, and Luís F. García, "The Secular Increase in Test Scores Is a

'Jensen effect,'" *Personality and Individual Differences* 30 (2001): 553–58; and Manuel Juan-Espinosa and others, "Individual Differences in Large-Spaces Orientation: *g* and Beyond?" *Personality and Individual Differences* 29 (2000): 85–98, for much stronger correlations between *g* loadings and IQ gains. Jensen, *The g Factor*, pp. 320–21 (see note 6), reviews a number of studies of the relation between subtests gains and *g* loadings, all of which show weak positive correlations. J. Philippe Rushton, "Secular Gains in IQ Not Related to the *g* Factor and Inbreeding Depression—unlike Black-White Differences: A Reply to Flynn," *Personality and Individual Differences* 26 (1999): 381–89, finds that a measure of *g* developed on the Wechsler Intelligence Scale for Children has loadings that are negatively correlated with subtest gains in several countries. But see James R. Flynn, "The History of the American Mind in the 20th Century: A Scenario to Explain IQ Gains over Time and a Case for the Irrelevance of *g*," in *Extending Intelligence: Enhancement and New Constructs*, edited by P. C. Kyllonon, R. D. Roberts, and L. Stankov (Hillsdale, N.J.: Erlbaum, forthcoming.) for an argument that IQ gains are greatest on tests of fluid *g* rather than crystallized *g*. He finds a positive (though statistically insignificant) correlation between a measure of fluid *g* he develops and IQ gains in the data used by Rushton. Olev Must, Aasa Must, and Vilve Raudik, "The Flynn Effect for Gains in Literacy Found in Estonia Is Not a Jensen Effect," *Personality and Individual Differences* 33 (2001); and Olev Must, Aasa Must, and Vilve Raudik, "The Secular Rise in IQs: In Estonia the Flynn Effect Is Not a Jensen Effect," *Intelligence* 31 (2003): 461–71, find no correlation between *g* loadings and gains on two tests in Estonia, but these are achievement tests with a strong crystallized bias.

26. Plomin and others, *Behavioral Genetics*, pp. 173–77 (see note 2).

27. Irving Lazar and Richard Darlington, "Lasting Effects of Early Education: A Report from the Consortium for Longitudinal Studies," *Monographs of the Society for Research in Child Development* 47, nos. 2–3 (1982).

28. William T. Dickens and James Flynn, "Heritability Estimates versus Large Environmental Effects," *Psychological Review* 108, no. 2 (2001).

29. This is not to say that there are no permanent or long-lasting environmental effects on cognitive ability. The effects of brain damage can be severe and permanent. However, such permanent environmental effects evidently explain only a small fraction of normal variation in cognitive ability. Shared family environment plays a large role in explaining variance in cognitive ability when children are spending most of their time in the home, with their activities strongly influenced by their parents. But that effect fades as they spend more of their time away from home and in self-directed activities.

30. Eric A. Hanushek and others, "Does Peer Ability Affect Student Achievement?" Working Paper 8502 (Cambridge, Mass.: National Bureau of Economic Research, 2001); Caroline Hoxby, "Peer Effects in the Classroom: Learning from Gender and Race Variation," Working Paper 7867 (Cambridge, Mass.: National Bureau of Economic Research, 2001); Dan M. Levy, "Family Income and Peer Effects as Determinants of Educational Outcomes," Ph.D. diss., Northwestern University, 2000; Donald Robertson and James Symons, "Do Peer Groups Matter? Peer Group versus Schooling Effects on Academic Achievement," *Economica* 70 (2003): 31–53; Bruce Sacerdote, "Peer Effects with Random Assignment: Results from Dartmouth Roommates," *Quarterly Journal of Economics* (May 2001): 681–704; David J. Zimmerman, "Peer Effects in Academic Outcomes: Evidence from a Natural Experiment," *Review of Economics and Statistics* 85 (2003): 9–23.

31. Michael A. Boozer and Stephen E. Cacciola, "Inside the 'Black Box' of Project STAR: Estimation of Peer Effects Using Experimental Data," Discussion Paper 832 (Economic Growth Center, Yale University, 2001).

32. In statistics this is referred to as the law of large numbers—that the variance of a mean falls as the number of items being averaged goes up. See Eugene Lukacs, *Probability and Mathematics Statistics: An Introduction* (New York: Academic Press, 1972). It applies whether or not the weights being put on the elements are equal. Because the variance and standard deviation of the mean fall, while the average difference stays the same, the difference in standard deviations grows. The example assumes that the effects are all uncorrelated with each other and that each has a normal distribution in the white and the black populations. If the effects were assumed to be correlated or the weights unequal, the results would be less dramatic, but with observed values for correlations of environmental factors, increasing the number of items to be averaged could produce the same results.

33. Dickens and Flynn, "Heritability Estimates vs. Large Environmental Effects" (see note 28).

34. Plomin and others, *Behavioral Genetics*, p. 201 (see note 2).

35. Eric Turkheimer and others, "Socioeconomic Status Modifies Heritability of IQ in Young Children," *Psychological Science* 14, no. 6 (2003). Their own study finds that shared family environment explains 60 percent of the variance of an IQ test score in low-socioeconomic-status seven-year-olds, which is a much larger share than other studies have found. For example, see Kathryn Asbury and others, "Environmental Moderators of Genetic Influence on Verbal and Nonverbal Abilities in Early Childhood" (Institute of Psychiatry, De Crespigny Park, London, 2004).

Neuroscience Perspectives on Disparities in School Readiness and Cognitive Achievement

Kimberly G. Noble, Nim Tottenham, and B. J. Casey

Summary

This article allows readers to look at racial and ethnic disparities in school readiness from a neuroscience perspective. Although researchers have traditionally measured gaps in school readiness using broad achievement tests, they can now assess readiness in terms of more specific brain-based cognitive functions. Three neurocognitive systems—cognitive control, learning and memory, and reading—are essential for success in school. Thanks to recent advances in brain imaging, it is now possible to examine these three systems, each located in specific areas of the brain, by observing them in action as children engage in particular tasks.

Socioeconomic status—already linked with how well children do on skills tests generally—is particularly closely linked with how well they perform on tasks involving these crucial neurocognitive systems. Moreover, children's life experiences can influence their neurocognitive development and lead to functional and anatomical changes in their brains. Noting that chronic stress or abuse in childhood can impair development of the brain region involved in learning and memory, the authors show how the extreme stress of being placed in an orphanage leads to abnormal brain development and decreased cognitive functioning.

More optimistically, the authors explain that children's brains remain plastic and capable of growth and development. Targeted educational interventions thus have the promise of improving both brain function and behavior. Several such interventions, for example, both raise children's scores in tests of reading and increase activity in the brain regions most closely linked with reading. The brain regions most crucial for school readiness may prove quite responsive to effective therapeutic interventions—even making it possible to tailor particular interventions for individual children. The authors look ahead to the day when effective educational interventions can begin to close racial and socioeconomic gaps in readiness and achievement.

www.future of children.org

Kimberly G. Noble is an M.D./Ph.D. candidate at the Center for Cognitive Neuroscience, University of Pennsylvania, and a visiting graduate student at the Sackler Institute for Developmental Psychology of Weill Medical College of Cornell University. Nim Tottenham is a Ph.D. candidate at the Institute of Child Development, University of Minnesota, and a visiting graduate student at the Sackler Institute for Developmental Psychobiology. B. J. Casey is the director of the Sackler Institute for Developmental Psychobiology and the Sackler Professor of Psychobiology at Weill Medical College.

Kimberly G. Noble, Nim Tottenham, and B. J. Casey

Racial disparities in school readiness among America's preschoolers are strong and persistent. As elaborated elsewhere in this volume, many aspects of childhood experience, including health, parenting, stress, violence, and access to resources, contribute to these disparities. Many of these same experiences, including chronic stress and cognitive stimulation, also affect brain development in both animals and humans, suggesting a possible pathway between experience and ability.

To show how differences in brain development may ultimately link experience and academic achievement, we focus in this article on three core neurocognitive systems that are crucial for school readiness. Typical measures of school readiness such as achievement tests or even IQ tests are quite imprecise from the perspective of brain science.[1] These tests assess a diverse set of mental processes, involving many neural systems, without telling much about the specific systems of the child's mind and brain that are most involved in school readiness. Recent work in the field of cognitive neuroscience, however, has made it possible to assess the specific neurocognitive systems or brain regions involved in particular cognitive skills. Using new neuroimaging methods, researchers can design cognitive tests that assess a single system, enabling them to understand more precisely the cognitive processes and underlying brain regions whose development contributes to differences in achievement. Ultimately, specific neurocognitive systems might be differentially targeted by early educational interventions.

We begin by introducing the three neurocognitive systems, including the cognitive processes involved, the types of tests used for assessment, and the brain regions implicated.

We touch on the limited research into racial differences across these systems and discuss some links between socioeconomic background and neurocognitive performance. We then discuss research findings about how experience can influence development of these systems. We conclude by drawing implications for educational interventions on early brain and cognitive development in these systems.

Three Core Neurocognitive Systems

To illustrate how brain development can inform notions of readiness and achievement, we briefly describe three key neurocognitive systems involved in cognitive skills necessary for school success. Cognitive control, the ability to override inappropriate thoughts and behaviors, is associated with the prefrontal cortex, located in the front of the brain. Learning and memory involve the hippocampus, buried deep within the brain's temporal lobe. And reading (and its precursors in preliterate children) is associated with the temporo-parietal and temporo-occipital cortex, located on the left surface of the brain. Each of these brain regions changes and matures throughout childhood, and researchers are currently trying to understand how children's experiences influence such brain development. Scientists hope that this research will lead to insights that are promising for the design of specific educational interventions.

Cognitive Control

Cognitive processes attributed to the prefrontal cortex include the ability to allocate attention, to hold something "online" in memory, and to withhold an inappropriate response.[2] Such processes, collectively known as cognitive control, are important developmentally, as they underlie cognitive and social skills essential to academic success, such as the ability to ignore distracting events inside and outside the classroom. In the laboratory, researchers can design behavioral tasks to assess a child's ability to inhibit an inappropriate response. For example, a widely used paradigm known as the Go–No Go task presents a child with many "go" stimuli that require a rote button-press response, along with an occasional "no go" stimulus that requires the child to *withhold* a response.[3]

Now, thanks largely to developments in imaging methods, like magnetic resonance imaging (MRI), researchers can study cognitive skills in the developing human brain. More than a decade ago, Kenneth Kwong, Seji Ogawa, and others showed that magnetic resonance is sensitive to blood oxygenation changes in the brain that may reflect changes in blood flow and neuronal activity.[4] The discovery that MRI can assess activity in the human brain without the need for radioactive tracers required by other forms of brain imaging opened a new era in the study of human brain development and behavior. Since then, numerous functional magnetic resonance imaging (fMRI) studies have examined children engaged in cognitive control tasks and have found a characteristic age-related pattern in the development of neural activity in the prefrontal cortex.[5] In young children, cognitive control tasks are associated with diffuse patterns of prefrontal cortex activity, whereas by adolescence the pattern of activity is both more focal and more intense. In adulthood, activity remains focal, but somewhat less intense. Because increasing age is also linked with accuracy in performing a task, with experience, and with learning, one possible interpretation of these findings is that the age-related decrease in brain activity could reflect reduced recruitment of brain tissue as the task becomes easier. But studies that have matched children and adults on accuracy on

the Go–No Go task show that prefrontal activity differences represent maturational change, not difference in ability.[6]

Memory and Learning

The development of memory and learning is also clearly important to academic success. One aspect of learning is the ability to form new associations among events. In laboratory tasks that test the learning of new memories, children typically see or hear lists of words, stories, or scenes and then try to recollect the presented stimuli.[7] For very young children,

---

Now, thanks largely to developments in imaging methods, like magnetic resonance imaging (MRI), researchers can study cognitive skills in the developing human brain.

---

for whom a nonverbal memory assessment is preferable, researchers first familiarize the child with a stimulus and then present him or her with test trials pairing the familiar stimulus with a new one. Infants' known preference for novelty allows researchers to infer that an infant who spends a longer time looking at the new stimulus recognizes the familiar one.[8]

The ability to learn and remember is supported in part by the hippocampus, located deep inside the brain's temporal lobe.[9] A child's hippocampus increases in size with age, with a particularly sharp increase before the age of two.[10] During the course of those two years, a child's ability to learn and remember associations matures in terms of both how much information is remembered and how long it is retained.[11] Although research into the link between a child's memory and the functional neuroanatomical development of the hippocampus is still in its early stages, a recent imaging study showed that in both children and adults, the speed of learning a new association was correlated with hippocampal activity.[12] Interestingly, as with cognitive control and the prefrontal cortex, the activity associated with forming and remembering new associations was more diffuse and less focal in children than it was in adults.

Language and Reading

Both cognitive control and memory and learning are general cognitive abilities that a child brings to the academic environment. A more specific cognitive ability—one that is key to understanding the gap in school readiness—is reading, along with the precursor language skills that are critical for the development of reading. Ample evidence has shown that phonological awareness, or an understanding of the sounds of language, is crucial for reading.[13] Not only do preliterate children with better phonological awareness learn to read more quickly than children with less such awareness, but kindergarten phonological awareness predicts teenage reading ability better than kindergarten reading skill does.[14] Phonological awareness is measured behaviorally by tasks such as rhyming, blending sounds, and word-sound games that assess the ability to manipulate syllables or smaller units of speech known as phonemes.

A large swath of cortex known as the perisylvian region stretches along the left side of the brain and underlies most language functioning. Within this larger area, two regions are primarily responsible for the normal development of reading.[15] The first region, the supe-

rior temporal gyrus, is involved in phonological processing in normally reading adults and children.[16] Later childhood brings anatomical maturation of this region as measured by size, symmetry, and connectivity.[17] The second region, the fusiform gyrus, located along the bottom-left side of the brain, has been associated with the ability of skilled readers to perceive automatically a written word. Activity in the fusiform gyrus is positively correlated with both reading ability and age.[18] The two regions are functionally linked in that the development of the fusiform gyrus is thought to be influenced by phonological processing in the preliterate child.[19]

This sketch of these three neurocognitive systems illustrates how researchers have begun to understand the developmental course of several cognitive processes and their neural underpinnings. The challenge is to understand how an individual child's experiences, many of which may vary according to racial, ethnic, or socioeconomic background, may affect the developing brain. Focusing on these specific neurocognitive systems, rather than on the multiple systems measured by achievement tests, may make it possible both to understand the link between experience and brain development and to address the racial gap in school readiness by directly targeting the specific systems with interventions.

Racial and Socioeconomic Disparities in Neurocognitive Performance

Few researchers as yet have examined racial disparities in academic achievement in terms of specific neurocognitive systems. In fact, few studies of cognitive development explicitly examine race at all. One notable recent exception, a study of cognitive control, investigated a child's ability to suppress an inappropriate response as measured in a laboratory task.[20] The study found that children from higher socioeconomic backgrounds generally performed better on the test. It also found, after controlling for socioeconomic status, that African American and Hispanic children resisted the interference of competing demands better than white children did. Although this study needs to be replicated to confirm its findings, a preliminary interpretation might be that racial disparities in achievement, or at least in cognitive control, are in fact mediated by socioeconomic differences (and with associated differences in access to resources).

The suggestion that socioeconomic differences underlie racial differences in academic performance is supported by the fact that minorities are at much greater risk for growing up in poverty.[21] As detailed elsewhere in this volume, children from impoverished backgrounds are at heightened risk for poor academic readiness and achievement because of differences in their physical health, the quality of the cognitive and emotional stimulation they receive at home, their parenting, and their early childhood education.[22] Thus, although work on racial differences in cognitive development is limited as yet, researchers are beginning to examine the link between socioeconomic status (SES) and neurocognitive achievement.

So far this research has documented a strong and persistent connection between socioeconomic status—most commonly measured using education, occupation, and income—and childhood cognitive ability and achievement as measured by IQ, achievement test scores, and functional literacy.[23] In one study, for example, socioeconomic status accounted for some 20 percent of the variation in childhood IQ.[24] Another found that disparities in achievement due to socioeconomic status in-

crease with age: a child's cognitive ability at age ten is more closely linked to his socioeconomic status at age two than to his cognitive ability at age two.[25] But despite extensive work on the connection between socioeconomic status and cognitive performance as measured by standardized testing, researchers are only beginning to focus on the specific brain functions that link childhood experience and cognitive performance.

To address this gap in research, we recently examined the neurocognitive functioning of African American kindergartners from different socioeconomic backgrounds, using tasks

The suggestion that socioeconomic differences underlie racial differences in academic performance is supported by the fact that minorities are at much greater risk for growing up in poverty.

from the cognitive neuroscience literature to explore how childhood SES helps account for the normal variance in performance across different neurocognitive systems.[26] We recruited thirty middle-SES children and thirty low-SES children from public kindergarten classes in Philadelphia to participate in a battery of behavioral tasks, each specific to a particular neurocognitive system. The tasks were designed to assess the language, cognitive control, and memory systems, along with several others. The systems we selected were relatively independent of one another, had correspondingly distinct locations in the brain, and had substantial roles in cognition and school performance. We found that socioeconomic status was generally correlated with the children's performance on the battery of tasks as a whole, thus replicating the well-documented socioeconomic gap in global measures of cognitive performance. But we also found that socioeconomic status was disproportionately correlated with performance in certain systems. Specifically, children's performance in tasks tapping the left perisylvian (language) system and the

---

Socioeconomic status accounted for a good portion of the variance in performance in different aspects of cognitive control and in tasks involving several other systems, including learning and memory.

---

prefrontal (cognitive control) system varied widely according to their socioeconomic status, while their performance in tasks involving other systems showed either no differences or nonsignificant trends. The effects on the language and cognitive control systems were quite large. For the left perisylvian (language) system, the mean score of the group of middle-class children was 1.1 standard deviations higher than the mean score of the poorer children; for the prefrontal (cognitive control) system, the difference was 0.68 standard deviation.

When we replicated our preliminary study in a larger sample of 150 multiracial children,

we largely confirmed our original findings.[27] Socioeconomic status accounted for the most variance in performance in the language system. It also accounted for a good portion of the variance in performance in different aspects of cognitive control and in tasks involving several other systems, including learning and memory.

These two studies are the first ever to compare directly the extent to which socioeconomic factors account for the variance in children's performance on tasks involving different neurocognitive systems. Both found that the effect of socioeconomic status was not uniform, that it differs from system to system. In some systems, the effect was negligible. Effects were greatest on variations in language skills, but socioeconomic status also accounts for some of the variation in other systems, including cognitive control and possibly learning and memory, among others.

Because of the exceptional importance of reading skill for academic and life achievement, we were particularly interested in examining how socioeconomic status affects that particular aspect of language development. Correlations between socioeconomic background and word reading ability are typically fairly strong (they fall within the range of 0.3 to 0.7, with 1 being a perfect correlation).[28] Often, researchers attribute this close relationship to the link between socioeconomic status and reading-related experiences, such as the home literacy environment, degree of early print exposure, and quality of early schooling.[29] But, as noted, a largely separate line of research has provided abundant evidence that phonological awareness is causally related to reading development.[30] Despite independent work showing that socioeconomic background and phonological awareness are each associated with reading achievement, surprisingly few studies have explored how socioeconomic status relates to phonemic awareness in predicting individual differences in reading ability.[31]

We investigated this question and found that on several different types of reading tasks, socioeconomic status and phonological awareness each accounted for unique variance in skill.[32] Furthermore, in certain cases, we found that SES actually seemed to *modulate* the relationship between phonological awareness and reading. That is, at the highest levels of phonological awareness, children were on average reading well regardless of socioeconomic background. In contrast, at lower levels of phonological skill, a disparity emerged such that higher-SES children continued to read relatively well, whereas lower-SES children began to struggle.

Together, these findings imply that the relationship between socioeconomic background and reading does not simply reflect differences in the development of phonological awareness skills. In contrast, multiple factors play complex roles in the development of reading and in predicting whether a child will acquire this crucial skill easily or with difficulty. Put simply, disparate causes may lead to the same cognitive difficulties. Two different children may have similar problems in learning to read, but one may have inherently poor phonological awareness skills, while the other may be growing up in an environment with scant access to literacy materials and instruction. Is it possible then, that a child who struggles with reading in the context of a low-literacy environment might have difficulties that are fundamentally different from those of a child who struggles *despite* access to a higher-literacy environment? Might these two children respond differently to different types of intervention?

This brings us to a key application for neuroimaging. If similar low levels of performance in a skill such as reading may have different causes, then imaging the brain may help to tease such effects apart, extending our knowledge beyond the limits of behavioral data. It is now possible to examine whether similar behavioral profiles resulting from different causes could be rooted in different effects on brain development. It may be differences in brain development, rather than differences in behavioral performance, that ultimately predict an individual child's response to intervention. In the next section, we examine how differences in experience influence the development of neurocognitive systems crucial for academic success.

Experience and Brain Development

Thus far, we have focused on the developmental course of several core cognitive processes and their neural underpinnings, as well as on how cognitive achievement is associated with socioeconomic background and perhaps race. The next challenge is to understand how a child's experiences—many of which may reflect his or her socioeconomic, racial, or ethnic background—may affect the developing brain. Understanding how experience influences behavioral and brain development may make it possible to design educational curriculums to target the specific brain regions that underlie cognitive skills important for academic success.

Experience shapes brain development at many levels of organization, from molecules to larger brain systems.[33] Variations in such types of experience as cognitive stimulation and early life stress lead to functional and anatomical changes throughout the brain in both animals and people. Scientists can, for example, cause broad neural changes in animals by manipulating the laboratory environment, enriching or depriving the animals' experience in various ways.[34] In humans, stress has garnered much attention as one particular experience that may affect cognitive and academic achievement. Stressful life conditions have been associated with low socioeconomic status, and differences in emotional support in the home account for a significant portion of the variance in children's verbal, reading, and math skills, even when maternal education, family structure, prenatal care, infant health, nutrition, and mother's age are taken into account.[35] Such cognitive differences may be caused in part by biological responses to stress.

Children raised in chronically stressful or abusive situations demonstrate increased or irregular production of stress hormone.[36] In animals, such abnormal levels of stress hormone lead to adverse brain development, particularly in the hippocampus.[37] Reduced hippocampal volume has also been found in human adults in a variety of stress-related conditions, including post-traumatic stress disorder and major depression.[38] Given the critical role of the hippocampus in learning and memory, it is not surprising that changes in hippocampal activity caused by prolonged exposure to elevated stress hormone may lead to deficits in learning.[39]

Developmental studies of maltreated children find generalized intellectual and academic impairments, as measured by IQ or achievement tests.[40] Studies applying more specific neurocognitive methods suggest that these children also show deficits in cognitive control.[41] MRI studies of children suffering from post-traumatic stress disorder caused by maltreatment have found not only that their brains are smaller overall than those of children who have not been maltreated, but also

that their frontal lobe structure is abnormal.[42] These studies, however, cannot draw causal relationships between maltreatment and brain changes.

To sort out these findings, we have begun to examine how one extreme form of chronic childhood stress—being placed in an orphanage—affects a child's developing brain. Researchers have recognized for some time that both a child's age at placement and the duration of the placement affect the child's development.[43] We have recruited and collected preliminary data on fourteen children between the ages of five and eleven who spent time in an orphanage. The children were adopted between the ages of six months and five years, except for one boy, who was adopted at age eight. They were placed in the orphanage between birth and age two, with the exception of the same boy, who was placed at age five.

Of the fourteen children, seven have at least one clinical psychiatric diagnosis. Strikingly, the older the children were at adoption, the more likely they are to have symptoms, and ultimately a diagnosis. The healthiest children were placed in the orphanage young and adopted young, and they spent relatively less time in the orphanage overall.

Most of the children's general cognitive ability scores fell within the average range, but their estimated full-scale IQ scores were negatively correlated with time spent in the orphanage (see figure 1). The children who lived there a shorter time tended to have higher IQ scores.

To assess cognitive control in these children, we used the Go–No Go test.[44] The performance of the adopted children on the test differed from that of twelve age-matched con-

Figure 1. Time Spent in Orphanage and IQ

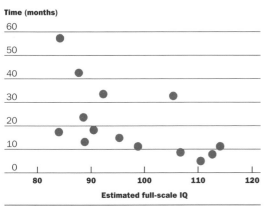

Figure 2. Cognitive Control and Age at Adoption

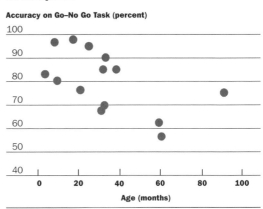

trols in overall accuracy. Performance was negatively correlated with age of adoption: children adopted at a younger age tended to score higher on the test (see figure 2). Thus stress associated with institutionalization appears to be linked with decreased cognitive ability as measured both by general intelligence tests and by specific measures of cognitive control. These findings are in line with those noted earlier, that traumatized children show abnormal maturation of prefrontal function.

How do these cognitive changes relate to brain changes? We examined the effects of institutionalization on brain development using magnetic resonance imaging on a subset of eight of these children. As seen in figure 3, MRIs of those children showed an association between total brain volume and estimated IQ, a trend that has been repeatedly demonstrated elsewhere.[45] The MRIs also showed a moderate association between the length of time a child spent in an orphanage and the child's prefrontal volume (after overall brain volume had been taken into account).

Because the hippocampus is implicated in memory and learning and because it is vul-

nerable to stress, we tested for a link between its volume and the length of time a child lived in the orphanage. As figure 4 shows, the volume decreased as a function of time spent in the institution. (We controlled for current age and overall brain volume.) These results, too, are in line with those noted in adults with post-traumatic stress disorder. Not surprisingly, we found that previously institutionalized children perform poorly on learning and memory tasks. Preliminary findings from our laboratory showed that these children were significantly slower than the control group to learn new stimulus-response associations and override old ones, an ability that correlates with hippocampal activity.[46] Hippocampal volume was also correlated with time spent with the adopted family: the longer a child lived with a stable family, the greater his or her hippocampal volume. This finding suggests a powerful effect of the positive experience of adoption from orphanage to home.

Although most research on stress and humans has focused on extreme—and rare—cases such as institutionalization, milder daily elevations in stress may have long-term effects as well. In children of low socioeco-

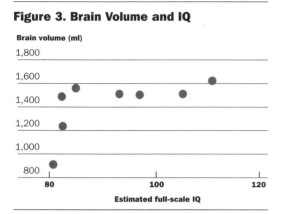

Figure 3. Brain Volume and IQ

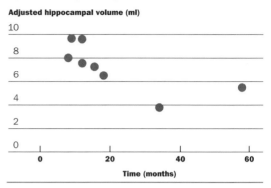

Figure 4. Hippocampal Volume and Time Spent in Orphanage

nomic status, for example, Sonia Lupien and her colleagues found increased levels of salivary cortisol, which were linked with depression in their mother.[47] This research is potentially quite relevant to understanding the biological and neural underpinnings of the achievement gap between children of different socioeconomic backgrounds.

As is evident from the effect of adoption in our study of children placed in an orphanage, experience need not be negative to shape a developing brain. On the contrary, positive differences in experience can quite powerfully lead to functional reorganization of the brain. One often-cited example is learning a second language. As has long been recognized, the older a person is when exposed to a second language, the less likely he or she is to be able to develop true, accent-free fluency. Recent neuroimaging studies have begun to elucidate the neurobiological basis for this experience.[48] Typically, the studies present children with written or spoken words in both their first and their second languages and examine differences in brain activity in response. In bilingual children who learn a second language before they turn seven, brain activity in response to the two languages is similar and takes place in overlapping regions of the left side of the brain. But in children

who learn a second language later, brain activity in response to the two languages occurs in nonoverlapping regions. In particular, the first language typically elicits the usual left-sided pattern of activity, whereas the second often causes a more variable pattern that is more likely to be localized to the right side. Although the brain retains plasticity for learning a second language, the specific pattern of plasticity appears to depend on the age when that language is learned, which may also reflect ultimate fluency.

Finally, discussions of experience-related plasticity in cognitive ability and brain development often evoke the issue of genetics. What is the role of genes in the development of cognitive abilities? Researchers have long agreed that both genes and experience influence cognitive outcomes. For instance, twin studies have shown that even when genetic effects are taken into account, violence in the home is linked with lower IQ.[49] Conversely, both genes and environment affect cognitive resilience to the effects of low socioeconomic status.[50] Adoption studies have also shown that the socioeconomic backgrounds of both biological and adoptive parents are independent predictors of adopted children's IQ, reflecting genetic and experiential influences on the child, respectively.[51]

But the nature-nurture question is more nuanced than merely being a matter of where the balance of influence lies. Researchers now recognize that genes and experience are not truly independent predictors, but that in many cases nature is in part *moderated* by nurture. Animal research, for example, has shown that naturally occurring variations in maternal care can alter the expression of genes that regulate the response to stress and that early social attachment relationships can modify the heritability of aggressive behavior.[52] Human research has drawn similar conclusions. Of particular relevance to understanding the gap in school readiness is a recent study showing that among families of lower socioeconomic status, variation in IQ is far more environmental than genetic in origin, whereas the converse holds in families of higher socioeconomic status.[53] That is, an impoverished child's background and experiences can so heavily influence his or her degree of achievement that his genetic makeup is nearly irrelevant in predicting his academic success. Optimistically, such a powerful role for experience suggests that intervention may be particularly successful among disadvantaged children.

Brain-Targeted Interventions

In this final section, we look ahead to the role that brain plasticity may play in developing and testing cognitive interventions in the three neurocognitive systems on which we have focused: memory and learning, cognitive control, and reading. It is premature to recommend specific interventions on the basis of brain evidence, but preliminary research in this nascent field is promising.

Researchers in brain plasticity have as yet done little work on memory training in humans. Although animal research has repeatedly shown that training on memory para-

digms can lead to improved learning and problem solving that is directly related to hippocampal plasticity, it is not yet clear whether similar effects could be observed in children.[54]

Cognitive control has received somewhat more attention. Several studies have shown not only that young children with attention deficit hyperactivity disorder (ADHD) can benefit from repeated training on laboratory tasks known to involve prefrontal function, but also that training on such tasks can improve performance on untrained tasks involving similar regions.[55] These studies did not directly measure brain function, relying instead on tasks already shown to engage prefrontal regions. Recently, however, M. R. Rueda and colleagues showed that four-year-olds who attended seven sessions of attention training showed significant improvement on abstract reasoning skills relative to children who received a control intervention of watching videos. Furthermore, during a cognitive control task administered after their training was complete, the children showed brain activity that was more adult-like than that of the control group.[56] These preliminary results suggest the possibility of designing broader educational interventions that specifically target cognitive control, which a recent study found to be the single best predictor of resilience among high-risk children, even controlling for age, gender, negative life events, chronic strain, abuse, nonverbal IQ, self-esteem, parental monitoring, and emotional support.[57] Of course, the feasibility of any intervention program must be assessed outside the laboratory before being implemented on a larger scale.

Reading has attracted by far the most attention from those scientists investigating intervention-related brain plasticity.[58] Many studies have provided behavioral evidence that children with mild to severe reading impairments can benefit from interventions that explicitly support phonological awareness and provide training in the alphabetic decoding skills necessary to convert print to sound.[59] Recent examinations of the neural effects of such behavioral studies provide a better understanding of how such programs improve skills, with the ultimate goal of targeting intervention to individual children's needs. Several investigators have used neuroimaging techniques to follow brain changes in children over the course of an intervention. One investigation found decreased brain activity in the left superior temporal gyrus region in eight children with reading difficulties, as compared with nonimpaired children.[60] Following a two-month intervention involving eighty hours of phonological processing work with one of two commercial packages (*Phono-Graphics* and *Lindamood Phoneme Sequencing*), the reading-impaired children's mean standardized reading scores improved from the 5th percentile to the 50th percentile. The children also showed increases in left superior temporal gyrus activity (as well as a decrease in right-sided activity). The eight nonimpaired children who did not participate in the intervention demonstrated stable brain responses over the same time span. Importantly, the study included no reading-impaired control group, making it impossible to tell whether changes were specific to the intervention or simply the result of generic tutoring or even schooling effects. Another interpretive difficulty was that before the intervention, the reading-impaired children showed very low accuracy in performing the task measured by the brain scanner. The changes in brain activity following the intervention, therefore, could have been due not to a change in brain function *per se* but rather to the children's engagement in a task to which they had previously not attended.

Similarly, Elise Temple and colleagues measured changes in functional activity in a group of reading-impaired children in whom pre-intervention functional magnetic resonance imaging indicated reduced activity in reading-related regions relative to children in a control group.[61] After the children in the experimental group participated in a six-week, forty-five-hour intervention, including a commercial computer-based training program (*Fast ForWord Language*) and a special school curriculum for children with dyslexia, their reading improved significantly. Changes in their post-test functional MRI results were widespread, extending to fourteen brain regions, some of which also changed in the nonimpaired group. Most of the regions undergoing change are thought to be typically involved in reading; several are not. The size of changes in regions associated with reading was correlated with improvements in oral language, but not with reading improvements. Again, this study is difficult to interpret because it lacked a reading-impaired control group randomized to a different intervention. To make interpretation even more complicated, in a separate randomized controlled study, more than 200 children in an urban school district received *Fast ForWord* but made no gains in reading compared with a control group of reading-impaired children who did not receive the program.[62] This finding underscores the need for a reading-impaired control group in imaging studies and suggests that the strict adherence to an intervention required in the laboratory setting may be unrealistic in the classroom.

Finally, a recent study followed a group of children who received an experimental intervention consisting of fifty minutes a day of individual tutoring focused on phonological awareness and the alphabetic principle and contrasted it with a "community intervention" group that received normal school-based remedial reading instruction.[63] The children were tested before and after eight months of intervention and were also compared with a control group of nonimpaired readers. Following the intervention, children in the experimental group had made significantly greater gains in reading fluency than had those in the community intervention group. They also showed brain activity during reading that looked remarkably similar to that of children in the nonimpaired control group—and they maintained this more typical pattern of activity for at least one year. The community intervention group showed less activity in the typical reading-related areas than did the other two groups.

Together, these three studies suggest that brain regions involved with reading in typically developing readers may prove to be quite malleable in response to effective therapeutic interventions. Brain activation patterns in these regions can change dramatically over the course of relatively short-lived interventions. As noted, successful interpretation of study results requires the rigorous use of control groups to examine both the behavioral efficacy and neural specificity of any intervention effects. In addition, improvements must be followed over time to verify that gains persist. Finally, interventions that succeed in the laboratory must be tested in real classroom environments before they can be widely implemented. Although it would be premature at this time to recommend a specific program for use, we are becoming more confident of the efficacy of combined training in phonological awareness and the alphabetic principle, as laboratory tests of that particular combination often show both

improved reading skills and patterns of brain activity that look more like those seen in typically developing readers.

But it is not enough for an intervention to improve reading skills on average. Ultimately, the goal is to tailor particular interventions for individual children. If, as we believe, similar low levels of reading performance—or any other neurocognitive skill—may result from different causes, then imaging the brain may help to tease such effects apart, extending our knowledge beyond the limits of behavioral data. We now have the ability to examine whether similar behavioral profiles associated with disparate risk factors might be rooted in different effects on brain development. In fact, it may be differences in brain development, rather than in behavioral performance, that ultimately predict an individual child's response to intervention.

Tantalizing preliminary evidence for this suggestion comes from a study showing that both socioeconomic status and a particular neuroanatomical measure (left-right asymmetry of the planum temporale in the temporal lobe) independently predicted reading ability.[64] The study suggests that researchers can predict a child's reading achievement levels better by using a combination of information about the brain and about social background than by using either type of information alone. By using both types of information, they might one day be able to design interventions that meet an individual child's needs in ways that simple behavioral measures alone cannot. Indeed, by thus honing the tools of intervention, they may ultimately reduce the gap in achievement so often observed for underserved groups.

Endnotes

1. Martha J. Farah and Kimberly G. Noble, "Socioeconomic Influences on Brain Development: A Preliminary Study," in *Developing Individuality in the Human Brain: A Tribute to Michael Posner*, edited by E. Awh, U. Mayr, and S. Keele (Washington: American Psychological Association, forthcoming).

2. B. J. Casey, Jay N. Giedd, and Kathleen M. Thomas, "Structural and Functional Brain Development and Its Relation to Cognitive Development," *Biological Psychiatry* 54, nos. 1–3 (2000).

3. B. J. Casey and others, "A Developmental fMRI Study of Prefrontal Activation during Performance of a Go–No-Go Task," *Journal of Cognitive Neuroscience* 9 (1997).

4. Kenneth K. Kwong and others, "Dynamic Magnetic Resonance Imaging of Human Brain Activity during Primary Sensory Stimulation," *Proceedings of the National Academy of Sciences, USA* 89 (1992); Seji Ogawa and others, "Intrinsic Signal Changes Accompanying Sensory Stimulation: Functional Brain Mapping with Magnetic Resonance Imaging," *Proceedings of the National Academy of Sciences, USA* 89, no. 13 (1992).

5. Silvia A. Bunge and others, "Prefrontal Regions Involved in Keeping Information in and out of Mind," *Brain* 124, no. 10 (2001); B. J. Casey and others, "Activation of Prefrontal Cortex in Children during a Non-Spatial Working Memory Task with Functional MRI," *Neuroimage* 2 (1995); B. J. Casey, Nim Tottenham, and John Fossella, "Clinical, Imaging, Lesion and Genetic Approaches toward a Model of Cognitive Control," *Developmental Psychobiology* 40 (2002); B. J. Casey and others, "A Developmental Functional MRI Study of Prefrontal Activation during Performance of a Go–No-Go Task," *Journal of Cognitive Neuroscience* 9 (1997); Sarah Durston and others, "The Effect of Preceding Context on Inhibition: An Event-Related fMRI Study," *Neuroimage* 16, no. 2 (2002); Torkel Klingberg, Hans Forssberg, and Helena Westerberg, "Increased Brain Activity in Frontal and Parietal Cortex Underlies the Development of Visuospatial Working Memory Capacity during Childhood," *Journal of Cognitive Neuroscience* 14, no. 1 (2002); Beatriz Luna and others, "Maturation of Widely Distributed Brain Function Subserves Cognitive Development," *Neuroimage* 13, no. 5 (2001); Kathleen M. Thomas and others, "A Developmental Functional MRI Study of Spatial Working Memory," *Neuroimage* 10 (1999).

6. Durston and others, "The Effect of Preceding Context on Inhibition"; Casey and others, "A Developmental fMRI Study of Prefrontal Activation during Performance of a Go–No-Go Task" (see note 5).

7. Susan E. Gathercole, "The Development of Memory," *Journal of Child Psychology and Psychiatry* 39, no. 1 (1998).

8. Charles A. Nelson and Sara J. Webb, "A Cognitive Neuroscience Perspective on Early Memory Development," in *The Cognitive Neuroscience of Development*, edited by Michelle de Haan and Mark H. Johnson (New York: Psychology Press, 2003).

9. Larry R. Squire, Frank Haist, and Arthur P. Shimamura, "The Neurology of Memory: Quantitative Assessment of Retrograde Amnesia in Two Groups of Amnesiac Patients," *Journal of Neuroscience* 9 (1989).

10. Jay N. Giedd and others, "Brain Development during Childhood and Adolescence: A Longitudinal MRI Study," *Nature Neuroscience* 2, no. 10 (1999); Hidetsuna Utsunomiya and others, "Development of the Temporal Lobe in Infants and Children: Analysis by MR-Based Volumetry," *American Journal of Neuroradiology* 20, no. 4 (1999).

11. Gathercole, "The Development of Memory" (see note 7).

12. Casey, Tottenham, and Fossella, "Clinical, Imaging, Lesion and Genetic Approaches toward a Model of Cognitive Control" (see note 5).

13. Marilyn J. Adams, *Learning to Read: Thinking and Learning about Print* (MIT Press, 1990); Lynette Bradley and Peter E. Bryant, "Categorizing Sounds and Learning to Read—a Causal Connection," *Nature* 301 (1983); Richard K. Wagner and Joseph K. Torgesen, "The Nature of Phonological Processing and Its Causal Role in the Acquisition of Reading Skills," *Psychological Bulletin* 101 (1987).

14. Wagner and Torgesen, "The Nature of Phonological Processing" (see note 13); G. Wayne MacDonald and Anne Cornwall, "The Relationship between Phonological Awareness and Reading and Spelling Achievement Eleven Years Later," *Journal of Learning Disabilities* 28, no. 8 (1995).

15. Bruce M. McCandliss and Kimberly G. Noble, "The Development of Reading Impairment: A Cognitive Neuroscience Model," *Mental Retardation and Developmental Disabilities Research Reviews* 9 (2003).

16. Barry Horwitz, Judith M. Rumsey, and Brian C. Donohue, "Functional Connectivity of the Angular Gyrus in Normal Reading and Dyslexia," *Proceedings of the National Academy of Sciences, USA* 95 (1998); Cathy J. Price and others, "Segregating Semantic from Phonological Processes during Reading," *Journal of Cognitive Neuroscience* 9, no. 6 (1997); Kenneth Pugh and others, "Cerebral Organization of Component Processes in Reading," *Brain* 119 (1996); Bennett A. Shaywitz and others, "Disruption of Posterior Brain Systems for Reading in Children with Developmental Dyslexia," *Biological Psychiatry* 52 (2002); Panagiotis G. Simos and others, "Dyslexia-Specific Brain Activation Profile Becomes Normal Following Successful Remedial Training," *Neurology* 58 (2002); Elise Temple and others, "Disrupted Neural Responses to Phonological and Orthographic Processing in Dyslexic Children: An fMRI Study," *NeuroReport* 12, no. 2 (2001).

17. Giedd and others, "Brain Development during Childhood and Adolescence" (see note 10); Elizabeth B. Sowell and others, "Mapping Sulcal Pattern Assymetry and Local Cortical Surface Gray Matter Distribution *in vivo*: Maturation in Perisylvian Cortices," *Cerebral Cortex* 12 (2002); Tomas Paus and others, "Structural Maturation of Neural Pathways in Children and Adolescents: In Vivo Study," *Science* 283 (1999).

18. Bradley L. Schlaggar and others, "Functional Neuroanatomical Differences between Adults and School-Age Children in the Processing of Single Words," *Science* 296 (2002); Shaywitz and others, "Disruption of Posterior Brain Systems for Reading in Children with Developmental Dyslexia" (see note 16).

19. McCandliss and Noble, "The Development of Reading Impairment: A Cognitive Neuroscience Model" (see note 15).

20. Enrico Mezzacappa, "Alerting, Orienting, and Executive Attention: Developmental Properties and Socio-Demographic Correlates in an Epidemiological Sample of Young, Urban Children," *Child Development* (forthcoming).

21. U.S. Bureau of the Census, *Statistical Abstract of the United States* (2000).

22. See also Theresa Hawley and Elizabeth R. Disney, "Crack's Children: The Consequences of Maternal Cocaine Abuse," *Social Policy Report* 6 (1992); Nancy K. Klein, Maureen Hack, and Naomi Breslau, "Children Who Were Very Low Birthweight: Development and Academic Achievement at Nine Years of Age," *Journal of Developmental and Behavioral Pediatrics* 10 (1989); Herbert L. Needleman and others, "The Long Term Effects of Low Doses of Lead in Childhood: An Eleven-Year Followup Report," *New England Journal of Medicine* 322 (1990); Robert H. Bradley and others, "The Home Environments of Children in the United

States, Part I: Variations by Age, Ethnicity and Poverty Status," *Child Development* 72, no. 6 (2001); Jeanne Brooks-Gunn, Pamela K. Klebanov, and Greg .J. Duncan, "Ethnic Differences in Children's Intelligence Test Scores: Role of Economic Deprivation, Home Environment, and Maternal Characteristics," *Child Development* 67 (1996); Vonnie C. McCloyd, "The Impact of Economic Hardship on Black Families and Children: Psychological Distress, Parenting, and Socioemotional Development," *Child Development* 61 (1990); W. Steven Barnett, "Long-Term Cognitive and Academic Effects of Early Childhood Education on Children in Poverty," *Preventive Medicine* 27 (1998).

23. Margaret E. Ensminger and Kate E. Fothergill, "A Decade of Measuring SES: What It Tells Us and Where to Go from Here," in *Socioeconomic Status, Parenting and Child Development*, edited by Marc H. Bornstein and Robert H. Bradley (Mahwah, N.J.: Lawrence Erlbaum Associates, 2003). Fong-ruey Liaw and Jeanne Brooks-Gunn, "Cumulative Familial Risks and Low-Birthweight Children's Cognitive and Behavioral Development," *Journal of Clinical Child Psychology* 23, no. 4 (1994); Judith Smith, Jeanne Brooks-Gunn, and Pamela K. Klebanov, "Consequences of Living in Poverty for Young Children's Cognitive and Verbal Ability and Early School Achievement," in *Consequences of Growing up Poor*, edited by Greg Duncan and Jeanne Brooks-Gunn (New York: Russell Sage, 1997); Jeanne Brooks-Gunn, Guang Guo, and Frank Furstenberg, "Who Drops out of and Who Continues beyond High School?" *Journal of Research on Adolescence* 3 (1993); Nazli Baydar, Jeanne Brooks-Gunn, and Frank Furstenberg, "Early Warning Signs of Functional Illiteracy: Predictors in Childhood and Adolescence," *Child Development* 64 (1993).

24. Allen W. Gottfried and others, "Socioeconomic Status in Children's Development and Family Environment: Infancy through Adolescence," in *Socioeconomic Status, Parenting and Child Development*, edited by Marc H. Bornstein and Robert H. Bradley (Mahwah, N.J.: Lawrence Erlbaum Associates, 2003).

25. Leon Feinstein, "Inequality in the Early Cognitive Development of British Children in the 1970 Cohort," *Economica* 70 (2003).

26. Kimberly G. Noble, M. Frank Norman, and Martha J. Farah, "Neurocognitive Correlates of Socioeconomic Status in Kindergarten Children," *Developmental Science* (forthcoming).

27. Kimberly G. Noble, Martha J. Farah, and Bruce M. McCandliss, "Normal Neurocognitive Development: Influence of Socioeconomic Status," paper presented to the Cognitive Neuroscience Society, San Francisco, 2004.

28. Karl R. White, "The Relation between Socio-Economic Status and Academic Achievement," *Psychological Bulletin* 91 (1982).

29. Steven A. Hecht and others, "Explaining Social Class Differences in Growth of Reading Skills from Beginning Kindergarten through Fourth Grade: The Role of Phonological Awareness, Rate of Access, and Print Knowledge," *Reading and Writing* 12, nos. 1–2 (2000).

30. See note 13.

31. Judith A. Bowey, "Socioeconomic Status Differences in Preschool Phonological Sensitivity and First-Grade Reading Achievement," *Journal of Educational Psychology* 87, no. 3 (1995); Hecht and others, "Explaining Social Class Differences in Growth of Reading Skills from Beginning Kindergarten through Fourth Grade" (see note 29); Ita S. Raz and Peter Bryant, "Social Background, Phonological Awareness and Children's Reading," *British Journal of Developmental Psychology* 8, no. 3 (1990).

32. Kimberly Noble, Martha J. Farah, and Bruce M. McCandliss, "The Effects of Socioeconomic Status and Phonological Awareness on Reading Development," paper presented to the Society for the Scientific Study of Reading, Amsterdam, The Netherlands, 2004.

33. William T. Greenough, James E. Black , and Christopher S. Wallace, "Experience and Brain Development," *Child Development* 58, no. 3 (1987); Sonia J. Lupien and others, "Child's Stress Hormone Levels Correlate with Mother's Socioeconomic Status and Depressive State," *Biological Psychiatry* 48 (2000); Bruce S. McEwen, "From Molecules to Mind: Stress, Individual Differences, and the Social Environment," *Annals of the New York Academy of Sciences* 935 (2001); Mark R. Rosenzweig and Edward L. Bennett, "Psychobiology of Plasticity: Effects of Training and Experience on Brain and Behavior," *Behavioral Brain Research* 78 (1996).

34. Rosenzweig and Bennett, "Psychobiology of Plasticity" (see note 33).

35. The association between stress and low SES is noted by Brooks-Gunn, Klebanov, and Duncan, "Ethnic Differences in Children's Intelligence Test Scores" (see note 22). The effects of emotional support in the home are documented by Sanders Korenman, Jane E. Miller, and John E. Sjaastad, "Long-Term Poverty and Child Development in the United States: Results from the NLSY," *Children and Youth Services Review* 17 (1995).

36. Mary Carlson and Felton Earls, "Psychological and Neuroendocrinological Sequelae of Early Social Deprivation in Institutionalized Children in Romaina," *Annals of the New York Academy of Sciences* 807 (1997); Megan R. Gunnar, "Early Adversity and the Development of Stress Reactivity and Regulation," in *The Minnesota Symposia on Child Psychology*, vol. 31: *The Effects of Early Adversity on Neurobehavioral Development*, edited by C. A. Nelson (Mahwah, N.J.: Lawrence Erlbaum and Associates, 2000); Michael D. De Bellis and others, "Developmental Traumatology, Part I: Biological Stress Systems," *Biological Psychiatry* 45 (1999).

37. Elizabeth Gould and others, "Neurogenesis in the Dentate Gyrus of the Adult Tree Shrew Is Regulated by Psychosocial Stress and Nmda Receptor Activation," *Journal of Neuroscience* 17 (1997); Elizabeth Gould and others, "Proliferation of Granule Cell Precursors in the Dentate Gyrus of Adult Monkeys Is Diminished by Stress," *Brain Research: Developmental Brain Research* 103 (1998); Patima Tanapat, Lisa A. Galea, and Elizabeth Gould, "Stress Inhibits the Proliferation of Granule Cell Precursors in the Developing Dentate Gyrus," *Journal of Developmental Neuroscience* 16 (1998).

38. J. Douglas Bremner and others, "MRI-Based Measurement of Hippocampal Volume in Patients with Combat-Related Posttraumatic Stress Disorder," *American Journal of Psychiatry* 152, no. 7 (1995); J. Douglas Bremner and others, "Hippocampal Volume Reduction in Major Depression," *American Journal of Psychiatry* 157, no. 1 (2000); Yvette I. Sheline and others, "Hippocampal Atrophy in Recurrent Major Depression," *Proceedings of the National Academy of Sciences USA* 93 (1996); David C. Steffens and others, "Hippocampal Volume in Geriatric Depression," *Biological Psychiatry* 43 (2000).

39. The role of the hippocampus in learning and memory is discussed by Squire, Haist, and Shimamura, "The Neurology of Memory" (see note 9). On the effects of prolonged exposure to stress hormones, see Robert M. Sapolsky, *Stress, the Aging Brain, and the Mechanisms of Neuron Death* (MIT Press, 1992).

40. Martha Augoustinos, "Developmental Effects of Child Abuse: A Number of Recent Findings," *Child Abuse and Neglect* 11 (1987); Normand J. Carrey and others, "Physiological and Cognitive Correlates of Child

Abuse," *Journal of the American Academy of Child and Adolescent Psychiatry* 34 (1995); John Money, Charles Annecillo, and John F. Kelly, "Abuse-Dwarfism Syndrome: After Rescue, Statural and Intellectual Catchup Growth Correlate," *Journal of Clinical Child Psychology* 12, nos. 279–83 (1983); Cynthia Perez and Cathy S. Widom, "Childhood Victimization and Longterm Intellectual and Academic Outcomes," *Child Abuse and Neglect* 18 (1994); Robert Pianta, Byron Egeland, and Martha F. Erickson, "Results of the Mother-Child Interaction Research Project," in *Child Maltreatment: Theory and Research on the Causes and Consequences of Child Abuse and Neglect*, edited by Dante Cicchetti and Vicki Carlson (Cambridge University Press, 1989); Penelope K. Trickett, Catherine A. McBride-Chang, and Frank W. Putnam, "The Classroom Performance and Behavior of Sexually Abused Girls," *Developmental Psychopathology* 6 (1994).

41. Sue R. Beers and Michael D. De Bellis, "Neuropsychological Function in Children with Maltreatment-Related Posttraumatic Stress Disorder," *American Journal of Psychiatry* 159 (2002); Ali R. Moradi and others, "Everyday Memory Deficits in Children and Adolescents with PTSD: Performance on the Rivermead Behavioral Memory Test," *Journal of Child Psychology and Psychiatry* 40 (1999).

42. Michael D. De Bellis and others, "Developmental Traumatology Part II: Brain Development," *Biological Psychiatry* 45 (1999); Victor G. Carrion and others, "Attenuation of Frontal Asymmetry in Pediatric Posttraumatic Stress Disorder," *Biological Psychiatry* 50 (2001).

43. H. Durfee and K. Wolf, "Anstaltspflege und Entwicklung im Ersten Lebensjahr," *Zeitschrift fur Kinderforschung* (translated in *Spitzer 1940*) 42, no. 3 (1933); Lawson G. Lowry, "Personality Distortion and Early Institutional Care," *American Journal of Orthopsychiatry* 10, no. 3 (1940).

44. Durston and others, "The Effect of Preceding Context on Inhibition" (see note 5).

45. Ian J. Deary and Peter G. Caryl, "Neuroscience and Human Intelligence Differences," *Trends in Neuroscience* 20 (1997); Larry A. Flashman and others, "Intelligence and Regional Brain Volumes in Normal Controls," *Intelligence* 25, no. 3 (1997); Bruce F. Pennington and others, "A Twin MRI Study of Size Variations in the Human Brain," *Journal of Cognitive Neuroscience* 12, no. 1 (2000); Uener Tan and others, "Magnetic Resonance Imaging Brain Size/IQ Relations in Turkish University Students," *Intelligence* 27, no. 1 (1999); John C. Wickett and others, "Relationships between Factors of Intelligence and Brain Volume," *Personality and Individual Differences* 29, no. 6 (2000).

46. Casey, Tottenham, and Fossella, "Clinical, Imaging, Lesion and Genetic Approaches toward a Model of Cognitive Control" (see note 5).

47. Lupien and others, "Child's Stress Hormone Levels Correlate with Mother's Socioeconomic Status and Depressive State" (see note 33).

48. Daphne Bavelier and Helen J. Neville, "Cross-Modal Plasticity: Where and How?" *Nature Reviews Neuroscience* 3 (2002).

49. Karestan C. Koenen and others, "Domestic Violence Is Associated with Environmental Suppression of IQ in Young Children," *Development and Psychopathology* 15 (2003).

50. Julia Kim-Cohen and others, "Genetic and Environmental Processes in Young Children's Resilience and Vulnerability to Socioeconomic Deprivation," *Child Development* 75, no. 3 (2004).

51. Christiane Capron and Michel Duyme, "Assessment of Effects of Socio-Economic Status on IQ in a Full Cross-Fostering Study," *Nature* 340, no. 6234 (1990).

52. Michael J. Meaney, "Maternal Care, Gene Expression, and the Transmission of Individual Differences in Stress Reactivity across Generations," *Annual Review of Neuroscience* 24 (2001); Stephen J. Suomi, "Gene-Environment Interactions and the Neurobiology of Social Conflict," *Annals of the New York Academy of Sciences* 1008 (2003).

53. Eric Turkheimer and others, "Socioeconomic Status Modifies Heritability of IQ in Young Children," *Psychological Science* 14, no. 6 (2003).

54. Rosenzweig and Bennett, "Psychobiology of Plasticity" (see note 33).

55. Kimberly A. Kerns, Karen Eso, and Jennifer Thomson, "Investigation of a Direct Intervention for Improving Attention in Young Children with ADHD," *Developmental Neuropsychology* 16, no. 2 (1999); Klingberg, Forssberg, and Westerberg, "Increased Brain Activity in Frontal and Parietal Cortex Underlies the Development of Visuospatial Working Memory Capacity during Childhood" (see note 5).

56. M. Rosario Rueda and others, "Training of Attention in 4 Year Old Children," paper presented to the Cognitive Neuroscience Society, San Francisco, 2004.

57. John C. Buckner, E. Mezzacappa, and W. R. Beardslee, "Characteristics of Resilient Youths Living in Poverty: The Role of Self-Regulatory Processes," *Development and Psychopathology* 15, no. 1 (2003).

58. Bruce M. McCandliss and Michael Wolmetz, "Developmental Psychobiology of Reading Disability," *Biological Psychiatry* (forthcoming).

59. Barbara R. Foorman and others, "How Letter-Sound Instruction Mediates Progress in First-Grade Reading and Spelling," *Journal of Educational Psychology* 83, no. 4 (1991); Joseph K. Torgesen and others, "Intensive Remedial Instruction for Children with Severe Reading Disabilities: Immediate and Long-Term Outcomes from Two Instructional Approaches," *Journal of Learning Disabilities* 34 (2001); Frank R. Vellutino and others, "Cognitive Profiles of Difficult-to-Remediate and Readily Remediated Poor Readers: Early Intervention as a Vehicle for Distinguishing between Cognitive and Experiential Deficits as Basic Causes of a Specific Reading Disability," *Journal of Educational Psychology* 88, nos. 601–38 (1996).

60. Simos and others, "Dyslexia-Specific Brain Activation Profile Becomes Normal Following Successful Remedial Training" (see note 16).

61. Elise Temple and others, "Neural Deficits in Children with Dyslexia Ameliorated by Behavioral Remediation: Evidence from Functional MRI," *Proceedings of the National Academy of Sciences, USA* 100, no. 5 (2003).

62. Cecilia E. Rouse and Alan B. Krueger, "Putting Computerized Instruction to the Test: A Randomized Evaluation of a 'Scientifically-Based' Reading Program," *Economics of Education Review* (forthcoming).

63. Bennett A. Shaywitz and others, "Development of Left Occipitotemporal Systems for Skilled Reading in Children after a Phonologically-Based Intervention," *Biological Psychiatry* 55 (2004).

64. Mark A. Eckert, Linda J. Lombardino, and Christiana M. Leonard, "Planar Asymmetry Tips the Phonological Playground and Environment Raises the Bar," *Child Development* 72, no. 4 (2001).

Low Birth Weight and School Readiness

Nancy E. Reichman

Summary

In the United States black women have for decades been twice as likely as white women to give birth to babies of low birth weight who are at elevated risk for developmental disabilities. Does the black-white disparity in low birth weight contribute to the racial disparity in readiness?

The author summarizes the cognitive and behavioral problems that beset many low birth weight children and notes that not only are the problems greatest for the smallest babies, but black babies are two to three times as likely as whites to be very small. Nevertheless, the racial disparities in low birth weight cannot explain much of the *aggregate* gap in readiness because the most serious birth weight–related disabilities affect a very small share of children. The author estimates that low birth weight explains at most 3–4 percent of the racial gap in IQ scores.

The author applauds the post-1980 expansions of Medicaid for increasing rates of prenatal care use among poor pregnant women but stresses that standard prenatal medical care cannot improve aggregate birth outcomes substantially. Smoking cessation and nutrition are two prenatal interventions that show promise. Several early intervention programs have been shown to improve cognitive skills of low birth weight children. But even the most promising programs can narrow the readiness gap only a little because their benefits are greatest for heavier low birth weight children and because low birth weight explains only a small share of the gap.

The author stresses the importance of reducing rates of low birth weight generally and of extending to all children who need them the interventions that have improved cognitive outcomes among low birth weight children. But because black infants are more likely to be born at the lowest birth weights, *preventing* low birth weight—when researchers learn how to—is likely to be more effective than early intervention in narrowing birth weight–related racial gaps in school readiness.

www.future of children.org

Nancy E. Reichman is associate professor of pediatrics at the Robert Wood Johnson Medical School, University of Medicine and Dentistry of New Jersey. She gratefully acknowledges eight continuous years of funding from the National Institute of Child Health and Human Development, without which this article would not have been possible. She also wishes to thank Nigel Paneth for his inspiring chart of survival rates of very low birth weight infants over time; Elana Broch for locating the 1980 vital statistics report and countless other materials over many years; Jennifer Borkowski for cheerfully and meticulously extracting, crunching, and compiling data from an assortment of historical vital statistics reports; Julien Teitler for numerous hours of brainstorming; Elaine Barfield, Kavita Bhanot, and Christopher Ramos for helping to synthesize portions of the literature; Anne Case and many others for helpful comments on an earlier draft; Rehan Shamim for compiling and formatting the references; Lenna Nepomnyaschy and Ofira Schwartz-Soicher for reviewing the final draft.

Nancy E. Reichman

In the United States, black women have for decades been twice as likely as white women to give birth to babies of low birth weight—those weighing less than 2,500 grams, or about 5.5 pounds. Not only is low birth weight a leading cause of infant mortality, but infants who survive are at elevated risk for many long-term health conditions and developmental disabilities that can impair school readiness. The black-white disparity in low birth weight is so large and so persistent that it raises the question of whether it contributes to racial disparities in children's cognitive abilities and in readiness.

This article, which focuses on the effect of low birth weight on the racial gap in test scores, consists of six sections. The first provides a brief overview of low birth weight in the United States—definition, trends, and associated rates of survival and child disability. The second discusses disparities in low birth weight by race, ethnicity, and nativity, as well as survival rates by race. The third section, the heart of the paper, examines the link between low birth weight and school readiness. It reviews the cognitive and behavioral problems that beset many low birth weight children, noting that the problems are greatest for the smallest babies and that black babies are much more likely than white babies to be very small. It also explores the effect of birth weight on the black-white gap in readiness and confirms earlier findings that the racial disparity in birth weight explains only a few percentage points of the aggregate gap. The fourth section looks at the determinants of low birth weight, focusing on those that vary by race. The fifth considers past efforts to tackle the problem of low birth weight through prevention or through amelioration of its adverse consequences. It highlights early intervention programs that have been shown to improve cognitive outcomes among low birth weight children and thus close at least a small portion of the readiness gap. The final section summarizes the article's key findings, highlights important implications, and offers recommendations.

Low Birth Weight in the United States

Low birth weight is a widely used and much studied marker of infant health.[1] It is well measured, reliably recorded, and readily available from vital statistics files and many other data sets. Birth weight is often categorized as very low (less than 1,500 grams, or about 3.3 pounds), low (less than 2,500 grams), or normal (2,500 grams or more). Further distinctions include extremely low (less than 1,000 grams) and moderately low (1,500–2,499 grams) birth weight. Births can also be characterized by gestational age: very preterm (less than 32 weeks), preterm (less than 37 weeks), and term (37 weeks or more). These terms and their definitions are summarized in table 1, along with the corresponding rates of births in the United States in 2000. Babies considered small for gestational age (SGA) or growth retarded are typically below the 10th percentile in sex-specific birth weight for gestational age. All low birth weight babies are preterm or growth retarded (they can be both), and virtually all very low birth weight babies are preterm.

Trends

Babies born in the United States are more likely to be low birth weight than those born in almost every other developed country.[2] Low birth weight is the second leading cause of infant mortality in the United States after birth defects, and surviving infants are at elevated risk for debilitating medical conditions and learning disorders.[3] Figure 1 shows rates of low birth weight, very low birth weight,

Table 1. Definitions of Low Birth Weight and Related Outcomes, United States

Term	Definition	Percent of live births, 2000
Normal birth weight	At least 2,500 grams	92.4
Low birth weight (LBW)	Less than 2,500 grams	7.6
Moderately low birth weight	1,500–2,499 grams	6.2
Very low birth weight (VLBW)	Less than 1,500 grams	1.4
Extremely low birth weight (ELBW)	Less than 1,000 grams	0.7
Preterm	Less than 37 weeks' gestation	11.6
Very preterm	Less than 32 weeks' gestation	1.9

Source: Joyce A. Martin and others, "Births: Final Data for 2000," *National Vital Statistics Reports* 52, no. 10 (Hyattsville, Md.: National Center for Health Statistics, February 12, 2002).

and infant mortality (death before age one) in the United States from 1980 to 2000. Thanks to increased specialization in delivering maternal and newborn health care and to advances in neonatal intensive care technology, the United States made substantial progress in reducing the infant mortality rate over this period, although its gains have lagged behind those of other developed countries.[4] Rates of low and very low birth weight, meanwhile, increased slightly, owing partly to the increasing prevalence of multiple births; the rate of low birth weight among singleton births has remained steady, at about 6 percent.[5]

Low birth weight babies are much more likely to survive today than they once were. Since 1960, survival rates have increased dramatically for very low and extremely low birth weight babies born in the United States (figure 2). Although less than 10 percent of extremely low birth weight singleton infants born in 1960 lived to their first birthday, that figure increased to 27 percent for those born in 1980 and to 57 percent for those born in 2000.[6] And while fewer than half of very low birth weight (defined here as 1,000–1,499 grams) singleton babies born in 1960 survived, by 2000 the share surviving had increased to

Figure 1. Low Birth Weight, Very Low Birth Weight, and Infant Mortality Rates, United States, 1980-2000

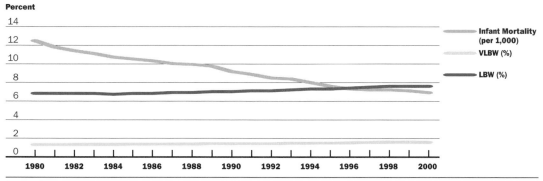

Source: Centers for Disease Control and Prevention, *Morbidity and Mortality Weekly Report,* vol. 51(27): 589–92 (www.cdc.gov/ mmwr/ preview/mmwrhtml/mm5127a1.htm).

Figure 2. One-Year Survival Rates of Singleton Low Birth Weight Infants, by Birth Weight, United States, 1960, 1980, and 2000

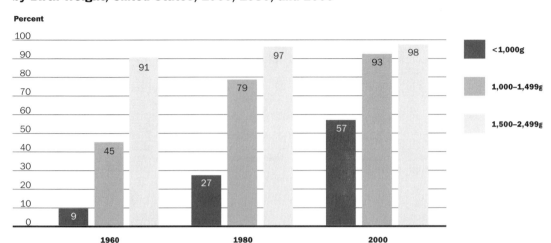

Sources: Data for 1960 are from U.S. Department of Health, Education, and Welfare, Public Health Service, Office of Health Research, Statistics, and Technology, "A Study of Infant Mortality from Linked Records, by Birth Weight, Period of Gestation, and Other Variables, United States, 1960 Live-Birth Cohort," (PHS) 79-1055 (Hyattsville, Md.: National Center for Health Statistics, May 1972). Data for 1980 are from U.S. Department of Health and Human Services, Public Health Service, "National Infant Mortality Surveillance (NIMS) 1980," (Atlanta: Centers for Disease Control, Center for Chronic Disease Prevention and Health Promotion, Division of Reproductive Health, December 1989). Data for 2000 are from National Center for Health Statistics, "Live Births, Infant Deaths, and Infant Mortality Rates by Plurality, Birthweight, Race of Mother, and Gestational Age: United States, 2000 Period Data," table LFWK 46 (www.cdc.gov/nchs/datawh/statab/unpubd/ mortabs.htm#Linked).
Notes: This figure was adapted from a slide provided by Nigel Paneth, M.D., M.P.H., Michigan State University. Only single births are used. The figures for 1960 were calculated using cutoffs of <1,001 grams and 1,001–1,500 grams.

more than 90 percent. Likewise, the survival rates of moderately low birth weight singleton infants increased from 91 percent in 1980 to 98 percent in 2000.[7] The new survivors, however, are at high risk for health and developmental problems, as discussed below.

Survival and Disability

The majority of moderately low birth weight infants thrive, suffering few or no problems. It is the lightest babies who are most at risk of disabilities, both cognitive and physical, that can impair school readiness. Of the many child health conditions associated with low birth weight, perhaps the most potentially disabling is cerebral palsy, a group of disorders characterized by the inability to control movement and often accompanied by cognitive impairments.[8] Preterm very low birth weight infants are up to 30 percent more likely to develop cerebral palsy

than are babies born at term.[9] Other serious conditions associated with low birth weight or preterm birth include mental retardation, respiratory distress syndrome (RDS), bronchopulmonary dysplasia (BPD), retinopathy of prematurity (ROP), and deafness. RDS and BPD can lead to feeding difficulty, recurrent respiratory infections, asthma, and growth delay.[10] ROP, a disorder caused by abnormal growth of blood vessels in the eye, can lead to blindness.[11] All these disabilities can impair learning and inhibit a child's school readiness. Almost without exception, the prevalence of these disabling conditions increases as birth weight decreases.

A recent review of forty-two studies of infants born after 1970 found no change between 1976 and 1990 in the prevalence of major neurodevelopmental disabilities among extremely immature (26 weeks or less) and extremely small (800 grams or less) survivors. Throughout that period, cerebral palsy affected 12 percent of extremely immature and 8 percent of extremely small survivors; mental retardation affected 14 percent of each group; 8 percent of each group was blind; and 3 percent of each group was deaf. Overall, 22 percent of extremely immature survivors and 24 percent of extremely small survivors had at least one major disability.[12]

Disparities in Low Birth Weight by Race, Ethnicity, and Nativity

The black-white disparity in low birth weight in the United States is glaring and persistent. In 2000, 13 percent of babies born to black mothers were low birth weight, compared to 6.5 percent of those born to white mothers.[13] (By contrast, rates of low birth weight for the other racial groups reported by the National Center for Health Statistics were close to that of whites: 6.8 percent among American Indians and 7.3 percent among Asians and Pacific Islanders.)[14] The two-to-one disparity between blacks and whites has persisted for more than forty years, exists at most maternal age ranges, cannot be explained by differences in rates of multiple births, and cannot be explained by socioeconomic status alone.[15] Even infants born to college-educated black women are at much greater risk than infants born to college-educated white women of being low birth weight.[16] Black mothers were 63 percent more likely to have preterm deliveries than white mothers (17.3 percent as against 10.6 percent) in 2000.[17] The rates of small-for-gestational-age births among infants born at term in 1998 were 17.4 percent among blacks and 9.0 percent among whites.[18]

Ethnicity

Rates of low birth weight also vary among women of different ancestral origins. The rate for women of Hispanic descent was 6.4 percent in 2000, on par with the rate for whites. But within that broad group, rates differ widely. In 2000, women of Cuban and Mexican descent had low birth weight rates of 6.5 percent and 6.0 percent, respectively, while Puerto Ricans had a rate of 9.3 percent.[19] The disparity between Puerto Ricans and Mexicans has baffled researchers because both groups are at high risk for adverse outcomes based on their socioeconomic status, and island-born Puerto Ricans, as U.S. citizens, have greater access than foreign-born Mexicans to Medicaid.[20] The disparity may have to do with unmeasured differences in culture, diet, stress, or lifestyle.[21] Researchers have termed the unexpectedly favorable rates among Mexican American women, despite their socioeconomic disadvantages and comparatively low use of prenatal care, the *epidemiologic* or *Hispanic paradox*.[22] Explaining this paradox could provide clues about how to blunt the negative effects of poverty on birth outcomes of other disadvantaged groups. Blacks of Puerto Rican or other Hispanic ethnicity have a lower probability of low birth weight than blacks who are non-Hispanic, but very few (3 percent) of the 622,598 births to black mothers in 2000 were to mothers who identified themselves as Hispanic.[23]

Several researchers, notably Gosta Rooth, have questioned the standard 2,500 gram cutoff for low birth weight, arguing that it does not account for variation in mean birth weights across countries that may be due to differences in, for example, maternal height.[24] That threshold may likewise not be appropriate for all racial and ethnic groups in the United States, but the "natural" underlying distributions are not known and may themselves be determined by factors such as health and socioeconomic status rather than

Figure 3. Extremely Low Birth Weight, Very Low Birth Weight, and Low Birth Weight Rates by Race, United States, 1980 and 2000

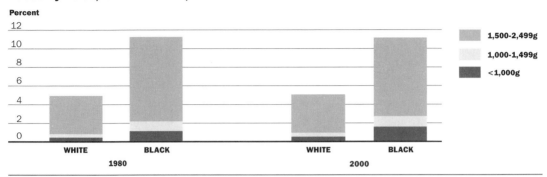

Sources: See figure 2.
Notes: Only single births are used. For 1980, race is based on both parents' races from birth certificates; for 2000, on mother's race from birth certificate.

biological predisposition. Nigel Paneth, in an excellent summary of this issue, suggests that there is not enough evidence to dismiss the glaring racial disparities in low birth weight in the United States as "normal."[25]

Nativity

In 2000 some 80 percent of U.S. births to white women and 88 percent of births to black women were to mothers born in the United States.[26] Many groups of immigrant mothers, particularly Mexicans, make less use of prenatal care and other health services than their U.S.-born ethnic counterparts because of multiple legal, language, socioeconomic, and cultural barriers.[27] Yet the birth outcomes of Mexican immigrants are even more favorable than those of U.S.-born Mexican mothers. In fact, for virtually every racial and ethnic group in the United States, immigrants have better birth outcomes than U.S.-born mothers.[28] Thus, although immigrants encounter numerous barriers to prenatal care, they have offsetting health, social, or lifestyle advantages that promote favorable birth outcomes.

Several studies have analyzed birth outcomes of black women by nativity.[29] Of particular in-

terest, Richard David and James Collins found that African-born black mothers have rates of low birth weight much closer to those of U.S.-born white mothers than to those of U.S.-born black mothers of predominantly African descent. This suggests that black-white disparities in low birth weight may be due to social and environmental factors rather than biological predisposition, although one cannot rule out the possibility that the differences are due to selective migration.

Low Birth Weight, Survival, and Race

Given the large disparity in low birth weight between blacks and whites and the small disparities between whites and other racial groups and between whites and Hispanics, in the remainder of this article I focus on black-white differences in school readiness. Whenever possible I focus on the lowest birth weight infants, because although they compose small proportions of all births, they suffer the highest rates of disability and therefore have the poorest long-term prognosis for school readiness and academic achievement. As figure 3 shows, the rate of low birth weight among blacks (single births) was the same in 2000 as in 1980; that for whites increased slightly.[30] The black-white disparity occurs across all low birth weight groups but is even larger for the lowest weight groups. And while the overall rates of low birth weight have remained constant, the shares of births in lowest weight groups have increased, particularly for blacks. Between 1980 and 2000 the rate of extremely low birth weight rose almost 50 percent among blacks and a third among whites, while the rate of very low birth weight rose about 25 percent among blacks and 15 percent among whites. These higher rates may reflect increased obstetric intervention that prevents fetal loss. Overall reported fetal deaths at 20 or more weeks' gestation declined 12 percent over 1990–2000 alone; the decreases for non-Hispanic whites and non-Hispanic blacks were 10 percent and 5 percent, respectively.[31]

The rate of infant mortality (death in the first year) has fallen steadily for both blacks and whites over the past twenty-five years. In 1980, 18 out of 1,000 black singleton babies did not live to their first birthday; by 2000 that figure had fallen to 12 out of 1,000. For white babies the comparable rates were 9 out of 1,000 in 1980 and 5 out of 1,000 in 2000.[32] As with low birth weight, the two-to-one black-white disparity in infant mortality has persisted over time, although the *percentage* decline in infant mortality has been greater among whites than among blacks.

Birthweight-specific survival rates are remarkably equivalent for black and white singletons. In the past, black low birth weight infants had a paradoxical survival advantage, perhaps owing to differences in fetal health and differential rates of fetal loss. In 1980, 83 percent of black and 76 percent of white singleton infants of very low birth weight (here, 1,000–1,499 grams) survived their first year;

for extremely low birth weight infants, the survival rates were 29 percent for blacks and 27 percent for whites. In 2000, survival rates for very low birth weight infants were 93 percent for whites and 94 percent for blacks; and for extremely low birth weight babies, 58 percent for whites and 57 percent for blacks. Even taking into account multiple births, recent figures show no indication of racial disparities in birth weight–specific survival or in birth weight–specific neonatal survival (the first 28 days of life).[33] The lifesaving advantages of neonatal care thus appear to be color-blind, at least in the aggregate. (These figures do not speak to whether there are disparities in newborn care more generally.) However, because black infants are much more likely to fall into the lowest weight groups, a disproportionate fraction of black survivors is at high risk for adverse health and developmental outcomes.

Among survivors born in 2000 (including multiple births), the share of black infants who were extremely low birth weight is 1.00 percent, more than three times that for whites (0.32 percent). The difference is similar for very low birth weight babies (2.31 percent for blacks, as against 0.89 percent for whites).[34] Thus among children born in 2000 who survived their first year of life, black children are more than two and a half times as likely as white children to have been extremely or very low birth weight—and therefore to be at risk of serious cognitive delays that could affect school readiness and academic achievement when they enter kindergarten in 2005.[35]

Low Birth Weight and School Readiness

Extensive research confirms that low birth weight children are at greater risk for cognitive and school performance problems than are their normal birth weight peers, and that the risk for adverse outcomes increases as birth weight decreases.[36] A meta-analysis of case control studies reported from 1980 to November 2001 found that the mean IQ for school-aged children born very preterm is approximately two-thirds of a standard deviation below that of controls who were born at term.[37] A population-based study using linked birth certificate and school records from Florida found that the risk of specific

---

Children born preterm have greater difficulty completing tasks involving reading, spelling, and math than their full-term peers.

---

school-identified disabilities increases as birth weight decreases.[38] Enrollment in special education also follows a birth weight gradient, with the lightest babies being most likely to be placed in such programs.[39] While all of these findings are based on cohorts born before the major advances in neonatal intensive care of the 1990s, research on later cohorts yields similar results.[40]

Children born preterm have greater difficulty completing tasks involving reading, spelling, and math than their full-term peers, though math scores are more consistently related to preterm birth or very low birth weight than are reading achievement scores.[41] Preterm children tend to have language difficulties related to grammar and abstraction.[42] They also tend to be more inattentive, aggressive, and hyperactive, as well as less able to handle leadership roles than their full-term peers.[43]

Some cognitive deficits are the direct result of medical disorders.[44] Compromised motor skills in many preterm infants, for example, may lead to learning disabilities and handicaps.[45] Studies of the brains of preterm and full-term children have identified areas that correspond to the cognitive deficits observed. Brain volume tends to be reduced, resulting in larger ventricles containing more cerebrospinal fluid, thinning of the corpus callosum (which indicates less white matter), and a reduction in gray matter. The sensorimotor cortex, amygdala, and hippocampus are also often reduced.[46] These anatomical deficiencies are most likely a result of immaturity, physiological instabilities, or stressful experiences as neonates.[47]

Birth weight may also have indirect effects on cognitive development through parenting. The medical, developmental, and behavioral problems of a very light infant may heighten parental stress, which may in turn impair the child's learning. Research in this area is in its infancy. According to one recent study, mothers of very low birth weight infants suffered more psychological distress than mothers of term infants at one month, at two years, and at three years, with the severity of stress positively related to the child's developmental outcomes.[48]

Collectively, past studies based on hospital or regional cohorts have found that among extremely low birth weight infants, 8 to 18 percent have IQ scores under 70 (a cutoff often used to define mental retardation), and 25 to 29 percent have IQs in the 70–84 (borderline) range at school age (generally ages six or eight to ten). The corresponding figures for very low birth weight infants (here, 1,000–1,499 grams) are 5 percent and 19 percent; for moderately low birth weight infants, 5 percent and 17 percent; and for normal birth weight infants, 0 to 4 percent and 4 to 14 percent (the figures for very low and moderately low birth weight infants are based on only one study).[49]

Birth Weight and Socioeconomic Status

Birth weight is but one of many risk factors for cognitive impairment. One of the most salient risk factors is low socioeconomic status. Disentangling the effects of birth weight from those of the many socioeconomic disadvantages linked with low birth weight is difficult. Research to date indicates that very low birth weight (and—much less so—moderately low birth weight) does have independent deleterious effects on early cognitive outcomes, such as IQ and PIAT scores.[50] But while it might be interesting from a variety of vantage points to disentangle the effects of birth weight and socioeconomic status, the two are so highly correlated that it may not be relevant for policy purposes to do so.

Low Birth Weight and Aggregate Educational Outcomes

Clearly, individual children born low birth weight can be seriously disadvantaged with respect to schooling. But because most serious birth weight–related disabilities tend to occur at the lowest weight ranges and therefore affect a very small proportion of children, low birth weight may not explain much of the observed variation in educational attainment at the aggregate level. A recent study of children born in the 1958 British birth cohort, for example, found that children born at low birth weight passed significantly fewer O-level exams. But being born at low birth weight, or being born to a mother who smoked during pregnancy (also a predictor of poor educational outcomes), explained only 2.5 percent of the variation in O-level results.[51]

Low Birth Weight and the Black-White Gap in Test Scores

Only two studies of which I am aware have presented data indicating the potential effect of low birth weight on racial test score gaps. Yolanda Padilla and her coauthors, in a study using National Longitudinal Survey of Youth (NLSY) child data and focusing on the effects of the Mexican-American birth weight advantage on early childhood development, found that low birth weight explains less than 1 percent of the (unadjusted) black-white gap in scores on the Peabody Picture Vocabulary Test-Revised (PPVT-R) among three- and four-year-olds in the late 1980s and early 1990s.[52] Jeanne Brooks-Gunn and her coauthors presented a similar estimate in a recent analysis of the contributions of family and test characteristics to the black-white test score gap.[53] Also using NLSY child data, they found that low birth weight and gender together explain less than 2 percent of the unadjusted racial gap in PPVT-R scores at age five.

My own estimate of the potential impact of birth weight on the racial gap in one test of cognitive ability—full-scale IQ score—is similar, though somewhat higher. My subject is all black and white infant survivors born in 2000, including multiples. In contrast to Padilla and Brooks-Gunn I do not use the NLSY data, because although that data set has actual test scores, it may underrepresent the very lightest babies. Instead I use vital statistics data, which provide exact race-specific birth weight distributions for surviving infants in the United States, though test scores must be imputed. I assigned an IQ score to each survivor, based on the infant's birth weight. I then computed the racial gap in imputed IQ scores and divided this figure by the total observed racial gap in IQ scores, to compute the maximum proportion of the overall gap that can be explained by birth weight.[54] Using various distributions of IQ scores based on past research and a range of assumptions, I found that birth weight explains a maximum of 3 to 4 percent of the racial gap in IQ scores, or one-half a point in IQ.

Determinants of Low Birth Weight

Researchers have identified and analyzed many social, medical, and behavioral risk factors for low birth weight, some of which could contribute to racial disparities in low birth weight, and ultimately to school readiness. Many of these risk factors are intricately intertwined, and for the most part I will not attempt to establish or disentangle causal effects.

Socioeconomic Status

Women of low socioeconomic status are at increased risk for delivering low birth weight babies, whether socioeconomic status is defined by income, occupation, or education.[55] Education may also have independent effects, above and beyond income, because more highly educated mothers may know more about family planning and healthy behaviors during pregnancy. In 1998, the rate of low birth weight among mothers with less than a high school education was 9 percent, as against 7.9 percent among high school graduates, and 6.5 percent among mothers with at least some college.[56] In 2000, 78.6 percent of white women giving birth, and 74.5 percent of black women giving birth, had twelve or more years of education.[57] Black Americans are much more likely than whites to come from a disadvantaged socioeconomic background, but that does not fully explain the racial disparity in low birth weight.[58]

Marital Status

Marital status is also a key correlate of birth weight. In 1992, the rate of low birth weight babies among unmarried mothers in the United States was 10.4 percent, as against 5.7 percent among married mothers.[59] In 2000, 27.1 percent of low birth weight babies born to white mothers and 68.5 percent of low birth weight babies born to black mothers had unmarried parents.[60] The marital status disparity may reflect either the greater likelihood of unmarried mothers to be poor or other characteristics that vary by marital status.[61]

Maternal Age

In 2000, 19.7 percent of births to black women and 10.6 percent to white women in the United States were to teens. The rate of low birth weight babies among teen mothers was 35 percent higher than that among mothers aged twenty to twenty-nine (9.6 percent as against 7.1 percent). The rate among the youngest teens—those fifteen and younger—was 14.1 percent, higher than in any age group except forty-five to fifty-four.[62] Teen mothers' birth weight disadvantage has several explanations. A pregnant teenager who is still growing may compete for nutrients with the fetus. Becoming pregnant within two years after menarche increases the risk for preterm delivery.[63] Many teen pregnancies are unplanned, unwanted, or discovered late, and pregnant teens are more likely than older mothers to be poor, to be undereducated, or to lack access to resources or services—all, in themselves, risk factors for low birth weight.[64]

In 1992 Arline Geronimus found, surprisingly, that black teen mothers seem to have a paradoxical advantage in birth outcomes over older black mothers. She speculated that this finding may be due to "weathering" among black women—more rapid age-related deterioration in health than among white women because of greater cumulative exposure to harsh living conditions. Thus young maternal age may not be as much a risk factor among black mothers as it is among whites.[65] Unadjusted national figures for black mothers from 2000 do not reflect this pattern; low birth weight rates among black mothers were lowest among mothers in their twenties.[66] If the national sample were restricted to disadvantaged black mothers, however, the Geronimus weathering pattern might become apparent.

On the other end of the age spectrum, women who give birth in their late thirties or older are also at increased risk for having low birth weight babies. In 2000, 9.7 percent of births to black women and 13.9 percent of births to white women in the United States were to women aged thirty-five and over.[67] For these women the risks are biological: older ova and a greater likelihood of medical risk factors such as hypertension.[68] Older women also have more unintended pregnancies—itself a risk factor for low birth weight—than do women in their twenties and early thirties.[69]

One study found that women aged thirty and older are at greater risk for poor birth outcomes than teens of the same race, though offsetting factors such as higher socioecoomic status mask this risk.[70] That same study, which controlled for such socioeconomic characteristics as whether the birth was covered by Medicaid, found evidence of the Geronimus weathering phenomenon. Black mothers aged fifteen to nineteen were at lower risk of delivering low birth weight babies than were black mothers in their twenties. Given the complicated relation between maternal age and low birth weight, it is difficult to assess the extent to which black mothers are at increased risk in this regard.

Medical Conditions

Among the medical risk factors for low birth weight and preterm birth are prior low birth weight or preterm delivery, cervical abnormalities, hypertension, anemia, and bacterial infections.[71] Chronic physical or psychological stress also increases the risk.[72] Among the risk factors for fetal growth retardation are previous low birth weight births, infections, sexually transmitted diseases, poor maternal hematological status, hypertension-related complications, renal disease, heart disease,

---

One study found that women aged thirty and older are at greater risk for poor birth outcomes than teens of the same race, though offsetting factors such as higher socioeconomic status mask this risk.

---

third trimester bleeding, and sickle cell disease.[73] Nutritional inadequacy can also impair fetal growth.[74]

Most, but not all, of these medical risk factors are more prevalent among blacks than whites. Most are rare. In 2000, for example, 3.8 percent of black mothers and 2.1 percent of white mothers were anemic during pregnancy; 1.4 percent of black mothers and 0.7 percent of white mothers had chronic hypertension. Black mothers had higher rates of acute or chronic lung disease, genital herpes, hydramnios or oligohydramnios (too little or too much amniotic fluid), hemoglobinopathy (a blood disorder), pregnancy-associated hypertension, eclampsia, incompetent cervix, and previous preterm babies or growth-retarded infants. White mothers had higher rates of cardiac disease, renal disease, Rh sensitization, and uterine bleeding.[75] Bacterial vaginosis, a mild bacterial infection more common among black women than white women, has been linked with preterm delivery of low birth weight infants.[76]

Prenatal Substance Use

Maternal cigarette smoking during pregnancy decreases fetal growth rates and substantially increases the risks of spontaneous abortion, preterm delivery, low birth weight, placental ruptures, placenta praevia, and perinatal death. Prenatal alcohol and drug use are also linked with poor birth outcomes, though the relationships are less clear-cut and not as dose-response specific as that of smoking.[77] Substance abuse during pregnancy, particularly of alcohol and illicit drugs, is notoriously underreported. Based on reported rates of smoking, black mothers do not appear to be at increased risk for low birth weight. In 2000, 9.1 percent of black mothers and 13.2 percent of white mothers in the United States reported smoking cigarettes (at all) during pregnancy. The proportion of black and white mothers who reported consuming alcohol at all during pregnancy according to birth records in 2000 was virtually identical—about 1 percent of each group.[78] However, these rates are nowhere near the proportion (16.3 percent) of pregnant women aged eighteen to forty-four who reported alcohol consumption in the past month in the 1995 Behavioral Risk Factor Surveillance System.[79] For this reason, prenatal alcohol consumption has since been removed from the U.S Standard Certificate of Live Birth. In the 2001 National Household Survey on Drug Abuse, reported rates of current illicit drug use were similar among white (4.0 percent) and black (3.7 percent) pregnant women.[80]

Intergenerational Health

Several studies have found strong associations between parents' (generally mothers') birth weight and the birth weight of their child.[81] A recent study comparing maternal cousins (children whose mothers are sisters), and thus filtering out much of the confounding effect of socioeconomic status, found that maternal and paternal low birth weights together explain a much larger share of the racial disparity in low birth weight than do individual characteristics and socioeconomic variables combined.[82] This finding suggests that there is a biological transmission of low birth weight across generations, which may contribute to racial differences in low birth weight. This is an important finding that can be used to target interventions, but given the strong association between birth weight and socioeconomic status, it should not be used to dismiss racial disparities as immutable.

Promising Directions for Future Research on Risk Factors

Other risk factors warrant further study and ultimately may offer strategies for reducing rates of low birth weight and narrowing racial disparities in low birth weight and school readiness. For the most part, research on these risks is in its infancy, and the associations being explored should not be interpreted as causal.

MATERNAL LIFESTYLE. Despite the beneficial effects of employment on income, mothers who work in strenuous occupations, including those that involve prolonged standing, are at heightened risk for both preterm delivery and having low birth weight babies.[83] Occupational exposures to toxic substances and solvents have also been linked to preterm delivery.[84] Given that a greater share of black women than white women (in 2002, 9 percent as against 5 percent) in the United States work as operators, fabricators, and laborers, black mothers may be more likely than white mothers to encounter strenuous working conditions and toxic exposures.[85]

NEIGHBORHOODS. Living in a poor neighborhood may pose health risks above and beyond those associated with individual poverty. Houses and other buildings in poor neighborhoods tend to be old and in poor condition; environmental toxins tend to be high; and access to medical care and other services tends to be limited.[86]

One study of Chicago in 1990 found that living in different neighborhoods accounted for as much as 30 percent of the difference in mean birth weight between non-Hispanic blacks and whites, though it is unclear whether these "neighborhood effects" reflect social, economic, or physical characteristics of neighborhoods or unobserved individual-level risk factors that vary by neighborhood.[87] Neighborhood socioeconomic characteristics, such as census tract–level income, are important predictors of low birth weight, even after controlling for many individual-level characteristics.[88] In Chicago, violent crime in neighborhoods has been found to have a negative association with birth weight, while a combined measure of social interaction and community involvement has a positive association.[89] Many studies have linked low birth weight to residential environmental exposures, including air pollution, substances in drinking water, and industrial chemicals.[90] Three-quarters of the residents of high-poverty neighborhoods in the United States are minorities, and the number of blacks living in poor areas increased from 2.4 million

in 1970 to 4.2 million in 1990. Thus black women are at high risk for delivering low birth weight babies on the basis of the neighborhoods in which they live.[91]

PATERNAL FACTORS. Finally, a growing body of research suggests that paternal behaviors and occupational exposures before conception may affect infant health. Male reproductive toxicity can have three mechanisms—nongenetic (seminal fluid), genetic (gene mutations or chromosomal abnormalities), and epigenetic (effects on gene expression, genomic imprinting, or DNA methylation).[92] One study linked paternal drinking and low birth weight, but its finding has not been replicated.[93] Others have found associations between paternal smoking and low birth weight, although it is difficult to disentangle potential direct effects of paternal smoking from indirect effects through maternal exposure to secondhand smoke.[94] Paternal occupational exposures are also a risk factor. Excess rates of preterm delivery, growth retardation, and low birth weight have been found in occupations that involve paternal exposure to pesticides, solvents, and lead.[95] In 2002, 28 percent of employed black men, as against 16 percent of employed white men in the United States, worked as operators, fabricators, and laborers, perhaps making black fathers more likely than white fathers to be exposed to toxic substances at work.[96]

Interventions

Child health policymakers and practitioners have implemented many programs both to prevent low birth weight and to improve the life chances of low birth weight babies, especially in the areas of school readiness and achievement. To the extent that the programs succeed, they could help narrow racial gaps in school readiness by as much as 3 to 4 percent, as noted.

Preventing Low Birth Weight

Recognizing the close links between low birth weight and socioeconomic status, policymakers have emphasized a strategy of expanding prenatal care eligibility and services for poor pregnant women. The expansion of Medicaid eligibility and outreach to pregnant women in the late 1980s and early 1990s increased access to prenatal care, improved services, and helped more women begin care earlier in their pregnancies.[97] Rates of both early and adequate use

---

Nevertheless, the U.S. rate of low birth weight, even for singletons, has not declined—perhaps owing in part to the declining rate of fetal mortality—and remains higher than that of most other developed countries.

---

of prenatal care increased substantially between 1981 and 1998 for both blacks and whites, and, except for some groups of young mothers, racial disparities in the use of prenatal care decreased.[98] In 2000, 85.0 percent of white mothers and 74.3 percent of black mothers who gave birth in the United States began prenatal care in the first trimester of pregnancy; 3.3 percent of white mothers and 6.7 percent of black mothers had late or no prenatal care.[99] Nevertheless, the U.S. rate of low birth weight, even for singletons, has not declined—perhaps owing in part to the declining rate of fetal mortality—and remains higher than that of most other developed countries.

It is difficult to ascertain the effectiveness of prenatal care in reducing low birth weight.

Randomized controlled trials—the gold standard in such research—are rarely feasible because of ethical concerns about depriving women of care. In a rare randomized trial, Lorraine Klerman and colleagues compared augmented and standard prenatal care provided to Medicaid-eligible African American women. The augmented care improved women's satisfaction with care and knowledge about risk conditions but did not reduce the rate of low birth weight.[100]

Studies other than randomized controlled trials face several methodological challenges, including selection bias. With *favorable selection*, women with the best expected outcomes are the most likely to seek prenatal care and to do so early, so the estimated effect of care could be overstated. With *adverse selection*, women with the worst expected outcomes are most likely to seek care and to do so early, so the estimated effect of care could be understated.

Research on the effects of expanded Medicaid eligibility and services on birth weight has produced mixed findings. Collectively, studies indicate only modest positive effects, stronger among blacks than whites.[101] One reason for the inconsistent findings may be that prenatal care varies widely—in the services and interventions offered, in the settings in which it is provided, and in quality. Moreover, interventions targeted at low-income families often lose clients by attrition, and programs are not always implemented as intended. Two recent studies have found that legislated changes in providers—one through hospital desegregation in Mississippi in the Civil Rights era and another, more recently, through changes in Medicaid hospital payments in California—reduced rates of low birth weight among African American children.[102]

Unquestionably, prenatal medical care can benefit certain mothers and their babies enormously. All women, pregnant or not, should get preventive and regular medical care. But standard prenatal care cannot be expected to improve *aggregate* birth outcomes because most treatable medical conditions during pregnancy affect only a small proportion of women.[103] A recent comprehensive review found no evidence that prenatal educational or psychosocial services, home visiting programs, or any medical interventions, even those to prevent infections, prevented either preterm birth or fetal growth retardation.[104] Researchers have recently found that progesterone supplementation reduces preterm birth among women who have had a previous preterm birth, but studies of its effectiveness and safety are still ongoing.[105] One promising way to reduce aggregate rates of low birth weight is to reduce smoking.[106] Another is through better nutrition. Three recent studies found that participation in the Supplemental Nutrition Program for Women, Infants, and Children (WIC) raised birth weight.[107]

The point is not that prenatal care programs have no positive effects. Rather, variations in content, implementation, or compliance make it difficult to pinpoint their effects. They may improve maternal health by connecting mothers to the health care system. They may reduce fetal death. Those that include family planning and other psychosocial services that could affect future fertility and prenatal behaviors could, in turn, improve maternal or infant health and increase the use of pediatric care. At the minimum, women of childbearing age should receive standard medical care beginning well before pregnancy, as well as smoking cessation and nutritional services as needed. But prenatal care—even enhanced care—will not auto-matically offset a lifetime of maternal health disadvantages.

Improving Cognitive Outcomes Associated with Low Birth Weight

Practitioners have established many early intervention programs to enhance the cognitive development of low birth weight infants and to improve their school readiness. Many programs pertaining to low birth weight and school readiness have been designed as randomized clinical trials, making them relatively straightforward to evaluate.

A broad review of such interventions found modest success overall, with the most effective programs involving parents as well as children.[108] One such "two-generation" intervention, the Infant Health and Development Program (IHDP), targeted low birth weight premature infants at eight sites. In the treatment group, 377 children received two years of high-quality center-based care at ages two and three. Family support, including home visits and parent group meetings, was also provided. The 608 children in the control group received none of these services. Both groups received the same medical care.

Many researchers have examined the readiness-related effects, both cognitive and behavioral, of the IHDP. Jeanne Brooks-Gunn and her coauthors found that the mean IQ of the intervention group at age three was 93.6, while that of the control group was 84.2; and that heavier low birth weight infants benefited more than lighter infants (those weighing less than 2,000 grams).[109] For both black and white subsamples, children whose mothers had a high school education or less gained more from the intervention than those whose mothers had attended college, with the latter showing no significant enhancement in IQ scores at age three.[110] Several studies found that the intervention improved cognitive scores at ages twenty-four months and thirty-six months, and one found lower (more favorable) behavior problem scores at twenty-four and thirty-six months.[111] Children who had large gains on IQ score, cognitive skills, school achievement, and behavior at age three, however, generally did not sustain the gains at age eight, although the heavier low birth weight intervention group still outscored the control groups on measures of cognition and school achievement.[112] And another study found that children at age eight who had attended the program for at least 400 days scored 7 to 10 points higher on IQ tests than those in the control group. Again, effects were greater for the heavier low birth weight infants (about 14 points) than for the lighter low birth weight infants (about 8 points).[113]

Combining home visits with hospital-based intervention also appears to be effective in enhancing the cognitive function of low birth weight children. In a randomized controlled trial of an intervention in Vermont that provided four home visits and seven hospital sessions, the experimental low birth weight group scored higher on several standardized tests at age seven than did a control group that received no treatment; differences in outcomes first became statistically significant at age three.[114] The experimental group also scored as high as a normal birth weight comparison group. A recent review of interventions targeting socially deprived families concluded that home visits accompanied by early stimulation in the neonatal unit, as well as by preschool placement, appeared to improve the cognitive development of low birth weight and premature children.[115]

In sum, early intervention can improve the cognitive and behavioral development of low birth weight children. Two-generation programs, which serve both mothers and children, and those that combine home visits with either center-based day care or hospital-based therapy appear particularly effective, with more pronounced gains for heavier low birth weight children.

Implications and Recommendations

The message of this article is mixed and cautious. Although racial disparities in low birth weight are large and persistent, they explain, at most, 3 to 4 percent of the racial gap in IQ scores. Resolving the problem of low birth weight will thus close only a small portion of the racial gap in school readiness. The adverse cognitive outcomes associated with low birth weight are being addressed successfully by several types of early intervention programs, but their benefits are greatest for heavier children, whereas it is the lightest children who are at the greatest risk.

Overall, there is both good and bad news about low birth weight. The encouraging news is that over the past two decades

■ Infant mortality rates among both blacks and whites have declined.

■ Birth weight–specific survival rates of both black and white infants have increased dramatically.

■ Birth weight–specific survival rates show no racial disparities. Black and white infants appear to benefit equally in terms of survival, at least in the aggregate, from neonatal care technology.

■ Thanks to public health campaigns and the Medicaid expansions of the 1980s and 1990s, levels of prenatal care use are high among both blacks and whites.

The discouraging news is that

- Black babies continue to be twice as likely as white babies to die before their first birthday. Despite declining infant mortality rates among both blacks and whites, the infant mortality rate among blacks in 2000 was still higher than that among whites twenty years earlier. Although the absolute racial gap in infant mortality has narrowed somewhat, the proportional gap has increased by half.

- Rates of low birth weight in the United States have not declined over the past twenty years—overall, for blacks or for whites. This apparently bad news may be due, at least in part, to declining rates of fetal death. However, the aggregate rate of low birth weight in the United States exceeds that of most other developed countries.

- Black babies continue to be twice as likely as white babies to be low birth weight. Racial disparities are most pronounced at the lowest birth weight ranges—those associated with the poorest child health and developmental outcomes.

I offer several recommendations for improving maternal and child health generally and for combating low birth weight as a way to reduce racial disparities in school readiness. First, policymakers and practitioners must focus on maternal health risks well before conception. It is extremely difficult, if not impossible, to counteract a lifetime of disadvantage during the gestational period. The emphasis must be on women's health rather than on prenatal care. Many analysts have made

this same point, but its importance cannot be overemphasized. Second, researchers must pay more attention to maternal and paternal environmental exposures and to the biological role of fathers, more broadly, in infant health and child health and development. Third, reducing rates of low birth weight would improve cognitive and behavioral outcomes among the entire population of school-aged children. At the same time, it would narrow racial gaps in school readiness, particularly if it were part of a multipronged, integrative approach focusing on the many inputs to school readiness reviewed in this volume.

Although the 3 to 4 percent potential contribution of low birth weight to the racial gap in IQ scores may not seem large, eliminating one source of the disparity is a step in the right direction. Moreover, beyond the question of school achievement, low birth weight is a problem that must be addressed to meet the national goals of increasing quality and years of healthy life and eliminating racial, ethnic, and socioeconomic disparities in health.[116]

Early intervention can and has improved cognitive and behavioral outcomes among low birth weight children. Ideally, such interventions should be available to all children who could benefit. That said, they appear to be of greater benefit to heavier low birth weight children than to lighter ones. Because black infants are more likely than white infants to fall into the lowest weight ranges, *preventing* low birth weight—when we learn how to do so—is likely to be more effective than remedial intervention at narrowing racial gaps in school readiness.

Endnotes

1. See the special issue of *The Future of Children* (vol. 5, no. 1, Spring 1995) devoted to low birth weight.

2. UNICEF (United Nations Children's Fund), *The State of the World's Children* (Oxford University Press, 2003).

3. T. J. Matthews, Fay Menacker, and Marian F. MacDorman, "Infant Mortality Statistics from the 2001 Period: Linked Birth/Infant Death Data Set," *National Vital Statistics Reports* 52, no. 2. (Hyattsville, Md.: National Center for Health Statistics, September 15, 2003); Maureen Hack, Nancy K. Klein, and H. Gerry Taylor, "Long-Term Developmental Outcomes of Low Birth Weight Infants," *The Future of Children* 5, no. 1 (1995), 176–96.

4. Jeffrey D. Horbar and Jerold F. Lucey, "Evaluation of Neonatal Intensive Care Technologies," *The Future of Children* 5, no. 1 (1995): 139–16; Virginia M. Fried and others, *Chartbook on Trends in the Health of Americans* (Hyattsville, Md.: National Center for Health Statistics, 2003).

5. Joyce A. Martin and others, "Births: Final Data for 2000," *National Vital Statistics Reports* 52, no. 10 (Hyattsville, Md.: National Center for Health Statistics, February 12, 2002).

6. Data on singleton births allow for comparisons over time that are not confounded by changes in the prevalence of multiple births.

7. The survival rate for normal birth weight singleton infants was 99 percent in 1960, 1980, and 2000.

8. For an extensive review of child medical and developmental conditions associated with low birth weight, see Hack, Klein, and Taylor, "Long-Term Developmental Outcomes of Low Birth Weight Infants" (see note 3); National Institute of Neurological Disorders and Stroke, "NINDS Cerebral Palsy Information Page" (www.ninds.nih.gov/health_and_medical/disorders/cerebral_palsy.htm [July 14, 2004]).

9. March of Dimes Birth Defects Foundation, "Cerebral Palsy" (www.marchofdimes.com/professionals/681_1208.asp [April 5, 2004]).

10. University of California, San Francisco (UCSF) Children's Hospital, "Bronchopulmonary Dysplasia" (www.ucsfhealth.org/childrens/health_professionals/manuals/31_ChronicLungDis.pdf [April 5, 2004]); UCSF Children's Hospital, "Respiratory Distress Syndrome" (www.ucsfhealth.org/childrens/health_professionals/manuals/25_RDS.pdf [April 5, 2004]).

11. National Institutes of Health, National Eye Institute, "Retinopathy of Prematurity" (www.nei.nih.gov/health/ rop/#2 [April 6, 2004]).

12. John M. Lorenz and others, "A Quantitative Review of Mortality and Developmental Disability in Extremely Premature Newborns," *Archives of Pediatric and Adolescent Medicine* 152, no. 5 (1998): 425–35.

13. Martin and others, "Births" (see note 5).

14. Ibid.

15. In 2000 the 2:1 ratio was present in the following maternal age groups: twenty to twenty-four, twenty-five to twenty-nine, thirty to thirty-four, thirty-five to thirty-nine, and forty to forty-four. The disparities are narrower for very young and very old mothers. For mothers younger than fifteen, the black-white low birth weight ratio is 1.4, for mothers aged fifteen to nineteen it is 1.7, and for mothers forty-five to fifty-four it is

1.3. Among singleton births, the rate of low birth weight in 2000 was 4.99 percent among white mothers and 11.15 percent among black mothers; the corresponding rates in 1980 were 4.90 and 11.46 percent, respectively. Martin and others, "Births" (see note 5).

16. Kenneth C. Schoendorf and others, "Mortality among Infants of Black as Compared with White College Educated Parents," *New England Journal of Medicine* 326, no. 23 (1992): 1522–26.

17. Martin and others, "Births" (see note 5).

18. Cande V. Ananth and others, "Small-For-Gestational-Age Births among Black and White Women: Temporal Trends in the United States," *American Journal of Public Health* 93, no. 4 (2003): 577-79.

19. Martin and others, "Births" (see note 5).

20. W. Parker Frisbie and Seung-eun Song, "Hispanic Pregnancy Outcomes: Differentials over Time and Current Risk Factor Effects," *Policy Studies Journal* 31, no. 2 (2003), 237.

21. Jose E. Becerra and others, "Infant Mortality among Hispanics: A Portrait of Heterogeneity," *Journal of the American Medical Association* 265, no. 2 (1991): 217–21; Fernando S. Mendoza and others, "Selected Measures of Health Status for Mexican-American, Mainland Puerto Rican, and Cuban-American Children," *Journal of the American Medical Association* 265, no. 2 (1991): 227–32.

22. Kyriakos S. Markides and Jeannine Coreil, "The Health of Hispanics in the Southwestern United States: An Epidemiological Paradox," *Public Health Reports* 101, no. 3 (1986): 253–65.

23. Nancy E. Reichman and Genevieve M. Kenney, "The Effects of Parents' Place of Birth and Ethnicity on Birth Outcomes in New Jersey," in *Keys to Successful Immigration: Implications of the New Jersey Experience,* edited by Thomas J. Espenshade (Washington: Urban Institute Press, 1997): 199–230; Nancy E. Reichman and Genevieve M. Kenney, "Prenatal Care, Birth Outcomes and Newborn Hospitalization Costs: Patterns among Hispanics in New Jersey," *Family Planning Perspectives* 30, no. 4 (1998): 182–87; Martin and others, "Births" (see note 5).

24. Gosta Rooth, "Low Birthweight Revised," *Lancet* 1, no. 8169 (1980): 639–41.

25. Nigel Paneth, "The Problem of Low Birth Weight," *The Future of Children* 5, no. 1 (1995): 19–34.

26. Martin and others, "Births" (see note 5).

27. Stephen A. Norton, Genevieve M. Kenney, and Marilyn Rymer Ellwood, "Medicaid Coverage of Maternity Care for Aliens in California," *Family Planning Perspectives* 28, no. 3 (1996): 108–12; Julia M. Solis and others, "Acculturation, Access to Care, and Use of Preventive Services by Hispanics: Findings from HHANES, 1982–84," *American Journal of Public Health* 80, suppl. (1990): 11–19; Fernando M. Trevino and others, "Health Insurance Coverage and Utilization of Health Services by Mexican Americans, Mainland Puerto Ricans, and Cuban Americans," *Journal of the American Medical Association* 265, no. 2 (1991): 233–37; Patricia Moore and Joseph T. Hepworth, "Use of Perinatal and Infant Health Services by Mexican-American Medicaid Enrollees," *Journal of the American Medical Association* 272, no. 14 (1994): 1111–15; Sylvia Guendelman, "Mexican Women in the United States," *Lancet* 344, no. 8919 (1994): 352.

28. Nancy S. Landale, R. S. Oropesa, and Bridget K. Gorman, "Immigration and Infant Health: Birth Outcomes of Immigrant and Native-Born Women," in *Children of Immigrants: Health, Adjustment and Public Assistance*, edited by D. J. Hernandez (Washington: National Academy Press, 1999).

29. Howard J. Cabral and others, "Foreign-Born and U.S.-Born Black Women: Differences in Health Behaviors and Birth Outcomes," *American Journal of Public Health* 80, no. 1 (1990): 70–71; Richard J. David and James W. Collins, "Differing Birth Weight among Infants of U.S.-Born Blacks, African-Born Blacks and U.S.-Born Whites," *New England Journal of Medicine* 337, no. 17 (1997): 1209–14; Jing Fang, Shantha Madhavan, and Michael H. Alderman, "Low Birth Weight: Race and Maternal Nativity—Impact of Community Income," *Pediatrics* 103, no. 1 (1999): e5: 1–6; Gopal K. Singh and Stella M. Yu, "Adverse Pregnancy Outcomes: Differences between U.S. and Foreign-Born Women in Major U.S. Racial and Ethnic Groups," *American Journal of Public Health* 86, no. 6 (1996): 837–43.

30. Unless indicated otherwise, the analyses of trends in birth weight and survival are restricted to single live births, due to incomplete data for multiple births in 1980 and to allow for comparisons over time that are not confounded by changes in the prevalence of multiple births.

31. Wanda Barfield, "Racial/Ethnic Trends in Fetal Mortality—United States, 1990–2000," *Morbidity and Mortality Weekly Report* 53, no. 24 (2004) (www.cdc.gov/mmwr/preview/mmwrhtml/mm5324a4.htm [June 27, 2004]). These figures are not limited to singletons. The corresponding decreases for American Indians/Alaska Natives, Asians/Pacific Islanders, and Hispanics were 27 percent, 8 percent, and 16 percent, respectively.

32. Figures for singletons are computed from the same data sources as in figure 2. The corresponding infant mortality figures, including multiple births, for 1980 are 22 out of 1,000 and 11 out of 1,000 for blacks and whites, respectively; and for 2000, 14 out of 1,000 and 6 out of 1,000, respectively. Centers for Disease Control and Prevention, *Morbidity and Mortality Weekly Report* 51, no. 27 (2002): 589–92 (www.cdc.gov/mmwr/preview/mmwrhtml/mm5127a1.htm [April 1, 2004]).

33. Data sources on survival rates are the same as in figure 2. Race-specific survival rates were also virtually identical for moderately low birth weight and normal birth weight in 2000. T. J. Matthews, Fay Menacker, and Marian F. MacDorman, "Infant Mortality Statistics from the 2000 Period: Linked Birth/Infant Death Data Set," *National Vital Statistics Reports* 50, no. 12 (Hyattsville, Md.: National Center for Health Statistics, August 28, 2003). In 1999, 3.1 percent of births to white mothers and 3.3 percent of births to black mothers were multiples. Black mothers were slightly more likely to have twins, and white mothers were slightly more likely to have higher-order multiple births. Rebecca B. Russell and others, "The Changing Epidemiology of Multiple Births in the United States," *Obstetrics and Gynecology* 101, no. 1 (2003): 129–35.

34. See sources for figures 2 and 3.

35. In 2000, 85 percent of deaths up to age five were of children under one year of age. Centers for Disease Control, "Deaths by Single Years of Age, Race, and Sex: United States, 2000," *Year 2000 Mortality Statistics*, table 310 (www.cdc.gov/nchs/data/statab/wktbl310.pdf [April 1, 2004]).

36. Marie C. McCormick and others, "The Health and Development Status of Very Low-Birth-Weight Children at School Age," *Journal of the American Medical Association* 267, no. 16 (1992): 2204–08; Maureen Hack and others, "School-Age Outcomes in Children with Birth Weights under 750g," *New England Journal of Medicine* 33, no. 12 (1994): 753–59.

37. Adnan T. Bhutta and others, "Cognitive and Behavioral Outcomes of School-Aged Children Who Were Born Preterm: A Meta-Analysis," *Journal of the American Medical Association* 288, no. 6 (2002): 728–37.

38. Rachel Nonkin Avchen, Keith G. Scott, and Craig A. Mason, "Birth Weight and School-Age Disabilities: A Population-Based Study," *American Journal of Epidemiology* 154, no. 10 (2001): 895–901.

39. Jennifer Pinto-Martin and others, "Special Education Services and School Performance in a Regional Cohort of Low-Birthweight Infants at Age Nine," *Paediatric and Perinatal Epidemiology* 18, no. 2 (2004): 120–29.

40. Betty R. Vohr and others, "Neurodevelopmental and Functional Outcomes of Extremely Low Birth Weight Infants in the National Institute of Child Health and Human Development Neonatal Research Network, 1993–1994," *Pediatrics* 105, no. 6 (2000): 1216–26; Peter Anderson, Lex W. Doyle, and the Victorian Infant Collaborative Study Group, "Neurobehavioral Outcomes of School-Age Children Born Extremely Low Birth Weight or Very Preterm in the 1990s," *Journal of the American Medical Association* 289, no. 24 (2003): 3264–72.

41. Anderson and others, "Neurobehavioral Outcomes of School-Age Children Born Extremely Low Birth Weight or Very Preterm in the 1990s" (see note 40); Bhutta and others, "Cognitive and Behavioral Outcomes of School-Aged Children Who Were Born Preterm" (see note 37); Jennifer R. Bowen, Frances L. Gibson, and Peter J. Hand, "Educational Outcome at 8 Years of Children Who Were Born Prematurely: A Controlled Study," *Journal of Paediatrics and Child Health* 38, no. 5 (2002): 438–44; Hack and others, "School-Age Outcomes in Children with Birth Weights under 750g" (see note 36).

42. Glen P. Aylward, "Cognitive Function in Preterm Infants: No Simple Answers," *Journal of the American Medical Association* 289, no. 6 (2003): 752–53.

43. Anderson and others, "Neurobehavioral Outcomes of School-Age Children Born Extremely Low Birth Weight or Very Preterm in the 1990s" (see note 41); Bhutta and others, "Cognitive and Behavioral Outcomes of School-Aged Children Who Were Born Preterm" (see note 37).

44. Anderson and others, "Neurobehavioral Outcomes of School-Age Children Born Extremely Low Birth Weight or Very Preterm in the 1990s" (see note 40); Bhutta and others, "Cognitive and Behavioral Outcomes of School-Aged Children Who Were Born Preterm" (see note 37).

45. Anderson and others, "Neurobehavioral Outcomes of School-Age Children Born Extremely Low Birth Weight or Very Preterm in the 1990s" (see note 40); Jane L. Hutton and others, "Differential Effects of Preterm Birth and Small Gestational Age on Cognitive and Motor Development," *Archives of Diseases in Children* 76, no. 2 (1997): F75–F81; Susan A. Rose and Judith F. Feldman, "Memory and Processing Speed in Preterm Children at Eleven Years: A Comparison with Full-Terms," *Child Development* 67, no. 5 (1996): 2005–21.

46. Anderson and others, "Neurobehavioral Outcomes of School-Age Children Born Extremely Low Birth Weight or Very Preterm in the 1990s" (see note 40); Bradley S. Peterson and others, "Regional Brain Volume Abnormalities and Long-Term Cognitive Outcome in Preterm Infants," *Journal of the American Medical Association* 284, no. 15 (2000): 1939–47.

47. Bhutta and others, "Cognitive and Behavioral Outcomes of School-Aged Children Who Were Born Preterm" (see note 37).

48. Lynn T. Singer and others, "Maternal Psychological Distress and Parenting Stress after the Birth of a Very Low-Birth-Weight Infant," *Journal of the American Medical Association* 281, no. 9 (1999): 799–805.

49. Hack, Klein, and Taylor, "Long-Term Developmental Outcomes of Low Birth Weight Infants" (see note 3). A review of the more recent literature indicates that these rates have remained essentially unchanged.

50. There are as yet too few studies to derive reliable estimates of the size of these effects. See, for example, Thomas D. Matte and others, "Influence of Variation in Birth Weight within Normal Range and within Sib-

ships on IQ at Age 7 Years: Cohort Study," *British Medical Journal* 323, no. 7308 (2001): 310–14; Robert Kaestner and Hope Corman, "The Impact of Child Health and Family Inputs on Child Cognitive Development," Working Paper 5257 (Cambridge, Mass.: National Bureau of Economic Research, 1995); Jason D. Boardman and others, "Low Birth Weight, Social Factors, and Developmental Outcomes among Children in the United States," *Demography* 39, no. 6 (2002): 353–68.

51. Anne Case, Angela Fertig, and Christina Paxson, "The Lasting Impact of Child Health and Circumstance," *Journal of Health Economics* (forthcoming).

52. Yolanda C. Padilla and others, "Is the Mexican American 'Epidemiologic Paradox' Advantage of Birth Maintained through Early Childhood?" *Social Forces* 80, no. 3 (2002): 1101–23.

53. Jeanne Brooks-Gunn and others, "The Black-White Test Score Gap in Young Children: Contributions of Test and Family Characteristics," *Applied Developmental Science* 7, no. 4 (2003): 239–52.

54. See Brooks-Gunn and others, "The Black-White Test Score Gap in Young Children" (note 53), for the magnitude of the observed total gap (denominator).

55. Dana Hughes and Lisa Simpson, "The Role of Social Change in Preventing Low Birth Weight," *The Future of Children* 5, no. 1 (1995): 87–102.

56. U.S. Department of Health and Human Services, *Healthy People 2010*, 2nd ed. (Government Printing Office, 2000).

57. Fried and others, *Chartbook on Trends in the Health of Americans* (see note 4).

58. Bernadette D. Proctor and Joseph Dalaker, "Poverty in the United States: 2002," *Current Population Reports*, P60-222 (U.S. Census Bureau, 2003).

59. Stephanie J. Ventura and others, "The Demography of Out-of-Wedlock Childbearing," *Report to Congress on Out-of-Wedlock Childbearing* (U.S. Department of Health and Human Services, 1995).

60. Martin and others, "Births" (see note 5).

61. Proctor and Dalaker, "Poverty in the United States" (see note 58). Poverty, in this case, identifies families with a female householder and no husband present.

62. Martin and others, "Births" (see note 5).

63. Allison M. Fraser, John E. Brockert, and Ryk H. Ward, "Association of Young Maternal Age with Adverse Reproductive Outcomes," *New England Journal of Medicine* 332, no. 17 (1995): 1113–17.

64. Alan Guttmacher Institute, *Sex and America's Teenagers* (New York and Washington, 1994); Cheryl D. Hayes, ed., *Risking the Future: Adolescent Sexuality, Pregnancy, and Childbearing*, vol. 1 (Washington: National Academy Press, 1987).

65. Arline T. Geronimus, "The Weathering Hypothesis and the Health of African-American Women and Infants: Evidence and Speculations," *Ethnicity and Disease* 2, no. 3 (1992): 207-21; Arline T. Geronimus, "Black/White Differences in the Relationship of Maternal Age to Birthweight: A Population-Based Test of the Weathering Hypothesis," *Social Science and Medicine* 42, no. 4 (1996): 589-97.

66. Martin and others, "Births" (see note 5).

67. Ibid.

68. Robert L. Goldenberg and Lorraine V. Klerman, "Adolescent Pregnancy—Another Look," *New England Journal of Medicine* 332, no. 17 (1995): 1161–62.

69. Sarah S. Brown and Leon Eisenberg, eds., *The Best Intentions: Unintended Pregnancy and the Well-Being of Children and Families* (Washington: National Academy Press, 1995).

70. Nancy E. Reichman and Deanna L. Pagnini, "Maternal Age and Birth Outcomes: Data from New Jersey," *Family Planning Perspectives* 29, no. 6 (1997): 268–72, 295.

71. Institute of Medicine, Committee to Study the Prevention of Low Birth Weight, *Preventing Low Birth Weight* (Washington: National Academy Press, 1985); Charles J. Lockwood, "Predicting Premature Delivery—No Easy Task," *New England Journal of Medicine* 346, no. 4 (2002): 282–84.

72. Peter W. Nathanielsz, "The Role of Basic Science in Preventing Low Birth Weight," *The Future of Children* 5, no. 1 (1995): 57–70; Greg R. Alexander and Carol C. Korenbrot, "The Role of Prenatal Care in Preventing Low Birth Weight," *American Journal of Public Health* 5, no. 1 (1995): 103–20. For an up-to-date discussion of what is known about the process of preterm birth, see Donald R. Mattison and others, eds., "The Role of Environmental Hazards in Premature Birth," Workshop Summary, Roundtable on Environmental Health Sciences, Research, and Medicine, Board of Health Sciences Policy (Washington: Institute of Medicine of the National Academy, 2003).

73. Nathanielsz, "The Role of Basic Science in Preventing Low Birth Weight"; Alexander and Korenbrot, "The Role of Prenatal Care in Preventing Low Birth Weight" (for both, see note 72).

74. Virginia Rall Chomitz, Lilian W. Y. Cheung, and Ellice Lieberman, "The Role of Lifestyle in Preventing Low Birth Weight," *The Future of Children* 5, no. 1 (1995): 121–38.

75. Martin and others, "Births" (see note 5).

76. Sharon Hillier and others, "Association between Bacterial Vaginosis and Preterm Delivery of a Low-Birth-Weight Infant," *New England Journal of Medicine* 33, no. 26 (1995): 1737–42. Many studies have replicated this finding.

77. Chomitz, Cheung, and Lieberman, "The Role of Lifestyle in Preventing Low Birth Weight" (see note 74).

78. Martin and others, "Births" (see note 5).

79. J. Durham and others, "Alcohol Consumption among Pregnant and Childbearing-Aged Women: United States, 1991 and 1995," *Morbidity and Mortality Weekly Report* 46, no. 16 (April 25, 1997) (www.health. org/ nongovpubs/mmwr [April 1, 2004]).

80. Substance Abuse and Mental Health Services Administration (SAMHSA), "Drug Abuse in America: 2001," excerpted from the 2001 National Household Survey on Drug Abuse, September 5, 2002 (www. policyalmanac.org/crime/archive/drug_abuse.shtml [January 21, 2004]).

81. Irvin Emanuel and others, "The Washington State Intergenerational Study of Birth Outcomes: Methodology and Some Comparisons of Maternal Birthweight and Infant Birthweight and Gestation in Four Ethnic Groups," *Paediatric and Perinatal Epidemiology* 13, no. 3 (1999): 352–69; James W. Collins Jr. and others, "Low Birth Weight across Generations," *Maternal and Child Health Journal* 7, no. 4 (2003): 229–37; Dalton Conley, Kate W. Strully, and Neil G. Bennett, *The Starting Gate: Birth Weight and Life Chances* (University of California Press, 2003); Dalton Conley and Neil G. Bennett, "Is Biology Destiny? Birth Weight and Life Chances," *American Sociological Review* 65, no. 3 (2000): 458–67.

82. Conley, Strully, and Bennett, *The Starting Gate* (see note 81).

83. Ellen L. Mozurkewich and others, "Working Conditions and Adverse Pregnancy Outcome: A Meta-analysis," *Obstetrics and Gynecology* 95, no. 4 (2000): 623–35.

84. Boguslaw Baranski, "Effects of the Workplace on Fertility and Related Reproductive Outcomes," *Environmental Health Perspectives Supplements* 101, suppl. 2 (1993): 81–90; Sohail Khattak and others, "Pregnancy Outcome Following Gestational Exposure to Organic Solvents: A Prospective Controlled Study," *Journal of the American Medical Association* 281, no. 12 (1999): 1106–09; Eunhee Ha and others, "Parental Exposure to Organic Solvents and Reduced Birth Weight," *Archives of Environmental Health* 57, no. 3 (2002): 204–14.

85. Jesse McKinnon, "The Black Population in the United States: March 2002," *Current Population Reports*, P20-541 (U.S. Census Bureau, 2003). Corresponding figures for pregnant women alone are not available.

86. Council of Economic Advisers, *Changing America: Indicators of Social and Economic Well-Being by Race and Hispanic Origin* (September 1998) (www.access.gpo.gov/eop/ca/pdfs/ca.pdf).

87. Narayan Sastry and Jon M. Hussey, "An Investigation of Racial and Ethnic Disparities in Birth Weight in Chicago Neighborhoods," *Demography* 40, no. 4 (2003): 701–25.

88. See, for example, Jeffrey D. Morenoff, "Neighborhood Mechanisms and the Spatial Dynamics of Birth Weight," *American Journal of Sociology* 108, no. 5 (2003): 976-1017.

89. Ibid.

90. J. Felix Rogers and others, "Association of Very Low Birth Weight with Exposures to Environmental Sulfur Dioxide and Total Suspended Particulates," *American Journal of Epidemiology* 151, no. 6 (2000): 602–13; Sven E. Rodenbeck, Lee M. Sanderson, and Antonio Rene, "Maternal Exposure to Trichloroethylene in Drinking Water and Birth Weight Outcomes," *Archives of Environmental Health* 55, no. 3 (2000): 188–94; Akerke Baibergenova and others, "Low Birth Weight and Residential Proximity to PCB-Contaminated Waste Sites," *Environmental Health Perspectives* 111, no. 10 (2003): 1352–57.

91. Paul A. Jargowsky, *Poverty and Place: Ghettos, Barrios, and the American City* (New York: Russell Sage Foundation, 1997).

92. Jacquetta M. Trasler and Tonia Doerksen, "Teratogen Update: Paternal Exposures—Reproductive Risks," *Teratology* 60, no. 3 (1999): 161–72.

93. Ruth E. Little and Charles F. Sing, "Association of Father's Drinking and Infant's Birth Weight," *New England Journal of Medicine* 314, no. 25 (1986): 1644–45.

94. Jun Zhang and Jennifer M. Ratcliffe, "Paternal Smoking and Birthweight in Shanghai," *American Journal of Public Health* 83, no. 2 (1993): 207–10; Fernando D. Martinez, Anne L. Wright, and Lynn M. Taussig, "The Effect of Paternal Smoking on the Birthweight of Newborns Whose Mothers Did Not Smoke," *American Journal of Public Health* 84, no. 9 (1994): 1489–91.

95. David A. Savitz and others, "Male Pesticide Exposure and Pregnancy Outcome," *American Journal of Epidemiology* 146, no. 12 (1997): 1025–37; Petter Kristensen and others, "Perinatal Outcome among Children of Men Exposed to Lead and Organic Solvents in the Printing Industry," *American Journal of Epidemiology* 137, no. 2 (1993): 134–44; Maarja-Liisa Lindbohm, "Effects of Parental Exposure to Solvents on Pregnancy

Outcome," *Journal of Occupational and Environmental Medicine* 37, no. 8 (1995): 908–14; Shao Lin and others, "Does Paternal Occupational Lead Exposure Increase the Risks of Low Birth Weight or Prematurity?" *American Journal of Epidemiology* 148, no. 2 (1998): 173–81; Yi Min, Adolfo Correa-Villasenor, and Patricia A. Stewart, "Parental Occupational Lead Exposure and Low Birth Weight," *American Journal of Industrial Medicine* 30, no. 5 (1996): 569–78.

96. McKinnon, "The Black Population in the United States" (see note 85).

97. Janet Currie and Jonathan Gruber, "Saving Babies: The Efficacy and Cost of Recent Changes in the Medicaid Eligibility of Pregnant Women," *Journal of Political Economy* 104, no. 6 (1996): 1263–96; Lisa Dubay and others, "Changes in Prenatal Care Timing and Low Birth Weight by Race and Socioeconomic Status: Implications for the Medicaid Expansions for Pregnant Women," *Health Services Research* 36, no. 2 (2001): 373–98.

98. Greg R. Alexander, Michael D. Kogan, and Sara Nabukera, "Racial Differences in Prenatal Care Use in the United States: Are Disparities Decreasing?" *American Journal of Public Health* 92, no. 12 (2002): 1970–75. Although timing of care is widely used as a measure of prenatal care use, it captures neither the intensity nor the quality of care received. The Adequacy of Prenatal Care Utilization (APNCU) Index, which is based on both the timing of prenatal care and the number of visits, does a better job of capturing the intensity of care; for a description and comparison with earlier indexes of the adequacy of prenatal care, see Milton Kotelchuck, "An Evaluation of the Kessner Adequacy of Prenatal Care Index and a Proposed Adequacy of Prenatal Care Utilization Index," *American Journal of Public Health* 84. no. 9 (1994): 1414–20. Even these indexes do not capture the *quality* of care received, however.

99. Martin and others, "Births" (see note 5).

100. Lorraine V. Klerman and others, "A Randomized Trial of Augmented Prenatal Care for Multiple-Risk, Medicaid-Eligible African American Women," *American Journal of Public Health* 91, no. 1 (2001): 105–11.

101. Currie and Gruber, "Saving Babies" (see note 97); Dubay and others, "Changes in Prenatal Care Timing and Low Birth Weight by Race and Socioeconomic Status" (see note 97); Arnold M. Epstein and Joseph P. Newhouse, "Impact of Medicaid Expansion on Early Prenatal Care and Health Outcomes," *Health Care Financing Review* 19, no. 4 (1998): 85–99; Nancy E. Reichman and Maryanne J. Florio, "The Effects of Enriched Prenatal Care Services on Medicaid Birth Outcomes in New Jersey," *Journal of Health Economics* 15, no. 4 (1996): 455–76; Theodore Joyce, "Impact of Augmented Prenatal Care on Birth Outcomes of Medicaid Recipients in New York City," *Journal of Health Economics* 18, no. 1 (1999): 31–67.

102. Douglas Almond and Kenneth Y. Chay, "The Long-Run and Intergenerational Impact of Poor Infant Health: Evidence from Cohorts Born during the Civil Rights Era" (National Bureau of Economic Research, 2003) (www.nber.org/~almond/cohorts.pdf [July 25, 2004]); Anna Aizer, Adriana Lleras-Muney, and Mark Stabile, "Access to Care, Provider Choice, and Racial Disparities in Infant Mortality," Working Paper 10445 (Cambridge, Mass.: National Bureau of Economic Research, 2004).

103. Alexander and Korenbrot, "The Role of Prenatal Care in Preventing Low Birth Weight" (see note 72).

104. Michael C. Lu and others, "Preventing Low Birth Weight: Is Prenatal Care the Answer?" *Journal of Maternal-Fetal and Neonatal Medicine* 13, no. 6 (2003): 362–80.

105. Paul J. Meis and others, "Prevention of Recurrent Preterm Delivery by 17 Alpha-Hydroxyprogesterone Caproate," *New England Journal of Medicine* 348, no. 24 (2003): 2379–85; American College of Obstetri-

cians and Gynecologists, Committee on Obstetric Practice, "Use of Progesterone to Reduce Preterm Birth," ACOG committee opinion 291, *Obstetrics and Gynecology* 102, no. 5 (2003):1115–16.

106. Alexander and Korenbrot, "The Role of Prenatal Care in Preventing Low Birth Weight" (see note 72); Lu and others, "Preventing Low Birth Weight" (see note 104).

107. Lori Kowaleski-Jones and Greg J. Duncan, "Effects of Participation in the WIC Program on Birthweight: Evidence from the National Longitudinal Survey of Youth," *American Journal of Public Health* 92, no. 5 (2002): 799–803; Nancy E. Reichman and Julien O. Teitler, "Effects of Psychosocial Risk Factors and Prenatal Interventions on Birth Weight: Evidence from New Jersey's HealthStart Program," *Perspectives on Sexual and Reproductive Health* 35, no. 3 (2003): 130–37; Marianne P. Bitler and Janet Currie, "Does WIC Work? The Effects of WIC on Pregnancy and Birth Outcomes," *Journal of Policy Analysis and Management* (forthcoming).

108. Cecilia M. McCarton, Ina F. Wallace, and Forrester C. Bennett, "Early Intervention for Low Birth-Weight Premature Infants: What Can We Achieve?" *Annals of Medicine* 28, no. 3 (1996): 221–25.

109. Jeanne Brooks-Gunn and others, "Early Intervention in Low Birth-Weight Premature Infants: Results through Age 5 Years from the Infant Health and Development Program," *Journal of the American Medical Association* 272, no. 16 (1994): 1257–62.

110. Jeanne Brooks-Gunn and others, "Enhancing the Cognitive Outcomes of Low Birth Weight, Premature Infants: For Whom Is the Intervention Most Effective?" *Pediatrics* 89, no. 6, part 2 (1992): 1209–15.

111. Jeanne Brooks-Gunn and others, "Enhancing the Development of Low Birth-Weight, Premature Infants: Changes in Cognition and Behavior over the First Three Years," *Child Development* 64, no. 3 (1993): 736-53. Clancy Blair, Craig T. Ramey, and Michael J. Hardin, "Early Intervention for Low Birthweight, Premature Infants: Participation and Intellectual Development," *American Journal of Mental Retardation* 99, no. 5 (1995): 542-54.

112. Cecilia M. McCarton and others, "Results at Age 8 Years of Early Intervention for Low-Birth-Weight Premature Infants: The Infant Health and Development Program," *Journal of the American Medical Association* 277, no. 2 (1997): 126–32.

113. Jennifer L. Hill, Jeanne Brooks-Gunn, and Jane Waldfogel, "Sustained Effects of High Participation in an Early Intervention for Low Birth-Weight Premature Infants," *Developmental Psychology* 39, no. 4 (2003): 730–44.

114. Thomas M. Achenbach and others, "Nine-Year Outcome of the Vermont Intervention Program for Low Birth Weight Infants," *Pediatrics* 91, no. 1 (1993): 45–55.

115. Dagmar Lagerberg, "Secondary Prevention in Child Health: Effects of Psychological Intervention, Particularly Home Visitation, on Children's Development and Other Outcome Variables," *Acta Paediatrica* 89, suppl. (2000): 43–52. This review expanded on an earlier review of randomized controlled trials of home visitation programs by including interventions that offered other forms of support than home visits and studies published after 1992. See David L. Olds and Harriet Kitzman, "Review of Research on Home Visiting for Pregnant Women and Parents of Young Children," *The Future of Children* 3, no. 3 (1993): 53–92.

116. U.S. Department of Health and Human Services, *Healthy People, 2010* (see note 56).

Health Disparities and Gaps in School Readiness

Janet Currie

Summary

The author documents pervasive racial disparities in the health of American children and analyzes how and how much those disparities contribute to racial gaps in school readiness. She explores a broad sample of health problems common to U.S. children, such as attention deficit hyperactivity disorder, asthma, and lead poisoning, as well as maternal health problems and health-related behaviors that affect children's behavioral and cognitive readiness for school.

If a health problem is to affect the readiness gap, it must affect many children, it must be linked to academic performance or behavior problems, and it must show a racial disparity either in its prevalence or in its effects. The author focuses not only on the black-white gap in health status but also on the poor-nonpoor gap because black children tend to be poorer than white children.

The health conditions Currie considers seriously impair cognitive skills and behavior in individual children. But most explain little of the overall racial gap in school readiness. Still, the cumulative effect of health differentials summed over all conditions is significant. Currie's rough calculation is that racial differences in health conditions and in maternal health and behaviors together may account for as much as a quarter of the racial gap in school readiness.

Currie scrutinizes several policy steps to lessen racial and socioeconomic disparities in children's health and to begin to close the readiness gap. Increasing poor children's eligibility for Medicaid and state child health insurance is unlikely to be effective because most poor children are already eligible for public insurance. The problem is that many are not enrolled. Even increasing enrollment may not work: socioeconomic disparities in health persist in Canada and the United Kingdom despite universal public health insurance. The author finds more promise in strengthening early childhood programs with a built-in health component, like Head Start; family-based services and home visiting programs; and WIC, the federal nutrition program for women, infants, and small children. In all three, trained staff can help parents get ongoing care for their children.

www.future of children.org

Janet Currie is professor of economics at the University of California at Los Angeles. She is affiliated with the National Bureau of Economic Research and is a research fellow at the Institute for the Study of Labor (IZA). She would like to thank Christina Paxson and Jack Shonkoff for their comments, as well as Michelle Hemmat for helpful discussions over the course of the year. The financial support of the Center for Health and Well-Being is gratefully acknowledged.

Every parent knows that a small child sick with an earache may not sit still to listen to a story, indeed may not listen at all, until she recovers. For some chronically ill children, the struggle to achieve academically may go on throughout childhood. This article explores some of the health conditions most common to American children, notes racial disparities in the health of children, and asks how much disparities in children's health might contribute to the racial gap in school readiness. Given the growing recognition that school readiness encompasses behavior as well as cognitive abilities, I highlight the effects of health on both domains.

Health problems can affect a child's school readiness both directly and indirectly. Lead poisoning, for example, directly impairs a child's cognition and causes behavior problems. Poor health can also affect readiness indirectly by crowding out beneficial activities and changing the way the family treats a child. For example, parents who perceive a child as frail or vulnerable may be overly protective. They may coddle or inadequately discipline the child or may discourage him or her from engaging in activities that could hone both academic and social skills. Maternal health conditions and health-related behaviors may also have consequences for a child's school readiness.

Clearly, health conditions can impair school readiness in individual children. Whether racial health differences are responsible for a large fraction of the black-white gap in school readiness is a more complex question. For health problems to affect the gap, three conditions must hold. First, the health problem must affect many children. Severe illnesses like childhood cancer are mercifully rare and

thus cannot explain the overall readiness gap between black and white children. Second, there must be a link between the health condition in question and academic performance or behavior problems. Health disparities that do not affect children's academic achievement or behavior cannot contribute to gaps in achievement or behavior. Third, there must be a racial gap either in the prevalence of the health problem or in its effects.

These same considerations have guided my choice of which health problems to address. Because space constraints make it impossible to discuss the possible contribution of every health condition, let alone every type of health behavior, I focus on health conditions and behaviors that affect many children or that affect children in some racial groups much more than in others. I also focus on health conditions whose connection with school readiness has been documented by research. Racial disparities in childhood injuries, for example, are large, but little research links these gaps to school readiness. Finally, I focus on five broad health domains: mental health conditions, chronic conditions, environmental threats, nutrition, and maternal health and behaviors. Within those domains, the specific topics are attention deficit hyperactivity disorder (ADHD), asthma, lead poisoning, anemia and iron deficiency, breastfeeding, and maternal depression. I consider maternal health and behaviors because they may have larger effects on racial disparities in school readiness than do most of the children's health conditions.

Within each area, I highlight studies based on large samples and good research designs. I focus on black-white and poor-nonpoor gaps in health status because most studies of disparities in health discuss these contrasts. Poor-nonpoor gaps are relevant because black children tend to be poorer than non-black children. In 2002, for example, 37.5 percent of black children under the age of five were poor, compared with 15.5 percent of white children.[1]

Although some of the specific health conditions considered here have large effects on children's cognitive skills and behavior, most explain little of the overall racial gap in school readiness. Still, the total cumulative effect of health differentials summed over all conditions is significant. "Back-of-the-envelope" calculations indicate that racial differences in health conditions and in maternal health and behaviors together may account for as much as a quarter of the racial gap in school readiness.

Health Conditions and School Readiness

This section considers several specific types of health problems including child mental health problems, chronic physical conditions, environmental hazards, and poor nutrition. The impact of maternal health conditions and behaviors is considered in the next section.

Child Mental Health Problems

According to the 1999 U.S. surgeon general's report, approximately one in five children and adolescents in the United States has symptoms of mental or behavioral disorders. Attention deficit hyperactivity disorder, the most commonly diagnosed chronic mental health problem among young children, is the focus of this section. The disorder is characterized by an inability to pay attention (inattention) or by hyperactivity, or both.[2]

Children with ADHD are not school ready, almost by definition. They have great difficulty with basic tasks such as sitting still and listening to instructions. They are likely to be disruptive and to have trouble getting along with other children because, for example, they constantly interrupt and have trouble taking turns. The disorder is also often linked with cognitive impairments.

A diagnosis of ADHD has three main criteria. Six or more symptoms of inattention or of hyperactivity must persist for at least six months to a degree that is maladaptive and inconsistent with the child's developmental level. Some of the symptoms must be present before the child reaches the age of seven. And impairment from the symptom must be evident in two or more settings, such as home and school. This last criterion means that teachers are often important for the diagnosis of ADHD.[3]

Assessing the prevalence of ADHD is complicated. Most studies of its prevalence are based on diagnosed cases, but considerable controversy exists over whether the disorder is over- (or under-) diagnosed. Data from the National Institute of Mental Health's Epidemiology of Child and Adolescent Mental Health Disorders (MECA) study of 1,285 youths aged nine through seventeen indicate that 5.1 percent of the children had ADHD. A study of 21,065 children aged four to fifteen recruited from 401 family medical practices found that 9.2 percent had "attention deficit-hyperactivity problems" according to their clinician, but that the clinicians did not generally use standard diagnostic criteria.[4]

According to the hyperactivity subscale of the Strengths and Difficulties Questionnaire of the National Health Interview Survey, 4.19 percent of boys and 1.77 percent of girls have "clinically significant" ADHD symptoms. Among boys, the prevalence is highest among blacks, at 5.65 percent, as against 4.33 percent for whites and 3.06 percent for Hispanics. Prevalence is also higher (6.52 percent) in families with incomes less than $20,000 than in families with higher incomes (3.85 percent). When gender, race, age, income, and parental education are taken into account, the effect of income remains statistically significant, but there is no difference in prevalence between blacks and whites.[5]

Although drug therapy improves behavior for approximately 70 to 80 percent of ADHD children, the evidence that treatment affects academic performance is much less conclu-

---

Teachers were most likely to believe that white males had ADHD and least likely to think that white females had the disorder, with black students falling in between.

---

sive.[6] Treatment differs widely by race and income. Data from the National Health Interview Survey indicate that the share of parents who had ever been told that their child had ADHD was 7.5 percent for whites, 5.7 percent for blacks, and 3.5 percent for Hispanics. For poor children the rates were 7.1 percent as against 6.6 percent for nonpoor children. According to the 1997 Medical Expenditure Panel, 4.4 percent of whites but only 1.7 percent of blacks were treated for ADHD, though the probability of receiving treatment varied little by income. In a Maryland study of Medicaid patients, blacks were less than half as likely to have been prescribed psychotropic drugs as whites were, indicating that even among children with similar insurance coverage, treatment patterns differ by race.[7]

In one study, teachers were given profiles of students and asked whether they had ADHD. The race and gender assigned to the profiles were randomly varied. Teachers were most likely to believe that white males had ADHD and least likely to think that white females had the disorder, with black students falling in between. A study based on random telephone interviews found that in a sample of 381 high-risk children, 91 percent of the white parents and 85 percent of the black parents believed that their child had a problem. Fifty-one percent of the white children had been evaluated for ADHD as against only 28 percent of the black children. Rates of treatment were 31 percent for whites and 15 percent for blacks. Following up on children who were diagnosed but not treated, the researchers found that blacks were more likely than whites to cite negative expectations about the treatment (58 percent versus 34 percent), stigma (47 percent versus 32 percent), and financial constraints (32 percent versus 15 percent).[8]

Using survey data that followed a group of children from the United States and Canada, Mark Stabile and I show that children with ADHD not only perform more poorly than children without the disorder on cognitive tests, but also are at greater risk of having to repeat a grade and to enroll in special education, even after controlling for a wide range of potential confounders. ADHD affects cognition and behavior more than other chronic health conditions, such as asthma, or poor health generally. Our estimates imply that children with ADHD score at least a quarter of a standard deviation lower on standardized tests of mathematics and reading than other children. Surprisingly, the effect of ADHD on cognitive and scholastic outcomes is not strongly related to income in either country.[9]

How much of the racial gap in school readiness might be accounted for by ADHD? Suppose that a generic test has a mean of 50 and a standard deviation of 15 and that black children tend to score at least a half a standard deviation (8 points) lower than white children on this test. The studies discussed above suggest that ADHD lowers test scores by about a third of a standard deviation (5 points) and that about 4 percent of whites have the disorder, compared with 6 percent of blacks. Hence, if the difference in the prevalence of ADHD were the only difference between the black and white children, one would expect the average test score of a sample of white children to be 49.8, while the average test score of a sample of black children would be 49.[10]

This estimate, though crude, makes clear that the mean test scores of blacks and whites are driven by children who do not have any health conditions. That being so, any given health condition would have to have quite a large effect (or a very different prevalence for whites and blacks) before it could have much effect on mean differences in test scores.

Chronic Physical Health Conditions

Poor children are more likely than better-off children to suffer from a wide array of chronic health problems, particularly severe conditions such as mental retardation, heart problems, poor hearing, and digestive disorders. Chronic conditions affect school readiness in various ways. First, illness may simply crowd out other activities with doctor visits and treatment. Second, children with chronic conditions may experience more stress, fatigue, or pain that can interfere with cognitive development. Third, drugs used to treat some illnesses may have unanticipated effects. Fourth, illness may alter relations between children, parents, and others in a way harmful to the child's de-

velopment. Fifth, illnesses directly affect the ability to learn, by altering body chemistry.[11]

This section focuses on asthma. Not only is asthma one of the most common chronic conditions among children, but it is also the subject of much research focused both on black-white gaps in prevalence and on the relationship between asthma and measures of cognitive achievement and behavior.

Asthma is the leading cause of children's trips to the emergency room, of their being hospitalized, and of their being absent from school. An "asthmatic" child is one who has had an episode of blocked airways or who has a tendency toward such episodes. Doctors use different methods to diagnose asthma, and diagnosis depends on the child's either having an episode or being treated for breathing or wheezing problems. Children whose asthma is adequately managed should not have acute attacks. Prevalence surveys that focus on doctor diagnoses and those that focus on asthma attacks, therefore, lead to very different estimates.

According to the 2001 National Health Interview Survey (NHIS), 13 percent of children under age eighteen have been diagnosed with asthma, and 6 percent have had an asthma attack in the past twelve months. Prevalence rates in diagnosed asthma are higher for blacks (15.7 percent) than for whites (12.2 percent) but lowest for Hispanics (11.2 percent). Rates are also higher for poor children (15.8 percent) than nonpoor children (12 percent). Among black children, 7.7 percent had an attack in the past twelve months, as against 5.7 percent of whites and only 4 percent of Hispanics.[12]

The NHIS further shows that 1.6 percent of white children under age eighteen, and

Common Chronic Childhood Conditions

Three common chronic conditions—dental caries, allergies, and ear infections—are potentially implicated in cognitive and behavior problems in children, but research is not yet far enough along to make it possible to estimate how large those effects might be.

Dental caries (tooth decay) is the most common childhood chronic condition. Chronic pain from dental disease can affect both children's cognitive attainment and their behavior. According to the Centers for Disease Control, poor children have almost twelve times more restricted-activity days because of dental problems than do higher-income children, and untreated dental disease can lead to problems of eating, speaking, and learning. It is, however, difficult to get estimates of the size of these effects.[1]

Not only is tooth decay extremely common, but it also affect blacks more than whites, so that if it does significantly affect children's learning and behavior, then it could contribute to disparities in school readiness. White, black, and Hispanic children have about the same number of decayed, missing, or filled teeth, suggesting that the rates of tooth decay are similar. But among two- to five-year-old children, 14.4 percent of white children have untreated dental caries, as against 25.1 percent for black children and 34.9 percent for Hispanic children.[2]

Allergies are also extremely common. According to the 2002 National Health Interview Survey, 10.3 percent of children have hay fever, 12.3 percent have respiratory allergies, and 11.3 percent have other allergies. (These categories are not mutually exclusive, so the share of children with any allergy is less than the sum of these percentages.) Assessing the prevalence of allergies is complicated because of serious reporting problems. For example, the probability that a parent reports an allergy increases with income and education; it is lower for blacks than for whites even though asthma, which is often associated with allergies, is much more common among blacks. Given these problems, and the fact that allergies may range from mild to life threatening, it is difficult to say how much of the gap in school readiness might be attributable to allergies.[3]

Ear infections (otitis media) affect most young children at one time or another and are the most common reason why children visit a doctor. Like dental caries, they can be extremely painful, though more than 80 percent of infections resolve themselves within three days if untreated. Among children who have had acute otitis media, almost half have persistent effusion after one month, a condition that can cause hearing loss. Researchers estimate that at any given time roughly 5 percent of two- to four-year-old children have hearing loss because of middle ear effusion lasting three months or longer. And hearing loss can delay language development. But the prevalence of ear infections does not appear to differ between blacks and whites, which suggests that otitis media cannot be responsible for gaps in school readiness.[4]

1. Centers for Disease Control, *Preventing Chronic Diseases: Investing Wisely in Health, Preventing Dental Caries* (U.S. Department of Health and Human Services, April 6, 2004).

2. Linda M. Kaste and others, "Coronal Caries in the Primary and Permanent Dentition of Children and Adolescents Ages 1 to 17 Years: United States, 1988–1991," *Journal of Dental Research* 75 (February 1996): 631–41.

3. Achintya N. Dey and others, *Summary Health Statistics for U.S. Children: National Health Interview Survey, 2002*, Vital Health Statistics Series 10, no. 221 (Hyattsville, Md.: National Center for Health Statistics, March 2004).

4. Paddy O'Neill, "Acute Otitis Media," *British Medical Journal* (September 25, 1999); Richard Thrasher and Gregory Allen, *Ear, Otitis Media with Effusion* (www.emedicine.com/ENT/topic209.htm [December 13, 2002]).

5.7 percent of black children, had been hospitalized for asthma between 1998 and 1999. The disparity in hospitalizations is much greater than that in the number of attacks, suggesting that black children's asthma is either much more serious or much less likely to be controlled. This conclusion is supported by the finding that blacks were more likely than whites to have their activity limited because of asthma (32.7 percent compared with 21.4 percent). Similar disparities in morbidity were noted between poor and nonpoor children (33.2 percent vs. 20.8 percent), but poor black children were most likely to have activity limited because of asthma (49 percent as against about 20 percent for nonpoor black or white children or for poor white children).[13]

Consistent with these observations, several smaller-scale studies have noted that doctors are less likely to prescribe inhaled anti-inflammatory drugs for minorities than for whites. One study using nationally representative data from the National Health and Nutrition Examination Survey (NHANES) III focuses on children with moderate to severe asthma (defined as having been hospitalized or having two or more acute attacks or three or more episodes of wheezing over the past year) and finds that only 26 percent of these children were taking maintenance medication. In this group, children who have Medicaid insurance and who speak Spanish are more likely to be inadequately medicated for asthma. Race is not an independent factor.[14]

Many research papers suggest, perhaps surprisingly, that asthma has little effect on cognitive outcomes or schooling attainment. Most such studies, however, examine children whose asthma is well controlled. Indeed, the purpose of such studies is to see whether the medication children take to control their asthma affects their cognitive functioning. But several studies indicate that children with asthma are more likely than other children to have behavior problems, even when the asthma is controlled. For example, one study found that asthmatic children scored between two-thirds to one standard deviation below the normative value on a test of impulse control, while another found that asthma doubled the risk of behavioral problems. These changes in behavior may reflect relatively subtle effects of childhood illness on parenting and family functioning.[15]

One large population-based study using NHIS data found that asthma affected school absences, the probability of having learning disabilities, and grade repetition. Asthmatic children in grades one to twelve were absent from school an average of 7.6 days a year as against 2.5 days for well children. Nine percent of the asthmatic children (5 percent of the well children) had learning disabilities; 18 percent (15 percent of the well children) repeated a grade.[16]

In the only study to examine school readiness explicitly, Jennifer Halterman and her collaborators examine 1,058 children entering kindergarten in urban Rochester and find that asthmatic children had lower scores on a test of school readiness skills and that their parents were three times more likely to report that they needed extra help with learning. Tests of language, motor, and socioemotional skills showed no differences. The negative effects were concentrated among a group of children whose asthma was severe enough to limit their activity (suggesting that it was not adequately controlled), a group more likely to include boys than girls.[17]

One difficulty in interpreting all these studies is that because asthma is most prevalent among poor and minority children, the apparent effect of asthma on academic performance and behavior could reflect omitted third factors. But several studies of homogeneous groups of children also find differences in behavior, suggesting that asthma probably does have a causal effect at least on behavior problems and hence on school readiness.

A back-of-the-envelope calculation similar to that for ADHD can help determine whether these differences are large enough to affect the mean test score gap. The studies discussed above suggest that some 5 percent of black children, but only 3 percent of white children, have asthma severe enough to limit their activity. The major effect of asthma is on behavior, so I will assume that asthmatic children score a standard deviation higher on a behavior-problem index than do non-asthmatic children and that the index has the same characteristics as the generic test score assumed above (that is, mean of 50, standard deviation of 15, average black-white difference of 8). Under these assumptions, the average behavior-problem score among blacks would be 50.4; that among whites, 50.2. Again, although asthma has important effects on individual children, it cannot account for much of the racial gap in measures of school readiness.[18]

Environmental Exposures to Hazardous Substances

The literature on asthma strongly suggests that its greater prevalence among impoverished children could be due in part to characteristics of their housing. The degree of segregation by race, ethnicity, and income in American cities suggests that some groups are more likely than others to be exposed to environmental hazards. Moreover, to the extent that known environmental hazards are capitalized into housing prices, pollution will lower rents, making hazardous areas more attractive to poor people than to rich ones. Conversely, low land prices in poor neighborhoods may draw in new hazards. One environmental hazard whose effect on children's health has been studied extensively is lead.

Lead has long been known to be toxic. Blood lead levels above 45 micrograms per deciliter (microg/dl) can cause damage to the central nervous system and even death. For many years, the Centers for Disease Control set 30 microg/dl as the threshold "level of concern" for lead poisoning. But in response to evidence that levels as low as 10 microg/dl could affect children's cognitive functioning and behavior, the CDC lowered the threshold to 25 microg/dl in 1985 and to 10 microg/dl in 1991. Controversy now centers on whether even lower levels of lead endanger children, who are generally at higher risk from lead than adults. In adults only organic lead compounds can breach the blood-brain barrier; in children, both organic and inorganic lead can penetrate that barrier. And children who have diets deficient in calcium, iron, and zinc tend to absorb more lead.[19]

Before the federal government began to regulate lead, children were exposed to it in paints, in drinking water (from lead solder in pipes), in gasoline, and in canned food. According to the NHANES surveys, 88.2 percent of children aged one to five had lead levels above 10 microg/dl during 1976–80. That share plummeted to 8.6 percent during 1988–91 and fell further to 2.2 percent during 1999–2000—figures that imply that the number of children with unsafe lead levels fell from 13.5 million to less than half a million over this period.[20]

Still, lead remains in the soil, in paint in older homes, and in pipes. Some states still have lead "hot spots." One study reported that 68 percent of children attending a pediatric clinic in inner-city Philadelphia had unsafe levels of lead in their blood. Poor and black children are more likely than others to have unsafe levels.[21]

The NHANES data from 1999–2000 and data from state surveillance systems indicate that 60 percent of one- to five-year-old children with confirmed elevated blood lead levels between 1997 and 2001 were black, indicating a much higher prevalence among blacks than among whites. In 2001, 2 percent of white children and 8.7 percent of black children had confirmed high blood lead levels. The condition affects more boys than girls. In 2001, for example, 40,000 boys and 33,000 girls were confirmed to have high levels.[22]

Although some studies have found that increasing blood lead levels from 10 to 20 microg/dl reduces IQ scores by as much as 7 points (where one standard deviation is about 15 points), two reviews of many studies of blood lead levels conclude that such an increase would reduce IQ by about 2 points. Elevated lead levels have also been linked to hyperactivity and behavior problems, most famously by Herbert Needleman, who argues that lead exposure causes criminal behavior. In his study, a sample of delinquents was four times more likely to have high bone lead levels than a group of matched controls. But because lead exposure is increasingly strongly correlated with minority status, poverty, and residence in decaying older neighborhoods, it is possible that at least some of the observed correlations between lead levels and negative outcomes reflect omitted third factors. These estimates of the effects of low-level lead exposure should thus be regarded as upper bounds.[23]

A calculation similar to those made for ADHD and asthma suggests that differing

exposure to lead might be responsible for 0.2 point of the average eight-point racial gap in scores assumed above. If racial disparities in exposure to other environmental hazards have also grown, exposure to such hazards could be an increasingly important cause of disparities in school readiness.[24]

One study reported that 68 percent of children attending a pediatric clinic in inner-city Philadelphia had unsafe levels of lead in their blood. Poor and black children are more likely than others to have unsafe levels.

Nutrition

U.S. food and nutrition programs were created to ensure that children and other vulnerable people would get enough to eat. Only recently have researchers and policymakers begun to recognize that many if not most children eat too much of the wrong things and that obesity is a greater threat to child health than insufficient calories. In fact, children at risk of missing meals (those who are "food insecure") are more likely to be obese than other children, although they are also more likely to be lacking specific micronutrients. Similarly, poor children from birth to age five are twice as likely as better-off children to be obese, about a third more likely to be anemic, and about 20 percent more likely to be deficient in vitamin A. It is possible that many micronutrients will be found to affect cognitive development among young children. But because most research to date on the effects of nutrition on cognition has focused on iron-deficiency anemia, that will be the focus of this section.[25]

Among its many negative effects on health, iron deficiency impairs immune function, cognitive functioning, and energy metabo-

---

If iron deficiency impairs cognitive functioning, it could well be responsible for part of the test score disparities between blacks and whites and between poor and nonpoor children.

---

lism. Clinically, iron deficiency is defined as having an abnormal value on at least two out of three laboratory tests of iron status. Anemia, a more severe condition, is defined as iron deficiency plus low hemoglobin.

When infants are about four months old, they begin to deplete the stores of iron with which they are born. The widespread use of iron-fortified infant formula and cereals has made anemia much less of a problem in infants under one year. But toddlers may stop eating these iron-fortified infant foods before they begin to gain adequate iron from their diet.

According to the NHANES III, 9 percent of toddlers are iron deficient, as against 3 percent of three- to five-year-olds and 2 percent of six- to eleven-year-olds. Only 3 percent of toddlers are anemic, and less than 1 percent of children aged three to eleven are anemic. The NHANES 1999–2000 yields similar estimates. These anemia rates are down consid-

erably from 15–30 percent in the late 1970s and early 1980s, a decline variously attributed to iron-fortified foods and the growth of the Special Supplemental Nutrition Program for Woman, Infants, and Children (WIC), a federal program that offers food supplements to pregnant, lactating, and postpartum mothers, infants, and children younger than five.[26]

Iron deficiency is much more common among poor and black children than among other children. Twice as many black children as white children are iron deficient (16 percent versus 8 percent for toddlers), while poor children are more than 50 percent more likely to be deficient than nonpoor children. If iron deficiency impairs cognitive functioning, it could well be responsible for part of the test score disparities between blacks and whites and between poor and nonpoor children.

Sally Grantham-McGregor and Cornelius Ani reviewed observational studies that followed a group of children over time and found that conditional on measures of social background, gender, and birth weight, low hemoglobin levels in children aged two or younger are strongly linked to poor schooling achievement, cognitive development, and motor development in middle childhood. These studies, however, do not establish a causal relationship, given the strong association between iron deficiency and other factors that could affect development, such as poverty.[27]

Grantham-McGregor and Ani also survey studies of trials in which anemic or iron-deficient children were given iron supplements. They find that giving anemic children iron supplements for two to six months improves cognitive functioning, although not enough to allow school-age children to catch up to their non-anemic peers. Five small-scale studies (four in developing countries) that investigated the effect of iron supplementation on iron-deficient non-anemic children found little evidence of an effect on cognition, but it is possible that subtle effects of improving iron status in these samples of children without anemia might be detectable in larger samples.

In short, although the higher rates of iron deficiency among poor and minority children are a cause for concern, little concrete evidence links these disparities to gaps in cognitive outcomes or schooling attainment. Anemia itself, which has been more definitively linked to cognitive deficits and poorer schooling attainment, has become relatively rare, even among disadvantaged children. Although anemia may have contributed to the readiness gap in the past, it is unlikely to be a major contributor today.

The Importance of Maternal Health Conditions and Behaviors

In this section I focus on two aspects of maternal health conditions and behaviors that significantly affect children's cognitive and social functioning and that are also characterized by large racial disparities. Because many other maternal health behaviors could be considered, my purpose here is merely to illustrate how potentially important maternal behaviors can be.

Breast Feeding

The first behavior, breast feeding, exhibits large disparities by race. The American Academy of Pediatrics recommends that infants be breast fed exclusively for their first six months and that cow's milk not be introduced until after the first birthday. Some 70 percent of white infants, but only 40 percent of black infants, have ever been breast fed. At six months, 29 percent of white infants, but only 9 percent of black infants, are still being breast fed.[28]

Theoretically, breast feeding affects a child's cognitive development through three channels. First, it prevents diseases such as ear infections and may even prevent asthma. To the extent that poor physical health impairs children's performance, a lack of breast feeding could thus be implicated. Second, breast feeding provides nutrients, such as long-chain fatty acids that may affect infants' brain development, that are not adequately provided in most infant formula sold in the United States. Third, breast feeding may promote maternal-infant bonding that may, in turn, be beneficial for learning. Many studies link breast feeding positively with cognitive skills. Typically they find IQ gains of two to five points for healthy infants and up to eight points for low birth weight babies. Once again, however, given the strong relationship between breast feeding and various measures of socioeconomic status, it is unclear whether the association between breast feeding and cognition is causal.[29]

If, however, breast feeding does affect IQ scores, then the racial differences in prevalence are large enough to explain a significant part of the gap in the generic test score that I have been considering. Suppose, for example, that breast feeding for six months raises IQ by five points, or about one-third of a standard deviation. Then the fact that 29 percent of white infants, but only 9 percent of black infants, are breast fed for six months would generate a one point difference in average scores (with the assumed black-white gap being eight points).[30]

Maternal Depression

Although my emphasis in this article has been on child health, the mental health of the mother may be a key determinant of the health of the child. The difficulties associated with poverty or racism, or both, may leave some mothers more vulnerable to depression, and depressed mothers may be less able than healthy mothers to provide a stimulating and nurturing environment for their children. The hypothesis that differences in rates of maternal depression could be associated with group-level differences in the attainments of children, however, has not been directly tested, so it is necessary to go through each link in the causal chain.

Evidence abounds that poverty is associated with a higher risk of depression. The poor are 2.3 times more likely to be depressed than the nonpoor, adjusting for age, gender, ethnicity, and prior history of depression. This higher risk may be due both to heightened stress and to a lack of resources to cope with that stress. The incidence of pregnancy and postpartum depression in a sample of poor, inner-city women is about one-quarter, double the rate typically found among middle-class women. In the Infant Health and Development Study, 28 percent of poor mothers, as against 17 percent of nonpoor mothers, were depressed.[31]

Given that blacks are generally poorer than whites, one might expect a higher prevalence of depression among black mothers than among white mothers. But research findings are mixed. Some studies have shown higher rates of depressive symptoms among blacks than whites, but studies that use the diagnostic criteria for major depression generally find little racial difference in incidence. The National Comorbidity Study and Epidemiological Catchment Area Studies found that blacks were less likely than whites to be depressed, whereas another study found no racial difference in the incidence of depres-

sion in a sample of poor women. These findings suggest that although poor mothers may be at higher risk than others, race does not play an independent role in explaining the incidence of maternal depression. It is possible that both race and socioeconomic status affect whether, and how effectively, women are treated for depression, but there is little hard evidence that race, per se, is a factor.[32]

Studies of the relationship between maternal depression and child development can be divided into several groups. First, observational studies of the way depressed mothers interact with their infants find that they are often inconsistent and ineffective in disciplining their children, more likely to use force rather than compromise, and less likely to interact in a positive way. These problems are more apparent among impoverished mothers with depression than among their better-off counterparts. Second, many studies document a relationship between maternal depression and both current and future child behavior problems, insecure attachment, and cognitive problems. Maternal depression, they find, can reduce test scores by about a third of a standard deviation among preschool children.[33]

It is not clear that maternal depression *causes* these negative outcomes: the link between the two could also reflect shared genes or a shared response of the mother and child to other external causes. It is also unclear how pervasive or persistent child responses to maternal depression are. Several studies, for example, find the effects of postpartum depression confined to boys.[34]

With 37.5 percent of black children under five and 15.5 percent of white children in that same age group living in poverty, the socioeconomic gap in the incidence of maternal depression noted above—28 percent among the poor, 17 percent among the nonpoor—means that maternal depression will affect some 11 percent of black preschool children but only 3 percent of white preschool children. These differing exposures to maternal depression could account for a half a point of the assumed eight-point gap in our generic average test score.[35]

Potential Policy Responses

Potential policy responses considered here include measures aimed at reducing disparities in access to health care, early intervention programs, family services, and WIC (the Supplemental Nutrition Program for Women, Infants, and Children).

Reducing Disparities in Access to Health Care

Disadvantaged children are not only more likely than better-off children to have particular health conditions, they are also less likely to be treated for them. Could differences in access to care be responsible for differences in use of care? Although lack of insurance coverage remains a serious problem for many children, past expansions of public health insurance under Medicaid and the State Children's Health Insurance Program (SCHIP) mean that most poor and near-poor children are already eligible for public health insurance. This journal devoted its spring 2003 issue to a discussion of health insurance for children and concluded that "programs already in place have the potential to virtually eliminate uninsurance among low-income children."[36]

Making more children eligible for care is unlikely to reduce health disparities greatly because the most disadvantaged children are already eligible (though reductions in eligibility in many states could undo recent progress). More to the point, many eligible children are not signed up for public health insurance

until they have an urgent medical problem. Thus they do not get preventive care. A Medicaid-*eligible* child suffering an asthma attack will be treated, but if she is not *enrolled*, she may not receive the monitoring and medication needed to prevent another attack. The children with the poorest access to specialists

Although lack of insurance coverage remains a serious problem for many children, past expansions of public health insurance mean that most poor and near-poor children are already eligible for public health insurance.

are those in families with incomes between 125 percent and 200 percent of poverty, even though many are eligible for SCHIP.[37]

One way to improve access to care among children eligible for public health insurance may be to make it easier to sign up for, and to maintain, Medicaid coverage. When Jeffrey Grogger and I examined several state efforts to streamline the Medicaid application process, such as shortening application forms and allowing mail-in applications, we found little evidence that they were effective. By contrast, Anna Aizer found that paying community organizations to help families sign up for public health insurance in California increased enrollments among Hispanic and Asian families and reduced preventable hospitalizations. Because take-up of social programs is highest when enrollment is automatic, the best approach to the problem of eligible, unenrolled children may be to make all children eligible for Medicaid services and charge premiums on a sliding scale.[38]

But further expanding public health insurance is unlikely ever to eliminate all socioeconomic disparities in health. The famous 1980 Black report in Great Britain concluded that links between socioeconomic status and health became more pronounced following the advent of national health insurance in 1948—although it is possible that the socioeconomic gap would have widened even further in the absence of the National Health Service. Moreover, despite universal take-up of national health insurance in Britain, the rich receive more services than the poor, conditional on their health status. Health is also linked to household income in Canada, even though Canadians have universal health insurance.[39]

A final consideration is that health care providers are not always trained to offer the services that children and their mothers require. A recent study found that pediatricians rarely recognized depressive symptoms in most mothers, suggesting that increasing access to these providers would not necessarily help children whose problems were linked to maternal depression.[40]

Early Childhood Intervention Programs

Most early intervention programs include a significant health component, in the belief that they cannot address educational needs without also addressing health problems. Because many different children's programs already address specific health problems (for example, by screening for lead poisoning or by focusing on child nutrition), it may seem irrational to make health a major focus of educationally oriented early intervention programs. But to take advantage of existing health programs, parents must be knowledgeable and tireless advocates for their chil-

dren. And parents who are struggling to put bread on the table may not have the time or energy to get all the services their children need. Hence the potential value of quality infant and preschool programs that offer "one-stop shopping" for these services. Staff members in such programs may be better than parents at spotting problems and also more knowledgeable about community resources. But researchers have not yet systematically assessed the importance and effectiveness of the health services component of early intervention programs.[41]

Head Start, the federal program serving disadvantaged three- to five-year-old children, mandates that children receive the health assessments and services that they need. A 1984 Abt Associates study, now quite dated, randomly assigned children in four sites to Head Start treatments and non–Head Start controls and evaluated the health services the children received. The children entering Head Start had many and serious health problems. They had an average of 4.6 unfilled cavities; 34 percent scored below the 10th percentile for fine and gross motor skills for their age; 63 percent had a speech or language problem; and one-third failed the hearing test. Fourteen percent had active otitis media.[42]

Although the Abt study found that compliance with Head Start health performance standards was imperfect, the Head Start children were significantly more likely than the control children to have received medical screenings and necessary services. It is also worth stressing that Head Start has detailed performance standards for health services and that programs are regularly evaluated with respect to indicators such as the fraction of children who have received dental examinations, hearing and vision screenings, and immunizations.

Using data from Head Start budgets and from the National Longitudinal Survey of Youth, Matthew Neidell and I found that Head Start programs that spend a larger share of their budgets on health and education raise future child test scores more than do programs that spend higher shares on other types of programming, such as programs for parents.[43]

Given the large socioeconomic disparities in health in the United States, it may well be that the health services offered by early intervention programs play an important role in improving the cognitive functioning and future schooling attainments of impoverished children. The programs do not seem to duplicate services, but rather to help children get the services for which they are eligible through other programs.

Family-Based Services

Offering health services through programs such as Head Start will not reach all needy children, both because not all eligible children enroll and because not all needy children are eligible. Home visiting programs and other family-centered programs offer an alternative model for service delivery. The most successful of these programs are those associated with David Olds.[44]

Olds's programs, which focus on families at risk because the mother is young, poor, uneducated, and unmarried, involve nurse visits from the prenatal period until the child turns two. Evaluators have documented many positive effects on both maternal behavior and children's health. As of age two, children in one study site were much less likely than control children to have visited a hospital emergency room for unintentional injuries or ingestion of poisonous substances, although this finding was not replicated at other study

sites. As of age fifteen, children of visited mothers were less likely to have been arrested or run away from home, had fewer sexual partners, and smoked and drank less. These children were also less likely to have been involved in verified incidents of child maltreatment. There was little evidence of effects on cognition at four years of age (except among children of initially heavy smokers), though the reduction in delinquent behavior among teens could be expected to improve their school achievement. These studies suggest that locating children at risk and ensuring that they receive necessary services would be a useful complement to other strategies for reducing disparities in child health.

The Special Supplemental Nutrition Program for Women, Infants, and Children

The WIC program probably already plays a large role in remediating health disparities that could lead to gaps in school readiness. It has, for example, been credited with the dramatic decline in the incidence of anemia among young children between 1975 (shortly after it was introduced) and 1985. Several studies indicate that these improvements in nutrition affect children's behavior and ability to learn. Children whose mothers were on WIC during the prenatal period score higher than children not on WIC on the Peabody Picture Vocabulary Test, a good predictor of future scholastic achievement.[45]

In any given month in 1998, 58 percent of all infants were eligible for WIC and roughly 45 percent of all infants received benefits. Among children aged one to four, 57 percent were eligible for WIC and 38 percent of eligible children received benefits. Participation tends to drop off sharply after a child's first birthday, when WIC stops providing valuable infant formula.[46]

The program offers participants coupons that can be used only to purchase specific commodities that meet the nutritional needs of pregnant or nursing women, infants, and children under five. It is a promising vehicle for addressing health disparities in other respects as well. First, WIC agencies have frequent contact with participants, who typically come in at least once quarterly to pick up coupons and get nutritional counseling. Second, the agencies are required to help participants get preventive health care by providing services on-site or through referrals. Third, agencies teach pregnant women that "breast is best,"

Because WIC already serves many children who receive inadequate health care and because it is strongly linked to the provision of health services, it is worth considering whether WIC could do more to reduce health disparities.

although they may undermine this message by providing free infant formula to women who choose not to breast feed.

Because WIC already serves many children who receive inadequate health care and because it is strongly linked to the provision of health services, it is worth considering whether WIC could do more to reduce health disparities. Further promoting breast feeding would be particularly worthwhile, as would offering screenings and referrals for maternal depression. Keeping children in

the program beyond their first year could increase access to health screenings and reduce nutritional problems such as low iron levels.

Discussion and Conclusions

That there are pervasive differences in health between black and white children in the United States is beyond doubt. But do these disparities explain the racial gaps in school readiness? The evidence assembled here suggests that although many specific health conditions impair cognition and behavior in individual children, it is unlikely that any particular condition can explain much of the racial gap. For example, children with ADHD score a third of a standard deviation lower on test scores than children without the disorder. But because ADHD affects relatively few children and because racial differences in its prevalence are small, it explains little of the racial difference in school readiness. This does not mean that ADHD or other health conditions are unimportant. Clearly ADHD often has devastating effects on the 4 percent of boys and 2 percent of girls it affects even if it does not explain much of the racial gap in outcomes.

Moreover, summed over all health conditions, health differentials could well explain a sizeable portion of the racial gap. Three of the conditions evaluated here—ADHD, asthma, and lead poisoning—could explain up to 0.6 of a point in the hypothetical 8 point gap used for illustrative purposes. Not enough evidence is yet available to evaluate how much other common conditions such as injuries, ear infection, and dental caries could contribute. But it would not be far-fetched to suppose that differences in health conditions might together explain one point, or an eighth of the school readiness gap. And maternal health and behaviors may have even larger effects on racial gaps in school readiness because they affect more children. After all, the majority of children are in excellent health, which means that mean gaps in test scores are driven largely by children who do not have health problems.

Simply summing the various estimates in this paper suggests that as much of a quarter of the readiness gap between blacks and whites might be attributable to health conditions or health behaviors of both mothers and children. Summing yields an upper estimate, because some children may be affected by more than one condition or behavior. But these findings confirm once again that mind and body are intimately connected and that at least some of the persistent gap in school readiness between black and white children may reflect differences in their health.

Endnotes

1. U.S. Bureau of the Census, "People in Families with Related Children under 18 by Family Structure, Age, Sex, Iterated by Income-to-Poverty Ratio and Race" (http://ferret.bls.census.gov/macro/032003/pov/new03_000.htm [2003]).

2. U.S. Department of Health and Human Services, *Mental Health: A Report to the Surgeon General* (1999).

3. American Psychiatric Association, *Diagnostic and Statistical Manual of Mental Disorders*, 4th ed. (Washington, 1994).

4. Peter S. Jensen and others, "Are Stimulants Overprescribed? Treatment of ADHD in Four U.S. Communities," *Journal of the American Academy of Child and Adolescent Psychiatry* 38, no. 7 (July 1999): 797–804; Richard C. Wasserman and others, "Identification of Attentional and Hyperactivity Problems in Primary Care: A Report from Pediatric Research in Office Settings and the Ambulatory Sentinel Practice Network," *Pediatrics* 103, no. 3 (March 1999): e38.

5. Steven Cuffe, Charity Moore, and Robert McKeown, "ADHD Symptoms in the National Health Interview Survey: Prevalence, Correlates, and Use of Services and Medication," poster presented to the Fiftieth Anniversary Meeting of the American Academy of Child and Adolescent Psychiatry, Miami, October 20, 2003.

6. James M. Swanson and others, "Effects of Stimulant Medication on Learning in Children with ADHD," *Journal of Learning Disabilities* 24, no. 4 (April 1991): 219–30.

7. Barbara Bloom and others, *Summary Health Statistics for U.S. Children: National Health Interview Survey, 2001*, Vital and Health Statistics Series 10, number 216 (Hyattsville, Md.: National Center for Health Statistics, 2003); Mark Olfson and others, "National Trends in the Treatment of Attention Deficit Hyperactivity Disorder," *American Journal of Psychiatry* 160, no. 6 (June 2003): 1071; Julie M. Zito and others, "Methylphenidate Patterns among Medicaid Youths," *Psychopharmacology Bulletin* 33, no. 1 (1997): 143–47.

8. Kelly B. Raymond, *The Effect of Race and Gender on the Identification of Children with Attention Deficit Hyperactivity Disorder* (Ann Arbor, Mich.: UMI Company, 1997); Regina Bussing and others, "Prevalence of Behavior Problems in U.S. Children with Asthma," *Archives of Pediatric and Adolescent Medicine* 149, no. 5 (May 1995): 565–72.

9. Janet Currie and Mark Stabile, "Child Mental Health and Human Capital Accumulation: The Case of ADHD," Working Paper (University of California at Los Angeles, Department of Economics, August 2004).

10. For whites, the mean score would be $[(.96°50) + (.04°45)] = 49.8$, and for blacks the mean score would be $[(.94°50) + (.06°45)] = 49.7$.

11. Anne Case, Darren Lubotsky, and Christine Paxson, "Economic Status and Health in Childhood: The Origins of the Gradient," *American Economic Review* 92, no. 5 (December 2002): 1308–34; Janet Currie and Mark Stabile, "Socioeconomic Status and Health: Why Is the Relationship Stronger for Older Children?" *American Economic Review* 93, no. 5 (December 2003): 1813–23; Paul W. Newacheck, "Poverty and Childhood Chronic Illness," *Archives of Pediatric and Adolescent Medicine* 148 (1994): 1143–49.

12. Olfson and others, "National Trends in the Treatment of Attention Deficit Hyperactivity Disorder" (see note 7).

13. Lara J. Akinbami, Bonnie J. LaFleur, and Kenneth C. Schoendorf, "Racial and Income Disparities in Childhood Asthma in the United States," *Ambulatory Pediatrics* 2 (2002): 382–87.

14. Edwin D. Boudreaux and others, "Multicenter Airway Research Collaboration Investigators," *Pediatrics* 111, no. 5, part 1 (2003): 615–21; Tracy A. Lieu and others, "Racial/Ethnic Variation in Asthma Status and Management Practices among Children in Managed Medicaid," *Pediatrics* 109, no. 5 (May 2002): 857–65; Alexander N. Ortega and others, "Impact of Site of Care, Race, and Hispanic Ethnicity on Medication Use for Childhood Asthma," *Pediatrics* 109, no. 1 (January 2002); Jill S. Halterman and others, "School Readiness among Urban Children with Asthma," *Ambulatory Pediatrics* 1, no. 4 (July–August 2001): 201–05.

15. Scott Lindgren and others, "Does Asthma or Treatment with Theophylline Limit Children's Academic Performance?" *New England Journal of Medicine* 327, no. 13 (September 24, 1992): 926–30; Robert D. Annett and others, "Neurocognitive Functioning in Children with Mild and Moderate Asthma in the Childhood Asthma Management Program," *Journal of Allergy and Clinical Immunology* 105, no. 4 (April 2000): 717–24; Linda B. Gutstadt and others, "Determinants of School Performance in Children with Chronic Asthma," *American Journal of Diseases in Children* 143, no. 4 (April 1989): 471–75; Rachel Calam and others, "Childhood Asthma, Behavior Problems, and Family Functioning," *Journal of Allergy and Clinical Immunology* 112, no. 3 (September 2003): 499–504; Arlene M. Butz and others, "Social Factors Associated with Behavioral Problems in Children with Asthma," *Clinical Pediatrics* 34, no. 11 (November 1995): 581–90.

16. M. G. Fowler, M. G. Davenport, and Rekha Garg, "School Functioning of U.S. Children with Asthma," *Pediatrics* 90, no. 6 (December 1992): 939–44.

17. Halterman and others, "School Readiness among Urban Children with Asthma" (see note 14).

18. The asthma studies suggest that 15.7 percent of black children have asthma and that 32.7 percent of black asthmatics are limited by their condition. Among whites, the comparable figures are 12.2 percent and 22.4 percent. Together, these figures imply that approximately 5 percent of black children and 3 percent of white children are limited by asthma. Hence, the average behavior problems score among whites would be $[(.97°50) + (.03°58)] = 50.2$ compared with an average score among 100 black children of $[(.95°50) + (.05°58)] = 50.4$ (where for behavior problems a higher score is worse).

19. Philip O'Dowd, "Controversies Regarding Low Blood Lead Level Harm," *Medicine and Health, Rhode Island* 85, no. 11 (November 2002): 345–48; Robert G. Feldman and Roberta F. White, "Lead Neurotoxicity and Disorders of Learning," *Journal of Child Neurology* 7, no. 4 (October 1992): 354–59.

20. U.S. Centers for Disease Control, *Children's Blood Lead Levels in the United States* (www.cdc.gov/nceh/lead/research/kidsBLL.htm#Tracking BLL [March 12, 2003]).

21. Shoshana T. Melman, Joseph W. Nimeh, and Ran D. Anbar, "Prevalence of Elevated Blood Lead Levels in an Inner-City Pediatric Clinic Population," *Environmental Health Perspectives* 106, no. 10 (October 1998): 655–57.

22. Pamela A. Meyer and others, "Centers for Disease Control and Prevention Surveillance for Elevated Blood Lead Levels among Children: United States, 1997–2001," *Morbidity and Mortality Weekly Reports Surveillance Summary* 52, no. 10 (September 2003): 1–21.

23. Stuart J. Pocock, Marjorie A. Smith, and Peter A. Baghurst, "Environmental Lead and Children's Intelligence: A Systematic Review of the Epidemiological Evidence," *British Medical Journal* 309, no. 6963 (November 5, 1994): 1189–97; Richard L. Canfield and others, "Low-Level Lead Exposure, Executive Functioning, and Learning in Early Childhood," *Neuropsychology, Development, and Cognition, Section C Child*

Neuropsychology 9, no. 1 (March 2003): 35–53; Herbert S. Needleman and others, "Bone Lead Levels in Adjudicated Delinquents: A Case Control Study," *Neurotoxicology and Teratology* 24, no. 6 (November–December 2002): 711–17.

24. The prevalence of high lead exposure is 8.7 percent among blacks and 2 percent among whites. If high lead exposure were responsible for a five point decline in IQ scores, and this decline translated into roughly a third of a standard deviation fall in our generic test score, then we could make the following calculation: the mean score for blacks would be $[(.91°50) + (.9°48)] = 49.8$, while the mean score for whites would be $[(.98°50) + (.2°48)] \sim 50.0$.

25. Janet Currie, "U.S. Food and Nutrition Programs," *Means-Tested Transfer Programs in the United States*, edited by Robert Moffitt (University of Chicago Press for NBER, 2003); Jayanta Bhattacharya, Janet Currie, and Stephen Haider, "Food Insecurity or Poverty? Measuring Need-Related Dietary Adequacy," Working Paper 9003 (Cambridge, Mass.: National Bureau of Economic Research, June 2002).

26. Anne C. Looker and others, "Prevalence of Iron Deficiency in the United States," *Journal of the American Medical Association* 277, no. 12 (March 26, 1997): 973; Anne C. Looker, Mary E. Cogswell, and Elaine W. Gunter, "Iron Deficiency—United States, 1999–2000," *Morbidity and Mortality Weekly Report* 51(40) (October 11, 2002): 897–99; Bettylou Sherry, Zuguo Mei, and Ray Yip, "Continuation of the Decline in Prevalence of Anemia in Low-Income Infants and Children in Five States," *Pediatrics* 107, no. 4 (April 2001): 677–82.

27. Sally Grantham-McGregor and Cornelius Ani, "A Review of Studies on the Effect of Iron Deficiency on Cognitive Development in Children," *Journal of Nutrition* 131, no. 2S-2 (February 2001): 649S–66S.

28. Ruowei Li and others, "Prevalence of Breastfeeding in the United States: The 2001 National Immunization Survey," *Pediatrics* 111, no. 5 Supplement (May 2003); Renata Forste, Jessica Weiss, and Emily Lippincott, "The Decision to Breastfeed in the United States: Does Race Matter?" *Pediatrics* 108, no. 2 (August, 2001): 291–96.

29. Jacqueline H. Wolf, "Low Breastfeeding Rates and Public Health in the United States," *American Journal of Public Health* 93, no. 12 (December 2003); Daniel L. Drane and Jeri A. Logemann, "A Critical Evaluation of the Evidence on the Association between Type of Infant Feeding and Cognitive Development," *Pediatric Perinatal Epidemiology* 14, no. 4 (October 2000): 349–56; Anjali Jain, John Concato, and John M. Leventhal, "How Good Is the Evidence Linking Breastfeeding and Intelligence?" *Pediatrics* 109, no. 6 (June 2002): 1044–53.

30. The average score for white infants would be $(.29°50) + (.71°45) = 46.45$ and the average score for black infants would be $(.09°50) + (.91°45) = 45.45$.

31. Martha L. Bruce, David T. Takeuchi, and Philip J. Leaf, "Poverty and Psychiatric Status," *Archives of General Psychiatry* 48 (1991): 470–74; Stevan E. Hobfell and others, "Depression Prevalence and Incidence among Inner-City Pregnant and Postpartum Women," *Journal of Consulting and Clinical Psychology* 63, no. 3 (1995): 445–53; Fong-ruey Liaw and Jeanne Brooks-Gunn, "Cumulative Familial Risks and Low-Birth-weight Children's Cognitive and Behavioral Development," *Journal of Clinical Child Psychology* 23 (1994): 360–72.

32. Dan L. Tweed and others, "Racial Congruity as a Contextual Correlate of Mental Disorder," *American Journal of Orthopsychiatry* 60 (1990): 392–402; Ronald Kessler and others, "Lifetime and 12-Month Prevalence

of DSM-III-R Psychiatric Disorders in the United States," *Archives of General Psychiatry* 51 (1994): 8–19; Hobfell and others, "Depression Prevalence and Incidence among Inner-City Pregnant and Postpartum Women" (see note 31); Bruce L. Rollman and others, "Race, Quality of Depression Care, and Recovery from Major Depression in a Primary Care Setting," *General Hospital Psychiatry* 24 (2002): 381–90.

33. Carolyn Zahn-Waxler and others, "Antecedents of Problem Behaviors in Children of Depressed Mothers," *Development and Psychopathology* 2 (1990): 271–91; Grazyna Kochanska and others, "Resolution of Control Episodes between Well and Affectively Ill Mothers and Their Young Child," *Journal of Abnormal Child Psychology* 15 (1987): 441–56; Stephen M. Petterson and Alison B. Albers, "Effects of Poverty and Maternal Depression on Early Child Development," *Child Development* 72, no. 6 (November–December 2001): 1794–813; Cheryl T. Beck, "Maternal Depression and Child Behavior Problems: A Meta-Analysis," *Journal of Advanced Nursing* 29, no. 3 (1999): 623–29; Carla Martins and Elizabeth A. Gaffan, "Effects of Early Maternal Depression on Patterns of Infant-Mother Attachment: A Meta-Analytic Investigation," *Journal of Child Psychology and Psychiatry* 41, no. 6 (2000): 737–46; Stephen Cogill and others, "Impact of Postnatal Depression on Cognitive Development in Young Children," *British Medical Journal* 292 (1986): 1165–67; Lynne Murray and others, "The Impact of Postnatal Depression and Associated Adversity on Early Mother-Infant Interactions and Later Infant Outcomes," *Child Development* 67 (1996): 2512–26.

34. Deborah Sharp and others, "The Impact of Postnatal Depression on Boys' Intellectual Development," *Journal of Child Psychology and Psychiatry* 36 (1995): 1315–37; Murray and others, "The Impact of Postnatal Depression and Associated Adversity on Early Mother-Infant Interactions and Later Infant Outcomes" (see note 37); Sophie Kurstjens and Dieter Wolke, "Effects of Maternal Depression on Cognitive Development of Children over the First 7 Years of Life," *Journal of Child Psychology and Psychiatry* 42, no. 5 (2001): 623–36; Petterson and Albers, "Effects of Poverty and Maternal Depression on Early Child Development" (see note 33).

35. The average score for white children would be $(.03°45) + (.97°50) = 49.9$ and the average score for black children would be $(.11°45) + (.89°50) = 49.45$.

36. Eugene Lewit, Courtney Bennett, and Richard Behrman, "Health Insurance for Children: Analysis and Recommendations," *The Future of Children* 13, no 1 (Spring 2003): 1–4.

37. Karen Kuhlthau and others, "Correlates of Use of Specialty Care," *Pediatrics* 113, no. 3, part 1 (March 2004): e249-55.

38. Janet Currie and Jeffrey Grogger, "Medicaid Expansions and Welfare Contractions: Offsetting Effects on Prenatal Care and Infant Health," *Journal of Health Economics* 21 (March 2002): 313–35; Anna Aizer, "Low Take-up in Medicaid: Does Outreach Matter and for Whom?" *American Economic Review, Papers and Proceedings* (May 2003): pp. 238–41; Janet Currie, "The Take-up of Social Benefits," Working Paper 10488 (Cambridge, Mass.: National Bureau of Economic Research, May 2004).

39. Anna Dixon and others, "Is the NHS Equitable? A Review of the Evidence," Health and Social Care Discussion Paper 11 (London School of Economics, 2003); Lori J. Curtis and others, "The Role of Permanent Income and Family Structure in the Determination of Child Health in Canada," *Health Economics* 10 (4) (June 2001): 287–302.

40. Amy M. Heneghan and others, "Do Pediatricians Recognize Mothers with Depressive Symptoms," *Pediatrics* 106, no. 6 (December 2000): 1367–73.

41. Janet Currie, "Early Childhood Intervention Programs: What Do We Know?" *Journal of Economic Perspectives* 15, no. 2 (Spring 2001): 213–38.

42. Linda Fosburg and others, "The Effects of Head Start Health Services: Report of the Head Start Health Evaluation," AAI 84-13 (Cambridge, Mass.: Abt Associates Inc., March 15, 1984).

43. Janet Currie and Matthew Neidell, "Getting Inside the 'Black Box' of Head Start Quality: What Matters and What Doesn't," Working Paper 10091 (Cambridge, Mass.: National Bureau of Economic Research, November 2003).

44. David L. Olds and others, "Prenatal and Infancy Home Visitation by Nurses: Recent Findings," *The Future of Children* 9, no. 1 (Spring/Summer 1999): 44–65.

45. Ray Yip and others, "Declining Prevalence of Anemia among Low-Income Children in the United States," *Pediatrics* 258, no. 12 (1987): 1619–23; Lori Kowaleski-Jones and Greg Duncan, "Effects of Participation in the WIC Food Assistance Program on Children's Health and Development: Evidence from NLSY Children," Discussion Paper 1207-00 (Madison, Wis.: Institute for Research on Poverty, 2000). For an extensive review of the WIC literature, see Janet Currie, "U.S. Food and Nutrition Programs," in *Means Tested Transfer Programs in the United States*, edited by Robert Moffitt (University of Chicago Press for NBER, 2003).

46. Marianne Bitler, Janet Currie, and John Karl Scholz, "WIC Eligibility and Participation," *Journal of Human Resources* 38 (2003): 1139–79.

The Contribution of Parenting to Ethnic and Racial Gaps in School Readiness

Jeanne Brooks-Gunn and Lisa B. Markman

Summary

The authors describe various parenting behaviors, such as nurturance, discipline, teaching, and language use, and explain how researchers measure them. They note racial and ethnic variations in several behaviors. Most striking are differences in language use. Black and Hispanic mothers talk less with their young children than do white mothers and are less likely to read to them daily. They also note some differences in harshness.

When researchers measuring school readiness gaps control for parenting differences, the racial and ethnic gaps narrow by 25–50 percent. And it is possible to alter parenting behavior to improve readiness. The authors examine programs that serve poor families—and thus disproportionately serve minority families—and find that home- and center-based programs with a parenting component improve parental nurturance and discipline. Programs that target families with children with behavior problems improve parents' skills in dealing with such children. And certain family literacy programs improve parents' skills in talking with their children. Several interventions have significantly reduced gaps in the parenting behavior of black and white mothers.

Not all improvements in parenting translate to improved school readiness. Home-based programs affect the mother but do not appear to affect the child, at least in the short term. But center-based programs with a parenting component enhance both parenting and school readiness. And some family literacy programs also improve readiness.

Because these successful interventions serve a greater share of minority than nonminority families and have more positive effects for blacks than for whites, they offer promise for closing the ethnic and racial gaps in school readiness.

www.future of children.org

Jeanne Brooks-Gunn is Virginia and Leonard Marx Professor of Child Development and Education at Teachers College and the College of Physicians and Surgeons, Columbia University. Lisa B. Markman is associate director of the Education Research Section, Woodrow Wilson School of Public and International Affairs, Princeton University. They thank Eleanor Maccoby, the NICHD Research Network on Child and Family Wellbeing, and graduate fellows at the National Center for Children and Families at Teachers College, Columbia University.

"Everyone knows" that parenting powerfully influences a child's well-being. And volumes of research confirm that intuitive link.[1] Could parenting behavior also play a role in the ethnic and racial gaps in school readiness found by social scientists? Just as there are stark differences in the economic, educational, and demographic conditions in the homes of white children and of black and Hispanic children, as other articles in this issue report, there may also be racial and ethnic variation in parenting behaviors. If so, such differences may contribute to the gaps in achievement and readiness that show up when children reach elementary school. To explore these possibilities, we first describe parenting behaviors, as well as the ways in which researchers often assess parenting. Then, we ask to what extent parents matter. That question may come as a surprise, because parenting is so universally regarded as important. But social scientists have raised questions about the extent to which parents matter (does their behavior matter at all, and if so does it matter a little or a lot?), and we pursue them here.

Next we turn our attention to possible racial and ethnic differences in parenting behavior. When we find ethnic or racial differences in parenting—and we do—we provide examples of how specific parenting behavior translates into specific child behavior. We also consider the issue of equivalence in parenting measures across racial and ethnic groups. Then we investigate possible programmatic approaches to altering parenting behavior and ask how effective parenting programs are. Finally, we explore both how much parenting programs can enhance the school readiness of minority children and how much they can close the ethnic and racial gaps in school readiness.

What Is Parenting?

Parenting encompasses the literally hundreds of activities that parents engage in either with or for their children. Often, researchers divide parenting into categories of behavior. In this article we use seven: nurturance, discipline, teaching, language, monitoring, management, and materials.[2]

Nurturance

Nurturing behavior involves ways of expressing love, affection, and care. High nurturing behaviors include expressing warmth, being responsive to a child's needs, and being sensitive to changes in a child's behavior. Low nurturing behaviors include detachment, intrusiveness, and negative regard.[3]

Researchers measure nurturance by observing a parent interacting with her child (parents are not particularly good or accurate reporters of their own warmth, detachment, or intrusiveness). They observe naturally occurring interactions during a two- or three-hour home visit or during structured tasks that can be set up at home, at a preschool center, or at a pediatric clinic. For home visits, the Home Observation for the Measurement of the Environment (HOME) Inventory, for example, asks the observer to record whether she saw certain behaviors, such as a parent spontaneously praising a child's qualities twice; caressing, kissing, or cuddling a child; or using a term of endearment.[4] The structured tasks range from free play with a specific set of toys to problem solving with unique materials (for example, getting a toy from a box using a rake or another utensil) to copying a puzzle or design. Often, researchers videotape the interactions so that they can code them later. Sometimes they code very detailed behaviors (marking the presence or absence of up to fifteen parent and child behaviors every five to ten seconds); other systems involve more global coding of a number of constructs, such as sensitivity to a child's cues, expressed warmth, intrusiveness, and detachment. Training of coders is intensive (often for as long as six weeks) to ensure their reliability.

In semistructured videotaped free play sessions, the observer gives parents and young children toys to play with, leaving instructions deliberately vague. In several studies, she places three toys in separate bags, so that the mother uses one toy at a time, and observes the parent and child for ten to fifteen minutes.[5] The observer rates the session after repeatedly viewing videotapes of behaviors, including detachment (low involvement with and lack of attention to the child), intrusiveness (over-control and over-involvement in the child's play), negative regard (anger, rejection), sensitivity (extent to which the parent perceives the child's signals and responds appropriately), and positive regard (demonstration of love, respect, and admiration).[6]

Sometimes, these behaviors are treated separately, because they measure different aspects of nurturance. At other times, they are clustered together to identify different groups of parents. For example, we have identified several groups of parents—we term them sensitive, directive, uninvolved, and harsh—based on the coding of behaviors in the three-bag free play.[7]

Discipline

Discipline involves parents' responses to child behaviors that they consider appropriate or inappropriate, depending on the child's age and gender and on parental beliefs, upbringing, and culture.[8] Observers sometimes measure discipline from what they see during the course of a home visit. They would describe discipline as harsh or punitive if the parent spanked, slapped, or yelled at the child during the visit.[9] Because parents may be less likely to spank a child with an observer in the home, observers often ask parents about frequency of spanking. They also ask about their use of other discipline strategies, such as time out, explanations, and taking away toys or food. In a few studies, they give parents a scenario. For example, they ask what a mother would do if her child had a temper tantrum in the market; or, if her child had had a tantrum, what she did in response. Sometimes they calculate a severity-of-punishment score or a use-of-reason score.[10]

Teaching

Teaching typically includes didactic strategies for conveying information or skills to the child. Observers set up interaction situations such as putting together a puzzle that is slightly difficult for the child; drawing a complex figure; learning a skill such as tying a shoe or buttoning a coat; or sorting building blocks by shape or color, and then observe teaching behaviors. Often, they rate the strategies in terms of quality of assistance. For example, when helping her child with a puzzle, a mother might do any of the following: take over and put most of the pieces in the puzzle; wait until the child runs into difficulty and then take over; not assist the child at all; provide cues or prompts ("What would happen if you turned that puzzle piece around?") to help the child find the right place for a piece; provide an overall strategy ("Can you find all the pieces that go on the edges of the puzzle?"). Observers would code the latter two examples as high in quality of assistance.[11]

The HOME Inventory includes items related to teaching—does the parent encourage the child to learn colors, songs, or numbers or to read a few words—that can be used to create a scale called Provision of Learning or Learning

Stimulation.[12] These reports are based on parental report, rather than direct observation.

Language

Researchers have extensively studied language use between parents and young children. The most comprehensive studies have transcribed hundreds of hours of mother-child conversations.[13] From those transcriptions, observers can code the sheer amount of language heard by and directed to the child, as well as the number of different

---

When parents read to their children, they vary in how often they ask the child questions, expand on what is in the story, and see whether the child understands the meaning of a word.

---

words, length of sentences, questions asked, elaborations on the child's speech, and events discussed. Observers also frequently elicit parent language by having parents read to their children.[14] Parents vary in how often they ask the child questions, expand on what is in the story, and see whether the child understands the meaning of a word.[15] They also vary in how much they engage in what Katherine Snow has called nonimmediate talk, or going beyond the information given in the story, and in their style of reading.[16]

The HOME Inventory includes several items indicative of reading: child has access to at least ten children's books; at least ten books are visible in the home; family buys and reads a daily newspaper; child has three or more books of his or her own.[17] These items are tapping something different from frequency of book reading or style of reading as measured through direct observation. The underlying premise is that children who are exposed to more reading materials live in households where reading, both adult reading and parent-child shared reading, is more common.

Materials

The term *materials* refers to the cognitively and linguistically stimulating materials provided to the child in the home. This category can overlap with language and with teaching. For example, some scholars categorize number of books in the home, number of children's books, and number of magazine subscriptions as materials rather than as language because they do not know whether parents use them to foster reading. Other items included here are toys and books for learning the alphabet and numbers, educational toys, musical instruments, push-pull toys, drawing materials, and the like. The extensiveness of material items in the home is associated with family income, which is not surprising, given that most are purchased.[18]

Monitoring

Monitoring is what might be called "keeping track." With young children, monitoring refers to parental watchfulness. For example, if a child is playing in a room alone, a parent might periodically check to see what she is doing or call out to her; if a child is watching television alone, a parent might keep track of what program he is watching and change the channel if it seems inappropriate. Studies using time-use diaries of children's days try to distinguish between time when the parent is directly interacting with the child and time when the parent is in the home and responsible for the child even though the two are doing different things.[19] Occasionally the distinction is difficult to make, such as when a child is watching television and the mother is in the room, sometimes watching and talking about a program with the child and sometimes doing housework. With older children, monitoring involves knowing what the child is doing and with whom he is doing it when he is outside the home.

Management

Management encompasses scheduling events, completing scheduled events, and the rhythm of the household. Most studies of young children either do not measure management at all or assess it with only one or two short questions, even though management tasks consume huge amounts of parenting time. Most national studies do ask about two health-related areas: getting the recommended number of well-child visits and getting immunizations on time. Sometimes studies note the appearance of the child (dirty, not dressed, clothes do not fit) as a possible indicator of child neglect. Studies do not always assess taking children to scheduled activities outside the home (even though time diary studies suggest that fathers spend the greatest proportion of their weekend time with their preschoolers in such activities), but often do assess taking children to the park and to visit relatives.[20]

Researchers sometimes tap the rhythm of the household, typically through questions about the regularity of bedtime, bedtime routines (reading, singing, praying), how many meals the family eats together, the breakfast routine (whether breakfast is eaten at all, whether the television is on).[21]

Does Parenting Matter?

Despite all the studies reporting links between parenting and child well-being, we still need to question whether parenting matters.[22] Our premise is as follows. Even though the literature is voluminous, it also has its limits, all of which comes down to the same problem: we do not know, in most cases, whether the so-called effects of parenting are caused by parental behavior or by something else that may complicate the causal link. We consider four different factors: family social, educational, and economic conditions; genetic similarities between parent and child; child characteristics; and other unmeasured characteristics (which we believe might be operating but have not measured, or do not know how to measure well). Although all four factors influence links between parenting and child well-being, they do not account completely for these links. (Another line of evidence supporting the premise that parents matter, reviewed later in this article, has to do with the potential of intervention programs to alter parenting.)

Parenting and Correlated Family Conditions

First, we know that parents differ in their social, economic, and educational backgrounds. And we know that variations in parenting are associated with such characteristics. The link between parental talking and child vocabulary is one example.[23] Parents who talk a lot to their children, ask questions, use many different words, and discuss events are also more likely to be highly educated, to have high incomes, and to have few children, as well as to have children with large vocabularies. And these latter characteristics are themselves associated with child vocabulary. Thus in reality parental education might account for the link between parental talking and child language. If parents who talk a lot are more likely to be highly educated, we need to adjust for parental education to be sure the link between parental language use and child vocabulary is not inflated. It is relatively easy to measure parental education and make statistical adjustments to see if the link between parental talking and child vocabulary still exists, just as it is for other characteristics like family structure, income, parity (number of children), age, and the like. Studies that make such adjustments find that the link exists independent of parental education.

At the same time, the purpose of such studies is often to show how parental education, for example, influences children's language. Clearly, in that case, the parental education effect would have to translate into a specific parenting behavior, such as talking to the child. So we often consider parenting (in this case parental talking) to be a pathway through which parental education influences child language. That suggests two types of intervention strategies. One is indirect: to try to increase maternal education in the hope that more schooling would cause a mother to talk more to her child. The other is direct: to try to increase her talking with the child. The latter would target behavior directed toward the child (talking), rather than a more general characteristic of the adult (more education). The assumption is that it is possible to pinpoint the specific parenting behaviors that contribute to a specific child outcome. High levels of parental warmth, in the absence of much parental talking, for example, would not be expected to increase child vocabulary. Neither would parental monitoring, unless it involved lots of talking.

Parenting and Correlated Genetic Characteristics

Second, perhaps the most widely heralded causal issue is that parents and children are genetically related, which can, in part, account for links between parenting and child well-being. To continue with our earlier ex-

ample, parents who talk a lot and have a large vocabulary are likely to have children who are predisposed toward language. That is, language facility is partly heritable.[24] Even in the absence of parenting behavior, parent language test scores would be linked with child language scores.[25] How can we tell to what extent the link is due to environment (here, language expressed to the child) and to what extent to genetics (here, the biological relationship between parent and child)? Studies informed by behavioral genetics are useful here.[26] Two examples, one from studies of adopted children and the other from work with identical twins (monozygotic twins, whose genetic material is identical, so that any differences between them must be environmental), demonstrate that parenting influences child well-being, over and above genetic relatedness of parents and children.

Studies of adopted children show striking increases in cognitive abilities when the children leave institutional care to be placed with adoptive parents.[27] Children in such studies, however, move from extremely deprived environments without consistent caregivers (orphanages) to stable, two-parent, largely middle-class homes. The studies speak to the powerful effect of having parents versus not having parents, but say little about the effects of varying levels of parenting behavior.

One study does address normal variation in parenting. Michel Duyme and colleagues identified a small sample of adopted children (fewer than seventy) from a review of more than 5,000 adoption cases in France.[28] They selected all children between the ages of four and six who had been placed in prescreened adoptive homes, removed from their birth parents because of abuse or neglect, and put in foster care before their adoption. The children were given cognitive tests before their adoption and again between the ages of eleven and eighteen. Overall, the children showed striking gains in IQ test scores from early childhood to adolescence, from a mean score of 77 to 91 (14 points or almost one standard deviation on a test with a mean of 100 and a standard deviation of 15). The authors classified the adoptive households as low, middle, or high socioeconomic status (SES), based on paternal occupation. The gains were largest for those placed in high SES families (19 points) and smallest for those in the low SES families (8 points).[29] The assumption is that the high SES families were providing more language, more teaching, and more materials, all of which facilitated the children's cognitive growth.

A study of children exposed to cocaine prenatally also illustrates the power of change in parenting.[30] The study recruited more than 400 mothers following delivery. All the new mothers were considered at high risk for cocaine use; about half had biological indications of cocaine use when they and their infants were tested at delivery. When the children were four years old, researchers gave them an IQ test, observed them in their homes, and gave their caregivers a vocabulary test. In the group of children who had been exposed to cocaine before birth, only 55 percent were living with their biological mothers at the follow-up, as against 95 percent of those in the group that had not been exposed. The cocaine-exposed preschoolers living with their mothers or with a relative had significantly lower IQ scores than their counterparts who were living with an adoptive or foster care mother—even though (not surprisingly) the latter group had been exposed to more cocaine than those who were not removed from the mother. Furthermore, the IQ scores of the exposed children living with an adoptive or foster mother were com-

parable to those of the children who were not exposed to cocaine prenatally. For example, the share of the cocaine-exposed children living with their mothers who had IQ scores under 70 (the mild mental retardation range) was 25 percent, as against 10 percent for the exposed children who lived with nonrelatives and 16 percent for the nonexposed children. As might be expected, the homes of the groups differed; cocaine-exposed children living with adoptive or foster mothers had more stimulating environments, and their mothers had higher vocabulary scores, than the cocaine-exposed children living with their biological mothers or relatives.[31]

The second class of studies does not rely on change in parents (from orphanage to family or from biological to adoptive parent). Instead, it uses genetic similarity to delve into parental effects. In a sample of 500 five-year-old identical twins, mothers were asked to talk about each of their children. Mothers tended to describe one twin in more negative terms than the other. When the children were in elementary school, their teachers were asked to rate their behavior.[32] Teachers reported that the twin for whom the mother had more negative feelings had more behavior problems than the other twin.[33] Because the children had identical genetic endowments, it is highly likely that maternal behavior accounted for the differences in behavior problems between the twins.

Parenting and Correlated Child Characteristics

A third causal issue is that parenting behavior may be in part contingent on the behavior of the child. That is, not only does parenting affect child behavior, but also children can influence parents.[34] We provide two examples, the first having to do with reading, the second with behavior problems.

Children of mothers who read to them frequently have large vocabularies, as countless studies have shown.[35] In an evaluation of the Early Head Start Program, Helen Raikes and her colleagues have found the expected links between shared book reading and child vocabulary in more than 1,000 children seen at age fourteen months, twenty-four months, and thirty-six months, even after adjusting for differences in mothers' verbal abilities.[36] (The adjustment is necessary because moth-

---

More shared reading at fourteen months was linked with higher vocabulary scores at twenty-four months, which affected the amount of reading at twenty-four and thirty-six months.

---

ers with higher verbal abilities are likely to enjoy reading more than other mothers, which could influence their shared book reading with the child, and because language ability is partly heritable.) Of more interest is their exploration of the pathways through which language at age thirty-six months was influenced. More shared reading at fourteen months was linked with higher vocabulary scores at twenty-four months, which affected the amount of reading at twenty-four and thirty-six months. Thus, mothers whose children knew and used more words were reading more to these children as they developed, over and above their reading levels at fourteen months.

One of the best-known examples of child-to-parent effects is an intervention geared to-

ward children with conduct disorders and their parents.[37] Half the children participated in a family program, which was effective in that the children displayed less aggression after the intervention. But the positive impact on the children was primarily due to changes in parenting behavior. That is, the parents in the intervention group stopped reacting negatively to their children's aggressive behavior by learning other techniques for dealing with outbursts. In contrast, the parents in the control group did not alter their responses to their children's outbursts, and therefore the children's problem behavior showed no change.

The point here is that child characteristics can influence parenting. But the existence of differences among children themselves does not totally account for parenting effects on children.

Parenting and Unmeasured Correlates

The final complicating causal issue involves possible correlates of parenting that have not been measured. Even studies that adjust for family conditions and child characteristics may fail to measure other sources of variation in parenting and children's school readiness, perhaps because of limits of cost or time or the lack of a reliable indicator.

One characteristic often associated with parenting and child outcomes is parents' mental health. Mothers who are diagnosed with clinical depression or as having high levels of depressive symptoms engage in less nurturance and more punitive discipline, as has been demonstrated countless times for preschoolers as well as older children.[38] And these mothers' preschool children have more behavioral problems and (sometimes but not always) lower cognitive test scores.[39] But even when analysts adjust for maternal depression, parenting still contributes to these indicators of child well-being. Indeed, maternal depression, as well as other measures of mental health (anxiety, irritability), is thought to act on children through its effect on parenting behavior.[40] Vonnie McLoyd, Rand Conger, and their colleagues have proposed a family stress model that traces the pathways from low income, financial instability, and material stress through parental mental health to parenting to child outcomes.[41] Jean Yeung and her colleagues have shown that this pathway is stronger for behavioral problems than for cognitive and language test scores in young children.[42]

Even if a study measures many potential correlates, it is impossible to be sure that it includes all that are relevant. So scholars use a variety of statistical techniques to minimize the likelihood that results are due to something besides parenting.[43] But the most convincing evidence is gleaned from experiments where families enter a treatment or a control group through random assignment. We present evidence from experiments designed to test the efficacy of parenting programs later in the article.

Do Ethnic and Racial Differences in Parenting Exist?

In this section we first ask whether measures of parenting are equivalent across ethnic and racial gaps. Next we consider whether there are ethnic and racial differences in the seven dimensions of parenting described earlier And, finding some, we compare their size with that of the ethnic and racial gaps in school readiness. For several domains of parenting, we find the sizes are similar. Using evidence of congruence in the strength and direction of links between parenting and school readiness for black, white, and Hispanic children, we ask whether the meaning of parenting behavior varies from one ethnic

or racial group to another. Although the dimensions of parenting seem to be equivalent across groups, the levels of particular behaviors do, in some instances, vary. At the same time, there are more similarities than differences in links between children's school readiness and parenting across racial and ethnic groups; when differences appear, they seem to be clustered in negative parenting behaviors.

Equivalence of Parenting Measures across Ethnic and Racial Groups

Any discussion of parenting gives rise to arguments about whether parenting behaviors are the same from one group to another and whether measures of parenting have the same meaning from one group to another. Three considerations are relevant: first, whether parenting behaviors are universal or specific to time and place; second, how representative the parenting behaviors typically measured and developed using middle-class white samples are of other groups; and third, whether a particular society "privileges" certain parenting behaviors.

Regarding the first point, many aspects of parenting described in this article are exhibited by parents in many societies.[44] That is, all parents have ways of nurturing, teaching, disciplining, monitoring, and managing their young children. All provide a linguistic environment as well as a material environment. But the expression of these parenting activities sometimes differs, and the emphasis among behaviors sometimes varies. In eastern Africa, for example, parents devote much time to working with and encouraging their toddlers to develop their motor skills. Not surprisingly, their children's motor skills are more advanced than those of U.S. children.[45] Parents in Western societies often value language and vocabulary skills (given their links to doing well in school), so the language output of Western children is often greater than that of children in other societies.[46] The point, however, is that parents across societies engage in teaching activities (as in the case of motor skills) and language activities (as in the case of vocabulary). The difference is in the level of a particular behavior, not its existence.[47]

On the second point, the parenting behaviors measured in most studies are said to be representative of middle-class families in the United States.[48] We agree with this proposition, given the samples from which most parenting measures were derived. Consequently, some parenting behaviors are probably not measured, or not measured well. And these may be behaviors that are more prevalent in black and Hispanic groups than in white groups. For example, some groups, such as recent Hispanic immigrants, may value compliance of toddlers more than do other groups.[49] Are we measuring compliance, and the parental behaviors that foster it, accurately?

Another example of imperfect measurement of parenting surfaced from our research group's work with a widely used coding scheme developed by Diana Baumrind, which distinguishes between authoritative parenting (warm, firm control) and authoritarian parenting (negative, harsh control).[50] Studies have found that black mothers are more authoritarian and less authoritative than white mothers, just as lower SES mothers are more authoritarian than higher SES mothers.[51] However, black graduate students in our laboratory felt that these codes did not represent what they had seen in black families. So we did an exploratory analysis using a sample of about 700 black and white mothers of toddlers, attempting to identify clusters of mothers based on our videotaped ratings on both domains. We identified not two but four

groups of mothers—those who were high in warm, firm control and low in negative, harsh control (the classic authoritative behavior); those who were high in negative, harsh control and low in warm, firm control (the classic authoritarian behavior); those who were relatively high in both (what we termed "tough love"); and those who were low in both (what we termed "detached"). More blacks than whites were in the tough love group. The classic authoritarian group was composed primarily of teenage mothers, both black and white, while the tough love group comprised mostly older black mothers with at least a high school education. Interestingly, children of mothers in the tough love group had higher IQ and vocabulary scores than children in the classic authoritarian or the detached group, suggesting that previous coding schemes had confounded two groups of black mothers by labeling them authoritarian—and assuming that their parenting had negative consequences for school readiness.[52] A further example of how difficult it can be to measure parenting relates to findings that spanking has less negative consequences for black than white children.[53] Spanking may be more normative for the black children, and it may occur in the context of warm parenting—that is, tough love.

As to the third point, perhaps the best evidence of the validity of a particular parenting behavior is how well it predicts school readiness. And given our focus on racial and ethnic differences, whether parenting predicts school readiness equally well in different groups is critical. In general, the parenting behaviors described in this article are related to school readiness in U.S. society at this time. They do not necessarily represent all parenting behaviors, or particular behaviors valued by certain groups, or behaviors that promote outcomes other than school readiness. In this sense, we are privileging more Western, middle-class parenting behaviors. If we are correct that these are the behaviors that contribute to school readiness, and if these are the behaviors that parenting interventions target because of their links to school readiness, then this privileging seems appropriate. It does not mean that these parenting behaviors are "good" while others are not.

Ethnic and Racial Differences in Parenting

There are ethnic and racial differences in parenting during early childhood. Evidence is available on five of the seven parenting dimensions: nurturance, discipline, teaching, language, and materials. In all cases, when differences occur, black mothers have lower scores on parenting measures than do white mothers. Similar differences often exist between Hispanic and white mothers as well, although the research base for this comparison is much smaller. In general, the effect sizes for the ethnic and racial differences range from one-fifth to three-fifths of a standard deviation—similar to but slightly smaller than school readiness measures, which are roughly two-fifths to four-fifths of a standard deviation.[54] These parenting differences would translate into 3 to 9 points on a test that had a mean of 100 and a standard deviation of 15 (as many tests of vocabulary and intelligence have). All references to test points in the rest of the article refer to a test with such characteristics. School readiness measures on such a test show racial gaps of 6 to 12 points, depending on the aspect of readiness being measured.

Evidence for racial and ethnic gaps in nurturance comes from several sources. On the first, the observational HOME Warmth Scale, black mothers sometimes have lower scores, although the differences are modest:

one-fifth of a standard deviation or less, or 3 points or less, using our reference test.[55] Hispanic mothers have scores comparable to whites in most cases.[56]

Another positive indicator of nurturance is the sensitivity of the mother, as expressed in mother-child free play or problem-solving situations. Black mothers are rated as having

---

Another positive indicator of nurturance is the sensitivity of the mother, as expressed in mother-child free play or problem-solving situations

---

somewhat lower levels of sensitivity—about one-fifth of a standard deviation—as coded from fifteen-minute videotaped sessions.[57]

Measures on the more negative end of the nurturance continuum are also gleaned from mother-child interchanges recorded on the videotapes, which have documented racial differences in negative regard, intrusiveness, and detachment, with black mothers scoring slightly higher than white mothers. The black-white differences are around one-fifth to two-fifths of a standard deviation (3 to 6 points).[58]

Discipline also varies by racial and ethnic group. Black mothers are somewhat more likely to spank their children than are white mothers.[59] White mothers are more likely to use reasoning as a discipline technique, though the effects are modest, about one-fifth or less of a standard deviation (1 to 3 points).[60]

Perhaps the most striking differences are for language.[61] Transcriptions of naturally occurring mother-child conversations suggest that children's exposure to language and conversation varies widely across social class groups, as demonstrated in a sample of forty-two children from three different social class groupings.[62] As such differences accumulate over the first years of life, the children in families with a high socioeconomic background have engaged in literally thousands more conversations than children from lower socioeconomic backgrounds. Even when they begin speaking (around their first birthday), higher SES children have larger vocabularies than the children from middle and low SES families. By their second birthday, the children in the middle SES group have pulled away from those in the low SES group. And these differences *accelerate* over time. So by age three, vocabularies of the children in the low SES group are half the size of those in the high SES group and two-thirds the size of those in the middle SES group. Given the racial composition of the SES groups in this study (the majority of black families were in the low SES group), black-white differences were equally large.

Scholars have posited differences in family "speech cultures," which are associated, in part, with social class and race.[63] The educated middle- to upper-middle-class "speech culture" provides more language, more varied language, more language topics, more questions, and more conversation, all of which are linked with large vocabularies in toddlers and preschoolers. Repeated and varied, these parental speech patterns predict how fast young children learn words.[64] Little research has focused on whether the variations, if controlled, would reduce the racial or ethnic gap in school readiness.[65]

Analysts have also examined shared book reading as a vehicle for language input.[66]

Large national or multisite studies often ask about the frequency of reading.[67] From 40 to 55 percent of mothers report reading to their toddler every day.[68] Black mothers are about two-thirds as likely as white mothers to do so; Hispanic mothers, about half as likely.[69] Ethnic and racial differences in frequency of reading exist in population-based as well as low-income samples. Black and Hispanic children also come from homes with fewer reading materials (books, children's books, magazines, newspapers) than do white children.[70] The size of such differences is between one-fifth and three-fifths of a standard deviation.

Materials in the home also vary by ethnicity and racial group. Not only do black and Hispanic families have fewer reading materials in their homes, but typically they also have fewer educationally relevant materials of other types (as indexed by the HOME Learning Scale). Racial differences on the Learning Scale are large, from two-fifths to three-fifths of a standard deviation, or 6 to 9 points on our reference test.[71]

Reduction in Racial Gaps in School Readiness as a Function of Parenting

The racial differences in parenting do account for a portion of the racial gap in school readiness. In general, researchers who have conducted such analyses report that a 12 to 15 point gap between black and white children is reduced by 3 to 9 points when parenting is considered.

Most national studies that follow a group of the same children over time use the Learning Scale as a measure of parenting.[72] This particular measure of parenting is often posited to be one of the pathways through which parental income, education, marital status, and age affect children (just as language input and shared book reading are pathways through which family social class influences school readiness). Taking this measure into account narrows the racial gap in such early childhood outcomes by one-third to one-half.[73]

Do Parenting Interventions Work?

Is it possible to enhance parenting through intervention programs? And if so, do some of the beneficial effects on children of early childhood intervention programs operate through their effects on parenting? We consider evidence for each question. In general, programs focused on parenting can alter behavior, as has been demonstrated in several well-designed evaluations of experimental programs (those in which families are randomly assigned to treatment and control groups). And some—but not all—of the benefits that accrue to children seem to operate through changes in parenting behavior.

Effects of Parenting Interventions

Interventions for parents of young children fall into four categories: home-based (often termed home-visiting) programs, center-based early childhood education programs with a parenting component (often termed center plus programs), family literacy programs, and programs targeting child behavior problems by changing parental behavior (the latter are reviewed in a separate section).[74] We focus on programs initiated in the first four years of a child's life.[75]

HOME-VISITING AND CENTER PLUS. Almost all parenting programs target families in which parents are poor, have little education, are young, or are unwed. The programs are not universal. Some have operated in multiple sites (which assures that they can be transferred to other settings and that staff can be trained to deliver services and curriculum). Overall, programs have served more

black and urban families than white, Hispanic, or rural families, so we have more evidence of program efficacy for the former than the latter.

Program evaluations have focused mostly on nurturance, discipline, language, and materials. They have gathered little information about teaching and virtually none about monitoring and management (with the exception of health practices, which are not reviewed here).[76] Several programs also target parental mental health.[77] Fewer programs have effects on maternal depression than on nurturance, language, and materials, suggesting that it might be easier to alter parenting behavior than parental emotional state, at least using parenting interventions, rather than more focused treatment of depressive symptoms.[78]

Nurturance has received much attention, because one of the goals of many home- and center-based programs with a parenting component is to enhance sensitivity and reduce negativity (the same is not true of family literacy programs). Home-visiting programs are more likely to affect nurturance than other parenting behaviors. For example, eleven of thirteen home-visiting evaluations that reportedly observed mother-child interactions found positive benefits.[79] (One meta-analysis suggests that home-visiting programs are better at reducing parental insensitivity than at changing other aspects of the mother-child attachment relationship.)[80] Center-based programs with a parenting component, including Early Head Start, also report enhancing sensitivity and reducing negativity.[81]

Discipline has not been measured as frequently. When it has, both home-based and center-based programs with a parenting component have shown decreases in spanking and, in several cases, an increase in the use of reasoning.[82] Again, this aspect of parenting is not the focus of family literacy programs.

Teaching is often a part of intervention programs. One curriculum, LearningGames, has been used in the Infant Health and Development Program, the Abecedarian Program, and Project Care.[83] The object is to present age-appropriate activities for the child and the parent to do together, and to provide the parent role modeling and instruction in how

---

Language is most likely to be changed by family literacy programs that focus directly on shared book reading and other language settings.

---

to approach them. Center-based programs with a parenting component have reported improving parents' ability to assist in problem-solving activities.[84] Much less is known about home-visiting programs in this regard.

Home-based and center-based programs do not often target maternal language, at least not directly. We know almost nothing about whether they increase maternal language output. Because one determinant of a child's increased vocabulary is the mother's vocabulary, such a goal might be sensible.

A few literacy programs have tried to change how parents read with their children, with an implied goal of using more, and more varied language. Grover Whitehurst and his colleagues developed a program of dialogic reading that trained mothers and teachers to read with an emphasis on asking children questions, providing feedback to their re-

sponses, initiating conversations that went beyond the book's content, and delving into children's understanding of concepts.[85] The adult training was successful, and children in the treatment group had higher language scores than those in the control group. Several programs with a focus on literacy are now being evaluated.[86]

Many home-based and center-based programs have used the HOME Learning Scale to assess the parenting dimension that we call materials. About half of the center-based programs with a parenting component report higher scores on this scale after treatment; fewer home-based programs report such effects.[87] Even Start, a national literacy program, reported its most consistent treatment effect on reading materials in the home.[88]

In conclusion, home- and center-based programs with a parenting component have their largest and most consistent effects on nurturance. They have some effects on discipline and, in some instances, on materials. Little evidence exists, for or against, regarding effects on language. Indeed, language is most likely to be changed by family literacy programs that focus directly on shared book reading and other language settings.

PARENT BEHAVIOR TRAINING PROGRAMS. Yet another type of parenting program aims to alter the behavior of parents whose children exhibit problem behavior. Typically, children who are disruptive and aggressive and who act out in the preschool and early school years are likely to have high rates of delinquency and school drop-out during adolescence.[89] In the early school years, they are likely to spend little time engaging in classroom tasks and are often disliked by their peers and teachers.[90] To address these children's needs, researchers and clinicians have developed several types of programs, focusing variously on parents, teachers, the child's social skills in the classroom, or individual counseling.[91]

One parent training program, developed by Carolyn Webster-Stratton and her colleagues, crafts group discussions around videotaped vignettes of typical discipline situations in the home, often showing several ways to handle a particular situation.[92] This program has been found to reduce parents' negative discipline and nurturance behaviors and increase positive parenting behaviors in mothers. Webster-Stratton's Incredible Years Curriculum is often targeted to families in Head Start. As a result, it benefits poor families. When the parent program was expanded to include a teacher component, it reduced negative behavior and increased more supportive behavior in parents, and it enabled teachers to use more positive management techniques in their Head Start classrooms. Children in the program have lower rates of acting out and aggressive behaviors and are more engaged in their classrooms than are children in a control group.[93] Webster-Stratton's programs have effects on children of between one-half and two-thirds of a standard deviation, or 7 to 10 points on our reference test.

A few other programs offer a range of services, beginning with low-intensity services for all parents in a classroom and moving to more intensive services for parents whose children have moderate behavior problems and even more training and counseling for families whose children have severe behavior problems.[94] Most of these programs, however, have focused on kindergartners and first graders.

Our point is that parent training programs for children with moderate or severe behavior problems have been proven successful. Programs that include both parents and preschool teachers seem to be the most successful of all.

Parenting Impacts and Their Effects on Children

Do the interventions' positive effects on parenting make any difference in children's cognitive performance and school readiness? Two types of evidence are relevant, the first having to do with whether the programs have effects on the children and the second with whether any of the children's benefits are due to the effects of the programs on parenting.

The answer to the first question depends on the type of intervention. Few home-visiting programs have altered children's school readiness.[95] That being so, the positive parenting effects for home-based programs could not be translated into child effects. In our view, most home-visiting programs are not intensive enough, and home visitors are not trained or supervised enough, to be likely to enhance school readiness.[96]

In contrast, the center-based early childhood education programs with a parenting component have improved vocabulary, reading achievement, math achievement, and IQ, with some effects continuing through adolescence in some studies.[97] Although these programs have few effects on socioemotional development in preschool, two have lowered juvenile delinquency and teenage pregnancy rates.

Second, when programs affect both parents and children, does the enhanced parenting affect the child outcomes? This question is important, especially for center-based programs with a parenting component, because these programs could operate through the parent or through the center services received directly by the child. In the Infant Health and Development Program, the positive effects on the HOME Inventory accounted for a portion of the IQ benefit at age three.[98] In the Early Head Start Program Demonstration, about two-fifths to one-half of the treatment effect on child cognitive test scores operated through the program's effect on parenting behavior.[99] Center-based programs with a parenting component appear effective at enhancing parenting and school readiness, with some of the effect on the latter operating through the former. These programs are, in our opinion, a good bet for increasing child well-being.

The Whitehurst literacy program noted above also had positive child effects. Other family literacy programs should similarly yield benefits, with the effects assumed to operate through parental language use. Although we have fewer data on which to base our opinion, we believe that these programs also show promise for improving parenting and school readiness. The parent behavior training programs also have shown effects on children when targeted to families whose children have been identified as having problem behavior.

Can Parenting Interventions Close the Ethnic and Racial Gaps in School Readiness?

If parenting interventions are to narrow ethnic and racial school readiness gaps, they must meet one of several conditions. First, effective interventions should be offered to proportionately more minority than nonminority families. This could be achieved if such programs were offered to families with characteristics—for example, poorly educated mother, unwed mother, or mother with

poor mental health—that are more often found in minority than in white families. Second, even if programs were not provided to more minority than nonminority families, they could still reduce the racial gaps if they were more beneficial to black than white parents. Third, even if parenting programs were not more effective for black and Hispanic than white parents, they could still narrow ethnic and racial differences if they were more beneficial to mothers with certain characteristics, such as being young or poorly educated, that are more prevalent among black and Hispanic mothers than white mothers.

Evidence on the first condition is scanty; estimates of the shares of black, Hispanic, and white families receiving parenting programs do not exist. But more is known about the second and third conditions. Parenting programs sometimes do have more beneficial effects for blacks than for whites and, to a lesser extent, for younger than for older mothers. That being the case, parenting programs, if implemented, could reduce the racial gap in school readiness.

Who Receives Parenting Programs?
Parenting interventions are almost always targeted to specific groups, typically parents who are poor, poorly educated, young and unwed, live in impoverished communities, or have mental health problems.[100] As such, they are likely to serve a greater share of minority than nonminority families—a ratio of three to one (or higher)—given the differential prevalence of such conditions.[101] No estimates exist of the number of families with young children served by parenting programs, but two home-visiting programs that focus on parenting—the Nurse Home Visitation Model and the Healthy Start Model—have been initiated countrywide.[102]

In their article in this volume, Katherine Magnuson and Jane Waldfogel note that 30 percent of all U.S. children under the age of six are in some form of center-based child care and education. Breaking that figure down, they find 30 percent of white children, 22 percent of Hispanic children, and 40 percent of black children in center-based care. Some but not all child care programs also provide parenting classes or home visiting; publicly funded programs, such as Head Start, are most likely to do so.[103] Proportionately more black than white children attend Head Start; if these programs are effective in altering parenting behavior, then Head Start could reduce the racial gap in school readiness. Too few studies have examined its efficacy vis-à-vis parenting outcomes to make an inference about the probability of Head Start as a path to reducing racial gaps, but the program does seem to have positive effects on children.[104]

Differing Program Effects on Black and White Parents

If parenting interventions benefit black and Hispanic parents more than white parents, they could reduce gaps in school readiness. Few demonstration programs have examined this question, in large part because most parenting programs operate in one community or neighborhood, so that racial and ethnic variation in participants is quite limited. But two multisite demonstrations report larger effects on black than white mothers in some, but not all, aspects of parenting.

Through the Infant Health and Development Program (IHDP), an eight-site randomized control trial, about 1,000 families with low birth weight children born in 1985 were offered parenting-focused home-visit and center-based child care from birth through the child's third year of life. The program assessed HOME Inventory, mother-child free play, and problem-solving videotaped interactions, maternal mental health, and spanking.[105] According to analyses conducted for this article, black mothers benefited more from the program than did white mothers when their children were age three (that is, at the end of the intervention). Observers noted more learning and less punitive discipline in the homes of black mothers in the intervention than those of black mothers in the con-

If parenting interventions benefit black and Hispanic parents more than white parents, they could reduce gaps in school readiness.

trol group; effect sizes were about one-fifth to one-quarter of a standard deviation, or 3 to 4 points on our reference test. We found no corresponding treatment differences for the white mothers.[106] In both cases, the scores of black mothers in the treatment group were higher than those of their counterparts in the control group and were comparable to those of the white mothers in both the treatment and the control groups.

Researchers report similar findings in the Early Head Start Demonstration (EHS), a randomized seventeen-site evaluation of home- and center-based early childhood intervention for pregnant women and young children, conducted from the late 1990s into 2000.[107] Black mothers in the intervention group had more positive and fewer negative parenting behaviors than did black mothers in the control group; the effect sizes ranged from one-fifth to one-half of a standard deviation (3 to 7.5 points on our reference test).

Researchers found these effects in eight parenting behaviors measured at the end of the intervention, when the children were three years old. Hispanic mothers also benefited from Early Head Start, although not as much as black mothers and not in as many parenting behaviors. The program had almost no effect on the white mothers. The EHS intervention raised the parenting scores of the black mothers to levels similar to those of the white mothers, mirroring the IHDP results.

Differing Program Impacts by Maternal Age, Education, and Mental Health

Programs could also reduce the ethnic and racial gaps if they benefited mothers who were poorer, younger, or single more than other mothers, because these characteristics are more likely among black and Hispanic mothers than among white mothers. At least three lines of evidence exist, the first relating to maternal education, the second to maternal age, and the third to maternal mental health. We believe that it would be possible to reduce racial gaps in school readiness if the results described below could be replicated in large-scale programs.

First, early childhood education programs seem to have more benefits for children of mothers with a high school education (or less) than they do for children whose mothers have some postsecondary schooling.[108] Less information is available on whether such programs affect parenting. In the IHDP, even though children of less educated mothers benefited more, their mothers did not. The Early Head Start Demonstration had somewhat greater effects on the parenting behavior of the less educated than on that of the more educated mothers, as well as on child engagement and persistence in mother-child play sessions.[109] Effect sizes range from one-fifth to one-quarter of a standard deviation (3 to 5 points on our reference test). At the same time, only EHS mothers with more than a high school education showed significant increases in reading at bedtime and reductions in spanking. These mixed findings signal caution in accepting this pathway—larger effects for less educated mothers—to reducing the racial gap in school readiness.

Second, young and first-time parents might also benefit more from parenting interventions than older, more experienced parents. And, indeed, whenever benefits of treatment differ by parental age, they favor the younger, typically teenage and unwed mother.[110] Results are stronger for the Nurse Home Visitation Model than for EHS.

Third, although evidence is limited, parenting interventions do appear to have greater effects for mothers with low psychological resources. Of the seventeen sites in the EHS demonstration, eight asked mothers about depressive symptoms before the intervention began; those with more symptoms were more likely than those with fewer symptoms to see symptoms reduced during the intervention.[111] In IHDP, by contrast, all intervention mothers experienced reduced depression symptoms.[112] Early Head Start had somewhat greater effects on mothers' parenting behaviors for those with initially high depressive symptoms.[113]

David Olds and colleagues have reported that their Nurse Home Visitation Model had more positive effects on mothers with low psychological resources (a measure comprising mental health, sense of mastery, and intelligence obtained before the intervention) than on those with high psychological resources.[114]

Conclusion

Parenting influences young children in many different ways. The frequency of certain parenting behaviors, those often linked with school readiness, are lower for black and Hispanic mothers than for white mothers, though adjustment for differences in family conditions attenuates these differences to an extent. These racial and ethnic differences in parenting in large part parallel racial and ethnic differences in school readiness. When such parenting differences are controlled, the gaps in school readiness drop 25 percent to 50 percent.

It is possible to alter the parenting behavior of black and Hispanic mothers. In several instances, interventions have reduced the gaps in the parenting behavior of black and white mothers. In these cases, black children also benefited more than white children from the intervention. These successful programs have been high-quality and center-based with a parenting component (typically through home visiting). Exclusively home-based programs have not yielded comparable findings; they affect the mother but not the child and therefore (with a few exceptions) cannot narrow ethnic and racial gaps in school readiness. We cannot say from existing evidence whether all center-based programs should have a parenting component. There is little evidence documenting the effects of parenting components in publicly funded programs such as Head Start. In addition, because virtually all programs for children under age four involve the parent, it is not known whether a center-based program without a parenting component is as effective as one with such a component. The rise of the prekindergarten programs may provide some insight, because many such programs do not target the parent in any significant way. Whether such programs will show similar impacts on children without parental involvement remains to be seen. The exciting findings of the new family literacy programs and the parent behavior training programs also provide possible avenues for targeted parenting programs.

Endnotes

1. Marc H. Bornstein, ed., *Handbook of Parenting: Children and Parenting* (Mahwah, N.J.: Lawrence Erlbaum Associates, 2002); Eleanor Maccoby and John A. Martin, "Socialization in the Context of the Family: Parent-Child Interaction," in *Handbook of Child Psychology*, vol. 4, *Socialization, Personality and Social Development*, 4th ed., edited by E. Mavis Hetherington (New York: Wiley, 1983): p. 1.

2. There are other ways of categorizing parenting behaviors. See Lisa J. Berlin, Christy Brady-Smith, and Jeanne Brooks-Gunn, "Links between Childbearing Age and Observed Maternal Behaviors with 14-Month-Olds in the Early Head Start Research and Evaluation Project," *Infant Mental Health Journal* 23, no. 1 (2002): 104–29; Bornstein, *Handbook of Parenting* (see note 1); Tama Leventhal and others, "The Homelife Interview for the Project on Human Development in Chicago Neighborhoods: Assessment of Parenting and Home Environment for 3-15 Year Olds," *Parenting: Science and Practice* 4 (2004); Maccoby and Martin, "Socialization in the Context of the Family" (see note 1); Eleanor Maccoby, "The Role of Parents in the Socialization of Children: An Historical Overview," *Developmental Psychology* 28 (1992): 1006; Lawrence Steinberg and Ann S. Morris, "Adolescent Development," *Annual Review of Psychology* 52 (2000): 83–110.

3. Low nurturance is sometimes linked more closely with aggression or low self-control than with cognitive and language skills, while the opposite is true for high nurturance behaviors. Jean Ispa and others, "Maternal Intrusiveness, Maternal Warmth, Mother-Toddler Relationship Outcomes: Variations across Low-Income Ethnic and Acculturation Groups," *Child Development* (forthcoming); Rebecca Ryan, Ann Martin and Jeanne Brooks-Gunn, "Is One Good Enough Parent Good Enough? Patterns of Father and Mother Parenting and Their Combined Associations with Concurrent Child Outcomes at 24 and 36 Months," *Parenting: Science and Practice* (forthcoming).

4. Robert Bradley and Bettye Caldwell, *Home Observation for Measurement of the Environment* (University of Arkansas, 1984); Robert Bradley, "Home Environment and Parenting," in *Handbook of Parenting*, vol. 2, *Biology and Ecology of Parenting*, edited by Marc Bornstein (Hillsdale, N.J.: Lawrence Erlbaum Associates, 1995), p. 235; Jeffrey B. Bingenheimer and others, "Measurement Equivalence for Two Dimensions of Children's Home Environment," *Journal of Family Psychology* (forthcoming); Leventhal and others, "The Homelife Interview" (see note 2); Miriam Linver, Jeanne Brooks-Gunn, and Natasha Cabrera, "The Home Observation for Measurement of the Environment (HOME) Inventory: The Derivation of Conceptually Designed Subscales," *Parenting: Science and Practice* (2004). The HOME Inventory, developed in the 1980s, originally had more than fifty exemplars (items either observed in the home or reported upon by the mother) of home conditions or parental behaviors that, if absent, might put the child at risk for less than optimal development. The items were crafted to discriminate among those homes with quite adverse circumstances; HOME does not differentiate particularly well among homes and families within the wide range of acceptable to excellent circumstances (and was not designed to do so); see Robert Bradley, "Chaos, Culture, and Covariance Structures: A Dynamic Systems View of Children's Experiences at Home," *Parenting: Science and Practice* 4 (2004). Many variants of HOME have been developed; the variants have different numbers of items; forms have been developed for different age groups (the first HOME focusing on early childhood); some forms have been adapted to be more similar across age groups than earlier forms; and some forms separate scales with only observation and only parental report items; see Linver and others, "The Home Observation for Measurement of the Environment" (see above in this note). Ethnic and racial differences in the coherence of scales have been examined as well; see Robert H.

Bradley and others, "The Home Environment of Children in the United States, Part I: Variations by Age, Ethnicity, and Poverty Status," *Child Development* 72 (2001): 1844; Bradley, "Home Environment and Parenting," and Bingenheimer and others, "Measurement Equivalence" (see Bradley and Bingenheimer both above in this note). The HOME Inventory is the parenting measure that is used in most of the national, longitudinal studies in the United States, Canada, and Australia.

5. NICHD Early Child Care Research Network, "Child Care and Mother-Child Interaction in the First Three Years of Life," *Developmental Psychology* 35 (1999): 1399; Jeanne Brooks-Gunn and others, "Depending on the Kindness of Strangers: Current National Data Initiatives and Developmental Research," *Child Development* 71, no. 1 (2000): 257.

6. Berlin, Brady-Smith, and Brooks-Gunn, "Links between Childbearing Age" (see note 2); NICHD Early Child Care Network, "Child Care and Mother-Child Interaction" (see note 5); Ryan, Martin, and Brooks-Gunn, "Is One Good Enough Parent Good Enough?" (see note 3).

7. Christy Brady-Smith and Jeanne Brooks-Gunn, analyses prepared for this article using data from the Early Head Start Demonstration, 2004 (available from the National Center for Children and Families, Teachers College, Columbia University); Ryan, Martin, and Brooks-Gunn, "Is One Good Enough Parent Good Enough?" (see note 3).

8. Kirby Deater-Deckard and others, "Physical Discipline among African American and European American Mothers: Links to Children's Externalizing Behaviors," *Developmental Psychology* 32, no. 6 (1996): 1065; Sara Harkness and Charles Super, "Culture and Parenting," in *Handbook of Parenting*, vol. 2, *Biology and Ecology of Parenting*, edited by Marc Bornstein (Mahwah, N.J.: Lawrence Erlbaum Associates, 1995), p. 211.

9. Robert Bradley, "Environment and Parenting," *Handbook of Parenting*, 2nd ed., edited by Marc Bornstein (Hillsdale, N.J.: Lawrence Erlbaum Associates, 2002), p. 281; Judith Smith and Jeanne Brooks-Gunn, "Correlates and Consequences of Harsh Discipline for Young Children," *Archives of Pediatric and Adolescent Medicine* 151 (1997): 777; Leventhal and others, "The Homelife Interview" (see note 2); Allison Fuligni, Wen Jui Han, and Jeanne Brooks-Gunn, "The Infant-Toddler HOME in the Second and Third Years of Life," *Parenting: Science and Practice* 4 (2004).

10. John Love and others, *Making a Difference in the Lives of Infants and Toddlers and Their Families: The Impacts of Early Head Start* (U.S. Department of Health and Human Services, 2002).

11. Donna Spiker, Joan Ferguson, and Jeanne Brooks-Gunn, "Enhancing Maternal Interactive Behavior and Child Social Competence in Low Birth Weight, Premature Infants," *Child Development* 64 (1993): 754; Alan Sroufe, Byron Egeland, and Terri Kreutzer, "The Fate of Early Experience following Developmental Change: Longitudinal Approaches to Individual Adaptation in Childhood," *Child Development* 61, no. 5 (1990): 1363; Lindsay Chase-Lansdale, Jeanne Brooks-Gunn, and Elise Zamsky, "Young African-American Multigenerational Families in Poverty: Quality of Mothering and Grandmothering," *Child Development* 65, no. 2 (1994): 373.

12. Pamela K. Klebanov, Jeanne Brooks-Gunn, and Marie McCormick, "Does Neighborhood and Family Poverty Affect Mothers' Parenting, Mental Health and Social Support?" *Journal of Marriage and the Family* 56, no. 2 (1994): 455; Linver, Brooks-Gunn, and Cabrera, "The Home Observation for Measurement" (see note 4).

13. Eve Clark, *The Lexicon in Acquisition* (Cambridge University Press, 1993); Betty Hart and Todd Risley, *Meaningful Differences in the Everyday Experience of Young American Children* (Baltimore: Brookes, 1995); Janellen Huttenlocher and others, "Early Vocabulary Growth: Relation to Language Input and Gender," *Developmental Psychology* 27 (1991): 236; Zehava Weizman and Catherine Snow, "Lexical Input as Related to Children's Vocabulary Acquisition: Effects of Sophisticated Exposure and Support for Meaning," *Developmental Psychology* 37 (2001): 265.

14. Pia Rebello Britto and Jeanne Brooks-Gunn, "Beyond Shared Book Reading: Dimensions of Home Process," *New Directions for Child Development* 92 (2001):73; Anat Ninio, "Joint Book Reading as a Multiple Vocabulary Acquisition Device," *Developmental Psychology* 19 (1983): 445; Catherine Snow and Anat Ninio, "The Contracts of Literacy: What Children Learn from Learning to Read Books," in *Emergent Literacy: Writing and Reading*, edited by William Teale and Elizabeth Sulzby (Norwood, N.J.: Ablex, 1986), p. 116.

15. See note 13.

16. Catherine Snow, "The Theoretical Basis for Relationships between Language and Literacy Development," *Journal of Research in Childhood Education* 6 (1991): 5; Anat Ninio and Catherine Snow, *Pragmatic Development* (Boulder, Colo.: Westview, 1996); Catherine Haden, Elaine Reese, and Robyn Fivush, "Mothers' Extratextual Comments during Storybook Reading: Stylistic Differences over Time and across Texts," *Discourse Processes* 21, no. 2 (1996): 135; Pia Rebello-Britto, Allison Fuligni, and Jeanne Brooks Gunn, "An Open Book? Effects of Home-Based Approaches on Children's Literacy Development," in *Handbook of Early Literacy Research*, vol. 2, edited by David Dickinson and Susan Neuman (New York: Guilford, forthcoming).

17. Linver, Brooks-Gunn, and Cabrera, "The Home Observation for Measurement" (see note 4); Bradley and Caldwell, *Home Observation* (see note 4).

18. Pamela K. Klebanov and others, "The Contribution of Neighborhood and Family Income to Developmental Test Scores over the First Three Years of Life," *Child Development* 69 (1998): 1420–36; Susan Mayer, *What Money Can't Buy: Family Income and Children's Life Chances* (Harvard University Press, 1997). The HOME Inventory allows items such as pans, household objects, or cereal boxes to be counted when they are used as musical instruments, for counting and classification, or for alphabet learning. It is not clear how often such items are counted in any given study, however.

19. Allison S. Fuligni and Jeanne Brooks-Gunn. "Measuring Mother and Father Shared Caregiving: An Analysis Using the Panel Study of Income Dynamics-Child Development Supplement," in *Conceptualizing and Measuring Father Involvement*, edited by R. Day and M. Lamb (Mahwah, N. J.: Erlbaum, 2004).

20. Ibid.; Klebanov and others, "The Contribution of Neighborhood and Family Income" (see note 18).

21. W. T. Boyce and others, "The Family Routines Inventory: Theoretical Origins," *Social Science and Medicine* 17 (1983): 193; Love and others, *Making a Difference* (see note 10).

22. Bornstein, *Handbook of Parenting* (see note 1); W. Andrew Collins and others, "Contemporary Research on Parenting: The Case for Nature and Nurture," *American Psychologist* 55, no. 2 (2001): 218; Maccoby and Martin, "Socialization in the Context of the Family" (see note 1).

23. Betty Hart and Todd Risley, *The Social World of Children Learning to Talk* (Baltimore: Paul Brookes Publishing, 1999).

24. Robert Plomin, "Genetic and Environmental Mediation of the Relationship between Language and Nonverbal Impairment in 4-Year-Old Twins," *Journal of Speech, Language, and Hearing Research* 46, no. 6 (2003): 1271.

25. Thomas Bouchard Jr., "Genetic Influence on Human Psychological Traits: A Survey," *Current Directions in Psychological Science* 13, no. 4 (2004): 148.

26. Michael Rutter and others, "Testing Hypotheses on Specific Environmental Causal Effects on Behavior," *Psychological Bulletin* 127 (2001): 291; Michael Rutter, "Nature, Nurture, and Development: From Evangelism through Science toward Policy and Practice," *Child Development* 73 (2002): 1.

27. M. Schiff and others, "Intellectual Status of Working-Class Children Adopted Early into Upper-Middle-Class Families," *Science* 200 (1978):1503–04; Marie Skodak and Harold Skeels, "A Final Follow-Up Study of One Hundred Adopted Children," *Journal of Genetic Psychology* 75 (1949): 85.

28. Michel Duyme, Annick-Camille Dumaret, and Stanislaw Tomkiewicz, "How Can We Boost IQs of 'Dull' Children? A Late Adoption Study," *Proceedings of the National Academy of Sciences, USA* 96 (1999): 8790.

29. It is important to realize that test scores within these groups of children show some stability; correlations between test scores in early childhood and adolescence were around .30. This demonstrates that even when stability is found, meaning that the rank ordering of children is somewhat similar across age, it is possible to increase mean scores (see Dickens, this volume).

30. Lynn Singer and others, "Cognitive Outcomes of Preschool Children with Prenatal Cocaine Exposure," *Journal of the American Medical Association* 291, no. 20 (2004): 2448.

31. Earlier studies have used different classifications of living arrangements, often combining relative, adoptive, and foster care. Children in relative care are often in the same household as the mother (that is, the grandmother has custody of the child). One of these studies has a similar finding to that of Singer and others reported here; see Toosje Thyssen Van Beveren, Bertis Little, and Melanie Spence, "Effects of Prenatal Cocaine Exposure and Postnatal Environment on Child Development," *American Journal of Human Biology* 12 (2000): 417. Another does not; see Gideon Koren and others, "Long-Term Neurodevelopmental Risks in Children Exposed in Utero to Cocaine. The Toronto Adoption Study," in *Cocaine: Effects on the Developing Brain*, edited by Barry Kosofsky and others (New York: New York Academy of Sciences, 1998), p. 306.

32. The mothers' ratings could not be used, because they had already talked about their emotional feelings about each twin.

33. Avshalom Caspi and others, "Maternal Expressed Emotion Predicts Children's Antisocial Behavior Problems: Using MZ-Twin Differences to Identify Environmental Effects on Behavioral Development," *Developmental Psychology* 40 (2004): 149.

34. Collins and others, "Contemporary Research on Parenting" (see note 22); Gerald Patterson, Barbara DeBaryshe, and Elizabeth Ramsey, "A Developmental Perspective on Antisocial Behavior," *American Psychologist* 44, no. 2 (1989): 329; Sandra Scarr, "Developmental Theories for the 1990s, Development and Individual Difference," *Child Development* 63 (1992): 1.

35. See note 13.

36. Helen Raikes and others, "Mother-Child Bookreading in Low-Income Families: Correlates and Outcomes during the First Three Years of Life," unpublished, 2004. Early Head Start is a federal program offered by

the Administration on Children, Youth, and Families for pregnant woman and their children from birth to age three. Initiated in 1995 with 68 programs nationwide, as of 2004 it now serves 700 programs. The evaluation was a randomized control trial in seventeen sites, with about 3,000 families assigned to receive either Early Head Start services or not; Love and others, *Making a Difference* (see note 10).

37. Patterson, DeBaryshe, and Ramsey, "A Developmental Perspective on Antisocial Behavior" (see note 34).

38. For reviews, see Bornstein, *Handbook of Parenting* (see note 1), and G. Downey and James Coyne, "Children of Depressed Parents: An Integrative Review," *Psychological Bulletin* 108 (1990), p. 50.

39. Miriam Linver, Jeanne Brooks-Gunn, and Dafna Kohen, "Family Processes as Pathways from Income to Young Children's Development," *Developmental Psychology* 38, no. 5 (2002): 719; Jean Yeung and others, "How Money Matters for Young Children's Development: Parental Investment and Family Processes," *Child Development* 73, no. 6 (2002): 1861.

40. Glen H. Elder Jr., *Children of the Great Depression: Social Change in Life Experience* (Boulder, Colo.: Westview Press, 1999).

41. Vonnie McLoyd, "Socioeconomic Disadvantage and Child Development," *American Psychologist* 53, no. 2 (1998): 185; Rand Conger, Katherine Conger, and Glen Elder, "Family Economic Hardships and Adolescent Adjustment: Mediating and Moderating Processes," in *Consequences of Growing Up Poor*, edited by Greg Duncan and Jeanne Brooks-Gunn (New York: Russell Sage Foundation, 1997), p. 288.

42. Yeung and others, "How Money Matters" (see note 39).

43. Among these techniques are fixed-effects and longitudinal models, sibling models, and instrumental variable approaches.

44. Harkness and Super, "Culture and Parenting" (see note 8); Cynthia Garcia-Coll and others, "Ethnic and Minority Parenting," in *Handbook of Parenting*, vol. 2: *Biology and Ecology of Parenting*, edited by Marc Bornstein (Hillsdale, N.J.: Lawrence Erlbaum Associates, Inc., 1995).

45. Harkness and Super, "Culture and Parenting" (see note 8).

46. Patricia M. Greenfield and others, "Cultural Pathways through Universal Development," *Annual Review of Psychology* 54 (2003): 461.

47. Bornstein, *Handbook of Parenting* (see note 1).

48. Patricia Greenfield, "Cultural Change and Human Development," in *Development and Cultural Change: Reciprocal Processes*, edited by Elliot Turiel (San Francisco: Wiley, 1999), p. 37; Garcia-Coll and others, "An Integrative Model" (see note 69).

49. Gail A.Wasserman and others, "Psychosocial Attributes and Life Experiences of Disadvantaged Minority Mothers: Age and Ethnic Variations," *Child Development* 61 (1990): 566.; Gontran Lamberty and Cynthia Garcia-Coll, editors, *Puerto Rican Women and Children: Issues in Health, Growth, and Development* (New York: Guilford, 1994).

50. Maccoby and Martin, "Socialization in the Context of the Family" (see note 1).

51. Diana Baumrind, "An Exploratory Study of Socialization Effects on Black Children: Some Black-White Comparisons," *Child Development* 43 (1972): 261.

52. Jeanne Brooks-Gunn and Lindsay Chase-Lansdale, "Adolescent Parenthood," in *Handbook of Parenting*, vol. 3, *Status and Social Conditions of Parenting*, edited by Marc Bornstein (Mahwah, N.J.: Lawrence Erlbaum Associates, 1995), p. 113.

53. Deater-Deckard and others, "A Genetic Study of the Family Environment" (see note 8); Vonnie McLoyd and Julia Smith, "Physical Discipline and Behavior Problems in African American, European American, and Hispanic Children: Emotional Support as a Moderator," *Journal of Marriage and Family* 64 (2002): 40.

54. These effect sizes are reduced when characteristics such as maternal age, education, marital status, and income are controlled in regression analyses. These reductions range from 20 percent to 50 percent, depending on the parenting measure and the sample (that is, the reductions are much less in low-income samples, such as the Early Head Start Demonstration). Brady-Smith and Brooks-Gunn, analyses (see note 7); Pamela Klebanov and Jeanne Brooks-Gunn, analyses prepared for this article using data from the Infant Health and Development Program, 2004 (available from the National Center for Children and Families, Teachers College, Columbia University); Klebanov and others, "The Contribution of Neighborhood and Family Income" (see note 18); Klebanov, Brooks-Gunn, and McCormick, "Does Neighborhood and Family Poverty Affect Mothers' Parenting, Mental Health and Social Support?" (see note 12); Meredith Phillips and others, "Family Background, Parenting Practices, and the Black-White Test Score Gap," in *The Black-White Test Score Gap*, edited by Christopher Jencks and Meredith Phillips (Brookings, 1998), p. 103; Raikes and others, "Mother-Child Bookreading" (see note 36).

55. Jeanne Brooks-Gunn, Pamela Klebanov, and Fong-Ruey Liaw, "The Learning, Physical, and Emotional Environment of the Home in the Context of Poverty: The Infant Health and Development Program," *Children and Youth Services Review* 17, no. 1/2 (1995): 251; Klebanov, Brooks-Gunn, and McCormick, "Does Neighborhood and Family Poverty Affect Mothers' Parenting, Mental Health and Social Support?" (see note 12); Linver, Brooks-Gunn, and Cabrera, "The Home Observation for Measurement " (see note 4); Phillips and others, "Family Background," (see note 54); Raikes and others, "Mother-Child Bookreading" (see note 54).

56. Bingenheimer and others, "Measurement Equivalence" (see note 4); Robert Bradley and others, "Early Indications of Resilience and Their Relation to Experiences in the Home Environments of Low Birthweight, Premature Children Living in Poverty," *Child Development*, 65, no. 2 (1994): 346; Guang Guo and Kathleen Harris, "The Mechanisms Mediating the Effects of Poverty on Children's Intellectual Development," *Demography* 37 (2000): 431; Linver, Brooks-Gunn, and Cabrera, "The Home Observation for Measurement" (see note 4).

57. Klebanov and Brooks-Gunn, analyses (see note 54); Brady-Smith and Brooks-Gunn, analyses (see note 7).

58. Berlin, Brady-Smith, and Brooks-Gunn, "Links between Childbearing Age and Observed Maternal Behaviors" (see note 2); Brady-Smith and Brooks-Gunn, analyses (see note 7).

59. Smith and Brooks-Gunn, "Correlates and Consequences of Harsh Discipline" (see note 9); Bradley and others, "The Home Environment" (see note 4).

60. Love and others, *Making a Difference* (see note 10).

61. Less has been done vis-à-vis racial differences in teaching than in language. The limited evidence suggests that black-white differences exist, using measures such as quality of assistance in a teaching task; see Spiker, Ferguson, and Brooks-Gunn, "Enhancing Maternal Interactive Behavior" (see note 11).

62. A very small sample of black and white families was followed, including thirteen high SES children (whose parents were primarily professors, with one being black), twenty-three lower-middle-class children (from working-class families, with ten being black), and six children on welfare (all of whom were black). Consequently, race and social class are totally confounded at the upper and lower ends of the SES distribution. See Hart and Risley, *Meaningful Differences in the Everyday Experience* (see note 13); Hart and Risley, *The Social World* (see note 23).

63. Clark, *The Lexicon in Acquisition* (see note 13); Hart and Risley, *The Social World* (see note 23); Shirley Brice Heath, *Ways with Words* (Cambridge University Press, 1983).

64. Clark, *The Lexicon in Acquisition* (see note 13); David Dickinson and Patton Tabors, eds., *Beginning Literacy with Language: Young Children Learning at Home and School.* (Baltimore: Paul H. Brookes Publishing, 2001); Janellen Huttenlocher and others, "Early Vocabulary Growth" (see note 13).

65. Such studies do not exist because the cost of taping and transcribing mother-child conversations is prohibitive for large-scale studies. Thus, our knowledge of maternal language input and child language output is gleaned from studies that are unable to look directly at reductions in racial gaps.

66. Elaine Reese and Adell Cox, "Quality of Adult Book Reading Affects Children's Emergent Literacy," *Developmental Psychology* 35, no. 1 (1999): 20; Ninio and Snow, *Pragmatic Development* (see note 16).

67. Lisa McCabe and Jeanne Brooks-Gunn, "Pre- and Perinatal Home Visitation Interventions," in *Early Child Development in the 21st Century: Profiles of Current Research Initiatives*, edited by Jeanne Brooks-Gunn and others (Teachers College Press, Columbia University, 2003), p. 145.

68. Pia Rebello Britto, Allison S. Fuligni, and Jeanne Brooks-Gunn, "Reading, Rhymes, and Routines: American Parents and Their Young Children," in *Childrearing in America: Challenges Facing Parents with Young Children*, edited by Neal Halfon and others (Cambridge University Press, 2002), p. 117; Raikes and others, "Mother-Child Bookreading" (see note 36).

69. The differences between white and Hispanic mothers are not explained by the fact that many Hispanic mothers speak Spanish, and fewer Spanish than English children's books are available in the United States; see Cynthia Garcia–Coll and others, "An Integrative Model for the Study of Developmental Competencies in Minority Children," *Child Development* 67 (1996): 1891. In the Early Head Start Demonstration, both English-speaking and Spanish-speaking Hispanic mothers were less likely to read to their two- and three-year-olds than were white mothers; Raikes and others, "Mother-Child Bookreading" (see note 36).

70. Fuligni, Han, and Brooks-Gunn, "The Infant-Toddler HOME" (see note 9); Phillips and others, "Family Background" (see note 54); Raikes and others, "Mother-Child Bookreading (see note 36).

71. Brooks-Gunn, Klebanov, and Liaw, "The Learning, Physical, and Emotional Environment" (see note 55); Klebanov, Brooks-Gunn, and McCormick, "Does Neighborhood" (see note 12); Guo and Harris, "The Mechanisms Mediating" (see note 56); Phillips and others, "Family Background " (see note 54).

72. Jeanne Brooks-Gunn and others, "Depending on the Kindness of Strangers: Current National Data Initiatives and Developmental Research," *Child Development* 71 (2000): 257.

73. Guo and Harris, "The Mechanisms Mediating the Effects of Poverty" (see note 56); Mayer, *What Money Can't Buy* (see note 18); Phillips and others, "Family Background" (see note 54).

74. For reviews, see Jeanne Brooks-Gunn, Lisa Berlin, and Allison Sidle Fuligni, "Early Childhood Intervention Programs: What about the Family?" in *Handbook of Early Childhood Intervention,* 2nd edition, edited by Jack P. Shonkoff and Samuel J. Meisel (New York: Cambridge University Press, 2000); Jeanne Brooks-Gunn, Alison Fuligni, and Lisa Berlin, *Early Child Development in the 21st Century: Profiles of Current Research Initiatives* (Teachers College Press, 2003); Jeanne Brooks-Gunn, "Intervention and Policy as Change Agents for Young Children," in *Human Development across Lives and Generations: The Potential for Change*, edited by P. Lindsay Chase-Lansdale, Kathleen Kiernan, and Ruth Friedman (Cambridge University Press, 2004).

75. This article does not review the program impacts on children; see W. Steven Barnett, "Long-Term Effects of Early Childhood Programs on Cognitive and School Outcomes," *The Future of Children* 5, no.3 (1995): 25–50; April Benesich, Jeanne Brooks-Gunn, and Beatrice Clewell, "How Do Mothers Benefit from Early Intervention Programs?" *Journal of Applied Developmental Psychology* 13, no. 3 (1992): 311; Janet Currie, "Early Childhood Education Programs," *Journal of Economic Perspectives* 15, no. 2 (2001): 213; Lynn Karoly and others, *Investing in Our Children: What We Know and Don't Know about the Cost and Benefit of Early Childhood Interventions* (Santa Monica, Calif.: RAND, 1998); Magnuson and Waldfogel, this volume.

76. See Brooks-Gunn, Berlin, and Fuligni, "Early Childhood Intervention Programs" (see note 74).

77. Ibid.

78. Differential effects of parenting interventions for mothers who are and are not depressed are discussed in the section on differential impacts by maternal characteristics. Our premise is that programs might want to target services to families with mental health issues, because program effects might be largest for this group.

79. Brooks-Gunn, Berlin, and Fuligni, "Early Childhood Intervention Programs (see note 74).

80. Marinus Van IJzendoorn, Femmie Juffer, and Marja Duyvesteyn, "Breaking the Intergenerational Cycle of Insecure Attachment: A Review of the Effects of Attachment Based Interventions on Maternal Sensitivity and Infant Security," *Journal of Child Psychology and Psychiatry and Allied Disciplines* 36, no. 2 (1995): 225.

81. Seven out of eight programs reviewed by Brooks-Gunn, Berlin, and Fuligni, "Early Childhood Intervention Programs" (see note 74), report such effects, as does Early Head Start; John Love and others, *Making a Difference* (see note 10). Positive impacts are much more likely to be found from coding of mother-child interchanges than from using the Warmth Scale from HOME.

82. See Brooks-Gunn, Berlin, and Fuligni, "Early Childhood Intervention Programs" (see note 74); John Love and others, *Making a Difference in the Lives of Infants and Toddlers and Their Families: The Impacts of Early Head Start* (U.S. Department of Health and Human Services, 2002).

83. Joseph Sperling and Isabell Lewis, *Partners for Learning* (Lewisville, N.C.: Kaplan, 1994).

84. John Love and others, *Making a Difference* (see note 10); Spiker, Ferguson, and Brooks-Gunn, "Enhancing Maternal Interactive Behavior" (see note 11).

85. Grover Whitehurst and others, "Outcomes of an Emergent Literacy Intervention in Head Start," *Journal of Educational Psychology* 86 (1994): 542.

86. David Dickenson and Susan Neuman, editors, *Handbook of Early Literacy Research,* vol. II (New York: Guilford, forthcoming).

87. Brooks-Gunn, Berlin, and Fuligni, "Early Childhood Intervention Programs" (see note 74).

88. Robert St. Pierre and Janet Swartz, "The Even Start Family Literacy Program," in *Two Generation Programs for Families in Poverty: A New Intervention Strategy*, edited by Shelia Smith (Westport, Conn.: Ablex Publishing, 1995), p. 37.

89. Daniel Nagin and Richard Tremblay, "Parental and Early Childhood Predictors of Persistent Physical Agresssion in Boys from Kindergarten to High School," *Archives of General Psychiatry* 58 (2001): 389.

90. Bridget K. Hamre and Robert Pianta, "Early Teacher-Child Relationships and the Trajectory of Children's School Outcomes through Eighth Grade," *Child Development* 72 (2001): 625.

91. Allan E. Kazdin, "Treatment of Antisocial Behavior in Children: Current Status and Future Directions," *Psychological Bulletin* 102 (1987): 187.

92. Carolyn Webster-Stratton, Jamilia Reid, and Mary Hammond, "Preventing Conduct Problems, Promoting Social Competence: A Parent and Child Training Partnership in Head Start," *Journal of Child Clinical Psychology* 30 (2001): 283; Carolyn Webster-Stratton and Ted Taylor, "Nipping Early Risk Factors in the Bud: Preventing Substance Abuse, Delinquency, and Violence in Adolescence through Interventions Targeted at Young Children (0–8 years)," *Prevention Science* 2 (2001): 165; Carolyn Webster-Stratton, "Preventing Conduct Problems in Head Start Children: Strengthening Parenting Competences," *Journal of Consulting and Clinical Psychology* 66 (1998): 715.

93. Webster-Stratton, Reid, and Hammond, "Preventing Conduct Problems" (see note 92).

94. Matthew R. Sanders, Karen M. T. Turner, and Carol Markie-Dadds, "The Development and Dissemination of the Triple P—Positive Parenting Program: A Multilevel, Evidence-Based System of Parenting and Family Support," *Prevention Science* 3 (2002): 173–89; Conduct Problems Prevention Research Group, "Initial Impact of the Fast Track Prevention Trial for Conduct Problems I: The High Risk Sample," *Journal of Consulting and Clinical Psychology* 67 (1999): 631–47; Conduct Problems Prevention Research Group, "Initial Impact of the Fast Track Prevention Trial for Conduct Problems II: Classroom Effects," *Journal of Consulting and Clinical Psychology* 67 (1999): 648–57.

95. Barnett, "Long-Term Effects of Early Childhood Programs" (see note 75); Deanne Gomby and others, "Long-Term Outcomes of Early Childhood Programs: Analysis and Recommendations," *The Future of Children* 5, no. 3 (1995): 6. A notable exception is the Nurse Home Visitation Program, developed by Olds and his colleagues; impacts on young children's social-emotional well-being have been reported, as have some impacts on adolescent outcomes. See David Olds and others, "Effects of Nurse Home Visiting on Maternal Life-Course and Child Development: Age-Six Follow-Up of a Randomized Trial," *Pediatrics* (2004).

96. Researchers have conducted two comparative analyses of home-visiting programs. See Jean Layzer and others, "National Evaluation of Family Support Programs Final Report, vol. A, The Meta–Analysis," submitted to the Administration for Children, Youth, and Families (Cambridge, Mass.: Abt Associates, 2001) (ERIC no. ED462186); and Monica Sweet and Mark Appelbaum, "Is Home Visiting an Effective Strategy?: A Meta-Analytic Review of Home Visiting Programs for Families with Young Children," *Child Development* 75 (2004): 1435. Most recently Sweet and Applebaum examined sixty programs, both experi-

mental and nonexperimental. Programs varied in length, target population, services, child age, and type of home visitor (professional or para-professional), making it difficult to say much about specific components. Almost all focused on groups of families at risk for poor child outcomes. Virtually all programs listed parent education (98 percent) and child development (85 percent) as goals. The authors examined the efficacy of the programs on ten outcomes, including parenting behavior, child cognitive outcomes, and child emotional outcomes. The weighted effect sizes were significant for all three, but were much smaller (about two-thirds smaller) for the experimental than the nonexperimental programs. There was some evidence that cognitive effects were positive when programs lasted longer and included more home visits. We speculate that home-visiting programs will be most likely to affect child outcomes if they have a schedule similar to that of the Nurse Home Visitation Program and if they ensure that families receive the recommended "dose" of visits (most families get fewer than half the visits planned by the program); see Deanne Gomby and others, "Long-Term Outcomes of Early Childhood Programs" (see note 95). We believe—although evidence, either pro or con, is not available—that programs such as Whitehurst's dialogic reading program might be effective as part of a home-visiting program.

97. William Barnett, "Early Childhood Education," in *School Reform Proposals: The Research Evidence*, edited by Alex Molner (Greenwich, Conn.: Information Age Publishing, 2002), p. 1; Lynn Karoly and others, *Investing in Our Children* (see note 75); Craig Ramey and others, "Early Educational Interventions for High-Risk Children: How Center-Based Treatment Can Augment and Improve Parenting Effectiveness," in *Parenting and the Child's World: Influences on Academic, Intellectual, and Social-Emotional Development*, edited by Sharon Landesman Ramey and others (Mahwah, N.J.: Lawrence Erlbaum Associates, 2002), p. 125.

98. Robert Bradley and others, "Impact of the Infant Health and Development Program (IHDP) on the Home Environment of Infants with Low Birth Weight," *Journal of Educational Psychology* 86 (1994): 531.

99. Love and others, *Making a Difference* (see note 10).

100. Other countries have, or have had, more universal parenting programs. A series of home visits after the birth of a child are provided to all new mothers in several countries. See Shelia Kamerman, "Early Childhood Intervention Policies: An International Perspective," in *Handbook of Early Childhood Intervention*, edited by Samuel J. Meisels and others (Cambridge University Press, 2000), p. 613; Gomby and others, "Long-Term Outcomes of Early Childhood Programs" (see note 95).

101. See Duncan and Magnuson, this volume, and Currie, this volume.

102. Olds and others, "Effects of Nurse Home Visiting" (see note 95).

103. McCabe and Brooks-Gunn, "Pre- and Perinatal Home Visitation" (see note 67).

104. See Magnuson and Waldfogel, this volume.

105. Infant Health and Development Program, "Enhancing the Outcomes of Low-Birth-Weight, Premature Infants: A Multisite, Randomized Trial," *Journal of the American Medical Association* 263 (1990): 3035; Pamela K. Klebanov, Jeanne Brooks-Gunn, and M. C. McCormick, "Maternal Coping Strategies and Emotional Distress: Results of an Early Intervention Program for Low Birth Weight Young Children," *Developmental Psychology* 37, 5 (2001): 654; Spiker, Ferguson, and Brooks-Gunn, "Enhancing Maternal Interactive Behavior" (see note 11); Smith and Brooks-Gunn, "Correlates and Consequences of Harsh Discipline" (see note 9).

106. Klebanov and Brooks-Gunn, analyses (see note 54).

107. Love and others, *Making a Difference* (see note 10).

108. Fong-Ruey Liaw and Jeanne Brooks-Gunn, "Patterns of Low Birth Weight Children's Cognitive Development and Their Determinants," *Developmental Psychology* 29, no. 6 (1993): 1024; Jeanne Brooks-Gunn and others, "Enhancing the Cognitive Outcomes of Low Birth Weight, Premature Infants: For Whom Is the Intervention Most Effective?" *Pediatrics* 89, no. 8 (1992): 1209; Love and others, *Making a Difference* (see note 10).

109. Love and others, *Making a Difference* (see note 10). These results adjust for characteristics including maternal race, age, parity, income, and marital status.

110. David Olds and others, "Effects of Prenatal and Infancy Nurse Home Visitation on Surveillance of Child Maltreatment," *Pediatrics* 95 (1995): 365; Love and others, *Making a Difference* (see note 10).

111. Love and others, *Making a Difference* (see note 10).

112. Pamela Klebanov, Jeanne Brooks-Gunn, and Marie McCormick, "Maternal Coping Strategies and Emotional Distress: Results of an Early Intervention Program for Low Birth Weight Children," *Developmental Psychology* 37, no. 5 (2001): 654.

113. Love and others, *Making a Difference* (see note 10).

114. Harriet Kitzman and others, "Effects of Prenatal and Infancy Home Visitation by Nurses on Pregnancy Outcomes, Childhood Injuries, and Repeated Childbearing: A Randomized Controlled Trial," *Journal of the American Medical Association* 278 (1997): 644; David L. Olds and others, "Home Visiting by Paraprofessionals and by Nurses: A Randomized, Controlled Trial," *Pediatrics* (2002): 486-96.

Early Childhood Care and Education: Effects on Ethnic and Racial Gaps in School Readiness

Katherine A. Magnuson and Jane Waldfogel

Summary

The authors examine black, white, and Hispanic children's differing experiences in early childhood care and education and explore links between these experiences and racial and ethnic gaps in school readiness.

Children who attend center care or preschool programs enter school more ready to learn, but both the share of children enrolled in these programs and the quality of care they receive differ by race and ethnicity. Black children are more likely to attend preschool than white children, but may experience lower-quality care. Hispanic children are much less likely than white children to attend preschool. The types of preschool that children attend also differ. Both black and Hispanic children are more likely than white children to attend Head Start.

Public funding of early childhood care and education, particularly Head Start, is already reducing ethnic and racial gaps in preschool attendance. The authors consider whether further increases in enrollment and improvements in quality would reduce school readiness gaps. They conclude that incremental changes in enrollment or quality will do little to narrow gaps. But substantial increases in Hispanic and black children's enrollment in preschool, alone or in combination with increases in preschool quality, have the potential to decrease school readiness gaps. Boosting enrollment of Hispanic children may be especially beneficial given their current low rates of enrollment.

Policies that target low-income families (who are more likely to be black or Hispanic) also look promising. For example, making preschool enrollment universal for three- and four- year-old children in poverty and increasing the quality of care could close up to 20 percent of the black-white school readiness gap and up to 36 percent of the Hispanic-white gap.

www.future of children.org

Katherine Magnuson is assistant professor of social work at the University of Wisconsin–Madison. Jane Waldfogel is professor of social work and public affairs at Columbia University. They are grateful for funding support from *The Future of Children,* the Russell Sage Foundation, and the John D. and Catherine T. MacArthur Foundation. They received helpful comments on an earlier draft from Steve Barnett, Janet Currie, Elisabeth Donahue, Rebecca Maynard, and the journal editors and benefited from many helpful discussions with Marcia Meyers, Dan Rosenbaum, and Chris Ruhm. They also appreciate assistance from David Blau with the SIPP data.

For children growing up in the United States, early childhood care and education have become an increasingly common experience. Almost every child entering kindergarten today has been in care of some form, and a growing share of kindergartners has attended preschool or received center care. On average, preschool and center care develop young children's early academic skills through enriching activities and sometimes direct instruction.[1] Yet the type and quality of the care that children receive varies widely. Hispanic children, for example, are less likely, and black children are more likely, than white children to be enrolled in a preschool or in center care.

Do children's differing experiences of early childhood care and education affect racial and ethnic gaps in school readiness? If so, do they widen the gaps or narrow them? In this article, we review research on the effects of child care and education on young children's school readiness and look at racial and ethnic differences both in who receives early childhood care and education and in the amount and quality of care.[2] All three types of evidence are important: for early childhood care and education to influence racial and ethnic gaps in school readiness, the enrollment, intensity, or effects of these programs must differ by race or ethnicity.

Early care and education might *widen* racial and ethnic gaps if children from racial and ethnic minority groups are less likely to be enrolled in beneficial programs, spend less time in them, attend lower-quality programs, or benefit less from them. Conversely, preschool experiences might *narrow* racial and ethnic gaps if children from minority groups are more likely to be enrolled, spend more time in them, attend higher-quality programs, or benefit more.

In discussing racial and ethnic gaps, we focus on three groups: Hispanics, non-Hispanic whites (whites), and non-Hispanic African Americans (blacks). We note that these groups are socially constructed and heterogeneous categories that proxy for diverse ethnic and cultural groups.[3] Hispanic describes first-generation immigrants, refugees from Cuba, and Puerto Ricans, all of whom face different circumstances in U.S. society, including socioeconomic resources.[4] In the United States, the Hispanic and black categories serve as markers for minority status and its accompanying experiences of discrimination and disadvantage.[5] Hispanic and black children face much higher rates of poverty, particularly persistent poverty, than do white children.

In this article, we first review the main types of early childhood care and education and their effects on school readiness. We then summarize trends in enrollment and in the quality of care for Hispanic, white, and black children. We conclude by considering how early childhood care and education might help to narrow racial and ethnic gaps in school readiness and by discussing the implications for public policy.

Main Types of Early Childhood Care and Education

Early childhood care and education programs come in many forms. We categorize these into three broad types: parental care, informal care (by a relative, nanny, or babysitter in the child's own home or in a babysitter's or family day care provider's home), and center care or preschool (day care center, nursery school, preschool, Head Start program, or prekindergarten).

We focus most on the third category because a host of studies has found that children who attend center care or preschool programs enter school more ready to learn. As noted, this category includes many different types of programs, and it is important to distinguish between them.

Most children in preschool or center care attend private programs, for which their parents pay fees. Low-income working parents may receive child care subsidies that offset some of the costs, and other families with working parents may also receive financial assistance through tax provisions, including the child and dependent care tax credit and the dependent care assistance plan.[6] Some center care and preschool programs operate full-day and year-round; others, only part-time or during the school year.

Preschool attendance becomes more common as children approach school age. Approximately 60 percent of four-year-old children are in care during the year before they enter kindergarten, up from about 17 percent in care before their second birthday.[7]

The federal government does not regulate preschool programs, and state regulations vary widely in both stringency and enforcement.[8] One way to assess the quality of center care is through "structural" indicators, such as more highly educated teachers, smaller classes, and lower children-to-staff ratios.[9] Some studies suggest that caregiver education may be particularly important.[10] Quality varies widely from one program to the next, but, on average, the quality of center care programs, as measured by structural indicators, is probably just "mediocre."[11]

A second, arguably better, way to measure child care quality is for trained observers to rate the quality of the "process"—the warmth, responsiveness, and sensitivity of caregivers, as well as the physical environment and children's activities.[12] Thus measured, few center-based programs are high in quality; a substantial proportion rank low in quality.[13] The Cost, Quality, and Child Outcomes Study, conducted in 1993, found good or developmentally appropriate care in only 24 percent of centers serving preschool-age children. Quality was poor in 10 percent. Child-caregiver interactions were positive in less than half.[14] The National Institute of Child Health and Human Development (NICHD) Study of Early Child Care found similarly low rates of positive child-caregiver interactions in center care.[15]

A small but growing share of children attend publicly funded preschools, most commonly Head Start and prekindergarten (other public programs exist, but they serve few children). Head Start, the largest publicly funded early education program, began in 1965 as part of President Lyndon B. Johnson's War on Poverty. It serves children from families with incomes below the federal poverty threshold, as well as children with disabilities.[16] Under Head Start, federal grants are provided to local community organizations that offer early education and comprehensive health, nutrition, and family services to three- and four-year-old children.[17] In 2002 the federal government distributed $6.3 billion to local Head Start grantees, who served an estimated 65 percent of eligible three- and four-year-olds, some 10 percent of all children in that age group.[18]

To receive funding, Head Start programs must meet twenty-four federal performance guidelines. Centers undergo an on-site review at least once every three years. In 2000 about 85 percent of reviewed centers met the standards of adequate care. According to a recent study of Head Start, programs met or exceeded recommendations of the National Association for the Education of Young Children (NAEYC, a leading group of experts in the field) for class size and adult-to-child ratios. Judged by process quality, on average Head Start centers are on par with other types of center care.[19] Nevertheless, only one-third of Head Start teachers hold four-

Most state programs target disadvantaged three- and four-year-old children and serve a small but growing share of children, with an estimated 14 percent of four-year-olds enrolled in public school–based prekindergarten programs in 2002.

year college degrees, and experts worry that low pay and low levels of provider education constrain program quality.[20]

Prekindergarten programs, often funded through local school districts, are a more recent type of early education.[21] As the name suggests, they provide a year (or two) of education before children enter kindergarten. Publicly funded programs rely mainly on state dollars, although local school districts may also use federal Title 1, disability, or other types of funds. Prekindergarten programs may operate in public schools, but some states also directly fund, and school districts may subcontract with, other programs to provide early education services. Typically,

prekindergartens offer some services beyond education, including meals and transportation, but few provide a full array of services such as health screenings.[22]

Since 1990, state funding for prekindergarten has increased 250 percent, to approximately $1.9 million in 2002, but state spending varies widely.[23] In 2000, thirty-nine states had prekindergarten initiatives, but only seven (Connecticut, Georgia, Illinois, Kentucky, Massachusetts, Ohio, and Oklahoma) made substantial per capita investments in them.[24] Most state programs target disadvantaged three- and four-year-old children and serve a small but growing share of children, with an estimated 14 percent of four-year-olds enrolled in public school–based prekindergarten programs in 2002.[25] Only two states, Georgia and Oklahoma, and the District of Columbia offer such programs to all children; they serve slightly more than half of their four-year-olds.

Structural quality indicators suggest that prekindergarten programs provide relatively high-quality care.[26] Most states set guidelines for class size and child-to-caregiver ratios that meet or exceed NAEYC recommendations. The average size of general education prekindergarten classes in public schools is well within NAEYC guidelines.[27] Of school-based prekindergarten teachers, 86 percent have four-year college degrees, more than twice the rate among center care and Head Start teachers. Teachers' pay is also more likely to be commensurate with that of elementary school teachers (82 percent receive public school teacher salaries) and considerably higher than that of other child care workers.[28] State-funded prekindergarten programs in private preschools, however, appear to have lower structural quality than programs in public schools.[29]

Data on process quality in prekindergarten programs are in short supply. Because structural indicators are linked to process quality and are higher for prekindergarten than for other types of center care, prekindergarten classrooms could be expected to have higher process quality, too. Indeed, an evaluation of Georgia's universal prekindergarten found the classrooms to be of higher process quality than private preschool classrooms in that state and less likely than Head Start classrooms to be of poor quality.[30] But an evaluation of New Jersey's Abbott preschool program argues for caution, because it found classroom quality was lower than that in Georgia and lower than national estimates of center care quality.[31] The lack of information on prekindergarten classroom quality makes any general conclusions about process quality unwarranted.

Effects of Early Childhood Care and Education on Children's School Readiness

Can early childhood care and education raise children's test scores and promote school readiness? Because space does not permit a comprehensive review of the literature, we summarize the best evidence on preschool and center care, as well as informal and parental care.

The best estimates of the effects of early childhood care and education come from random-assignment experimental studies. These compare children in a particular program with children who were not in the program but were otherwise equivalent on important background characteristics, thus assuring that any differences in children's academic outcomes must be due to their experiences in care. Random-assignment studies, however, are rare. And researchers who conduct them typically evaluate high-quality programs that serve only a few children, often at a single site, making it hard to generalize findings to large-scale programs or more diverse populations of children.

Many nonexperimental studies consider the effects of more typical early childhood care and education on children's school readiness by taking advantage of naturally occurring variation in child care arrangements. But these observational studies may identify effects that in fact reflect unobserved factors, such as socioeconomic status, that cause children to receive a particular type of care. Because the analyses often include only a few statistical controls for such factors, their findings, although more generalizable to other programs and children, typically do not provide convincing evidence that an effect has been *caused* by the child's experience in care.[32]

Experimental Evaluations of High-Quality Model Programs

Over the past thirty years, researchers have conducted experimental evaluations of several high-quality model programs in compensatory early education. These model programs, which primarily enroll economically disadvantaged children, provide developmentally appropriate education, often in combination with health, nutrition, parenting education, and family support services. With highly trained teachers and low child-to-staff ratios, they offer quality far superior to most typical early education programs.

Not surprisingly, these programs enhance children's cognitive development and academic skills at school entry.[33] For example, in the Infant Health and Development Program (IHDP), which provided full-time high-quality center care to low birth weight children between birth and age three, the heavier low birth weight children had IQ scores close to 4 points higher than their counterparts in the comparison group at ages five and eight.[34] Children from the most disadvantaged backgrounds, as measured by maternal education, gained the most.[35]

The academic benefits of these model programs persist, although they fade over time. Children who in their first five years received high-quality care from the Carolina Abecedarian project continued to outperform a comparison group on IQ tests at ages eight and fifteen by just over one-third of a standard deviation.[36] Furthermore, exemplary programs reduce children's special education placement and grade retention.[37] Children who attended Perry Preschool, for example, received special education services for an average of 1.1 years, as against 2.8 years for comparison children.[38]

Because most programs were developed to improve children's academic skills and cognitive development, few studies have considered whether they also improve children's social skills and behavioral problems. Indeed, only the IHDP has documented short-term positive effects on children's behavior.[39] But several long-term follow-up studies have found lower rates of juvenile delinquency and antisocial behavior, as measured by criminal activity.[40] It is not yet clear whether long-term declines in problem behavior follow from positive effects on young children's behavior or emerge later in childhood.

Head Start

Clearly, high-quality model early childhood programs can enhance the school readiness of disadvantaged children, but what about other types of programs? Has Head Start done the same for the disadvantaged or disabled children it serves? Answering this question is dif-

ficult because the program has never been evaluated by a random assignment study (although one is now under way). Researchers using nonexperimental designs must find an appropriate comparison group, and as Head Start enrollees became increasingly disadvantaged during the 1980s and 1990s, constructing an appropriate comparison group may have become even more difficult.[41]

A series of observational studies with data collected during the 1970s and 1980s found generally modest, short-term positive effects of Head Start participation on disadvantaged children's school readiness.[42] For example, Valerie Lee and colleagues found that black children who attended Head Start gained 0.25 of a standard deviation more on a test of verbal skills by the end of first grade than did black children who attended no early education program.[43] Head Start also improved children's social competence.

The studies that have most successfully controlled for the disadvantaged background of the children enrolled in Head Start may be those that compare children who attended the program with their siblings who did not. Using this method, a series of parallel analyses across two large data sets finds that attending Head Start enhanced children's cognitive development. Six-year-old Head Start children scored close to 7 percentile points higher on a vocabulary test than their siblings who did not attend preschool.[44] The benefits appeared to persist through elementary school for white and Hispanic children, but not for black children.[45] Furthermore, follow-up analyses found that Head Start children engaged in less criminal activity as they grew older.[46]

Thus, Head Start appears to have beneficial cognitive and behavioral effects for the children it serves, though how large the effects are, how long they persist, and whether they vary by race and ethnic group remain unclear. Evidence from the random assignment study now under way should shed further light on these questions.

Quasi-Experimental and Observational Studies of Prekindergarten Programs

Do prekindergarten programs improve children's school readiness? In the absence of large-scale experiments, we cannot answer this question with certainty. Researchers have undertaken at least twenty evaluations of state prekindergarten programs, but many are so methodologically weak as to raise questions about their findings.[47] Several rigorous quasi-experimental and observational studies, however, suggest that school-based early education programs can enhance readiness.

The first of these studies evaluated the Chicago Child Parent Centers (CPC), a prekindergarten program provided by the Chicago public school system to predominantly African American children living in poor neighborhoods.[48] CPC, a part-day preschool for three- to four-year-olds, was staffed by teachers with college degrees and early childhood certification; it offered a follow-on program during the early elementary school years. The preschool program emphasized early language development, promoted parental involvement, and offered comprehensive services such as meals and health screenings. The follow-on program provided smaller classes and programming to keep parents involved in their children's schooling. Because the program was neighborhood based, the researchers were able to compare CPC children with children from poor communities that did not have CPC programs. Children who attended CPC during the year before kindergarten scored 0.64

of a standard deviation higher on an assessment of academic skills in the fall of kindergarten.[49] Accumulated evidence suggests that preschool contributed to lasting improvements in CPC children's reading and math achievement, as well as high school graduation.[50]

More recently, researchers evaluated the Tulsa prekindergarten program, part of Oklahoma's universal prekindergarten initiative. Tulsa's program offers part- or full-day early

Head Start appears to have beneficial cognitive and behavioral effects for the children it serves, though how large the effects are, how long they persist, and whether they vary by race and ethnic group remain unclear.

education to any child who turns four by September 1; classes are held at local public schools, and teachers have at least a college degree. Taking advantage of the program's strict age cutoff for entry, evaluators compared children at kindergarten entry who had met the age cutoff and attended prekindergarten with those who had missed the age cutoff. Prekindergarten boosted children's language skills by 0.39 of a standard deviation, with the largest effects for Hispanic and black children who attended full-day.[51]

Observational studies also find positive prekindergarten effects on school readiness.

One such study evaluated Georgia's universal prekindergarten program, delivered by private providers and public schools.[52] In our own analyses, we used national data from the Early Childhood Longitudinal Study—Kindergarten Cohort (ECLS-K). In this national sample of children entering kindergarten in 1998, the 17 percent who had attended prekindergarten scored 0.19 of a standard deviation higher on a reading and math skills assessment at school entry than otherwise comparable children who spent the previous year in exclusively parental care. The children who had attended prekindergarten also performed better at school entry than children who had attended other types of center care.[53] From their review of states' prekindergarten evaluations, William Gilliam and Edward Zigler conclude that although most studies are methodologically weak, evidence is accumulating that prekindergarten programs have positive short-term effects on children's academic skills.[54]

The evidence on the effects on social skills and behavior is more mixed. The CPC studies have not explored effects on children's social skills or problem behavior at school entry, but have found lower levels of adolescent delinquency, as measured by arrest records. The Tulsa prekindergarten evaluation found no effect on children's behavior as they entered school. Our own work with the ECLS-K finds that children who attend prekindergarten have more problem behavior at school entry than do children in parental care.[55] Likewise, evaluations of state prekindergarten programs do not consistently find improved behavior at school entry, though, as noted, many of these studies are methodologically flawed.[56]

Research on prekindergarten programs is still in its infancy, and much remains to be learned. Few studies follow children long enough to know whether benefits to school readiness are likely to persist. In addition, few studies describe well the quality of prekindergarten programs being studied or identify program characteristics that might contribute to or hinder children's school readiness. Finally, whether prekindergarten has short- or long-term effects on children's behavior is unclear.

Observational Studies of Other Types of Early Childhood Care and Education

Most children do not attend model programs, prekindergarten, or Head Start. What do we know about the effects of privately funded preschools, nursery schools, and day care centers, as well as informal care and parental care? Most observational studies lump together several care arrangements into broad categories, providing estimates, for example, of the effects of center-based care or informal care.

Whereas estimating the effects of Head Start is complicated by the disadvantaged background of the children, evaluating center-based care is problematic because of the children's relatively *advantaged* family backgrounds. The best observational studies use various techniques to reduce bias from the characteristics of children that cause or coincide with center care enrollment. Methodological concerns notwithstanding, these studies find that attending center care at, for example, a day care center, nursery school, or preschool, particularly at ages three and four, promotes children's academic skills and cognitive development.[57] Center care during a child's first three years may also enhance cognitive development, particularly for disadvantaged children, although evidence is less consistent for infants and toddlers than for preschool-age children.[58]

A particularly informative study, by Greg Duncan and colleagues, used data from the NICHD Study of Early Child Care to model changes in children's cognitive development as a function of time spent in child care.[59] By relying on intra-individual change to identify effects, the authors greatly reduced the likelihood of bias caused by the children's advantaged family backgrounds. They found that by attending center care at ages three and four, children gained between 0.22 and 0.33 of a standard deviation more on measures of academic achievement than children in parental or informal care. And children whose cognitive ability was lowest gained the most. Yet, they also found that attending center-based care from birth to age three was not consistently linked to higher academic achievement.[60]

We and our colleagues have used data from the Early Childhood Longitudinal Study— Kindergarten Cohort of 1998–99 to analyze the effects of center care on children's reading and math skills.[61] Children who attended center care (including prekindergarten) the year before entering school performed better on academic skills assessments than their peers. After controlling for a host of family background and other factors that might be associated with center care attendance, we found positive effects at school entry (effect sizes of about 0.14) that persisted into first grade (effect sizes of about 0.06). In most instances, the effects were largest (ranging from 0.16 to 0.23) for disadvantaged groups, measured by such indicators as family income, parental education, and family structure.

Center care may have some adverse effects. Observational studies link all types of nonmaternal care, including center care, with increased problem behavior and aggression in preschool and early school.[62] Effects are more pronounced for children who enter nonmaternal care at an early age, are in care for many hours, and attend center care. Although the links between center care and increased problem behavior are consistent, we are uncertain what to make of these findings, for several reasons. First, because all the evidence comes from observational studies, the links may not be causal. Second, the effects are relatively small. The NICHD study suggests that attending center care from birth to age fifty-four months would result in an increase of only 0.10 of a standard deviation in teacher reports of conflict, and most children in center care did not exhibit serious behavior problems or aggression.[63] Whether such small differences in children's behavior have any long-term implications for their well-being is unclear. Finally, researchers do not understand what explains the problem behaviors or how much effects may differ depending on program and child characteristics.

Some children attend no center care or preschool before starting formal education. They are cared for by their parents or informal caregivers, such as relatives, babysitters, nannies, or family day care providers. Informal child care is most prevalent during children's earliest years; it is the primary child care arrangement for about 38 percent of infants.[64] Again, studies of informal and parental care are limited by their reliance on observational, rather than experimental, data. Most find that, on average, informal care does not influence children's cognitive development or academic skills, though, as noted, it may be linked to increases in problem behavior. However, these average effects may mask considerable variability in effects because of differences in the quality of care. Research consistently links higher-quality informal care to better cognitive development and positive behavior.[65]

Figure 1. Preschool Enrollment of Three-Year-Olds, by Race and Ethnicity, 1968–2000

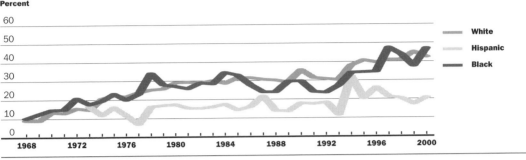

Source: Current Population Survey.

In the cohort of children in kindergarten in 1998–99, about 17 percent had been in parental care the year before, and 12 percent had been in informal child care (including care by a relative, babysitter, or nanny).[66] In terms of school readiness, children in parental and informal child care fared similarly. Compared with children who attended some form of preschool, children who had only parental or informal care entered school with lower reading and math scores, but with better behavior and self-control, even after a host of child and family characteristics had been taken into account.

Racial and Ethnic Differentials in Enrollment in Early Childhood Care and Education

To consider how children's experiences in early childhood care and education may be affecting racial and ethnic gaps in school readiness, we examine racial and ethnic differences in enrollment in different types of care. We start by comparing rates of Hispanic, black, and white children's enrollment in center care or preschool programs over time, making use of data from the October Current Population Survey (CPS) from 1968 to 2000.[67] Despite minor changes in question wording over the period, the October CPS provides fairly consistent data on the enroll-

ment of three- to five-year-olds in center care and preschool (including nursery schools, Head Start, and prekindergarten).[68] We focus on enrollment trends for three- and four-year-olds, because kindergarten is now almost universal for five-year-olds.

In recent decades, preschool enrollment has grown steadily for three- and four-year-olds from all racial and ethnic groups (figures 1 and 2).[69] Yet racial and ethnic differences in enrollment are still evident. From the late 1960s through the early 1980s, black three- and four-year-olds were slightly more likely than their white peers to attend preschool. Starting in the mid-1980s, however, black children's enrollment stagnated, while white children's enrollment continued to increase. Trends since the mid-1990s suggest that black children may have regained their enrollment advantage. Rates of preschool enrollment for Hispanic children have remained consistently below those of other children. In 2000, only 23 percent of Hispanic three-year-olds were in preschool compared with 49 percent and 43 percent of their black and white peers, respectively. Gaps are also apparent for Hispanic four-year-olds.

In fact, racial and ethnic differences in enrollment in center care or preschool pro-

Figure 2. Preschool Enrollment of Four-Year-Olds, by Race and Ethnicity, 1968–2000

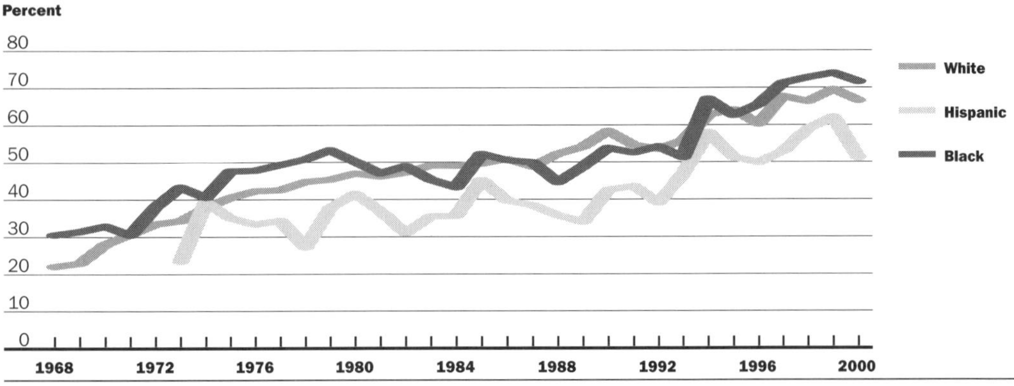

Source: Current Population Survey.

grams exist for young children in all age groups. Table 1 describes the care and education arrangements of children under age six in 1999.[70] As expected, young white children are somewhat less likely to be enrolled in center care or preschool than black children (panel A). Black children are more likely than white children to attend center care as their primary arrangement (33 percent versus 26 percent) or to attend any center care, whether as a primary or secondary arrangement (40 percent versus 30 percent). Again, Hispanic children are the least likely to be in center care (22 percent).

If one looks only at children with employed mothers (panel B), the patterns remain quite similar, suggesting that different rates of maternal employment do not explain the disparities in enrollment. Thus, the fact that black mothers are more likely to be employed full-time than white mothers is not the only reason why a greater share of black children is enrolled in center care.[71] Even within families with employed mothers, black children are more likely to be in center care than white children.[72]

As table 1 shows, the type of early childhood care and education also varies by family in-

come. Families with the highest incomes (at or above 200 percent of the poverty threshold) are most likely to use preschool or center care. Because child care subsidies and Head Start and prekindergarten programs are targeted to economically disadvantaged families, families in poverty are more likely to use center care than are those with incomes between 100 percent and 200 percent of the poverty threshold.

Although black children are more likely to be in center care than white children, they are not enrolled in the same types of programs. As noted, black and Hispanic children are more likely to be economically disadvantaged than white children, and thus are more likely to participate in publicly funded preschool programs. More than 20 percent of black and 15 percent of Hispanic three- and four-year-olds are enrolled in Head Start, compared with about 4 percent of white children.[73]

These racial and ethnic differentials in participation suggest that Head Start probably has played an important role in equalizing rates of black and white children's participation in early education. Assuming that children attending Head Start centers would not receive any center care in its absence, then relative to white

Table 1. Share of Children under Age Six in Child Care, by Type of Child Care, 1999

Percent

Race/ethnicity and poverty status of children	Primary care arrangement						
	Maternal care	Paternal care	Relative care	Other nonrelative care	Family day care	Center-based care and education	Any center-based care and education[1]
Panel A: All Children							
All children	28	12	21	7	7	25	30
Race/ethnicity							
White	29	13	18	8	7	26	30
Hispanic	37	10	25	4	6	19	22
Black	17	9	30	5	7	33	40
Other	30	11	32	2	5	20	27
Poverty status							
Below 100% poverty	38	6	23	3	6	23	27
100–200% poverty	33	12	25	4	5	20	24
Above 200% poverty	23	13	19	9	8	28	33
Panel B: Children of Employed Mothers							
All children	5	19	27	11	9	29	37
Race/ethnicity							
White	5	21	22	13	9	30	38
Hispanic	5	20	37	7	12	19	25
Black	3	13	34	5	8	38	45
Poverty status							
Below 100% poverty	5	16	34	6	10	28	36
100–200% poverty	5	23	34	7	8	23	30
Above 200% poverty	4	19	23	13	9	32	39
Other	4	19	45	3	7	23	5

Source: Authors' calculations of 1999 SIPP data. Distribution of children across primary care arrangements may not sum to 100 because of rounding of numbers.

1. Includes center-based care or education that was reported as a secondary care arrangement.

children gaps in enrollment might be as large as 9 percentage points for black children and 31 percentage points for Hispanic children.[74]

What does this imply for Head Start's effectiveness in narrowing the black-white achievement gaps? Answering this question requires an accurate estimate of Head Start's effects on children, which to date have not been established. We offer an upper bound of the possible effects by using estimates from the quasi-experimental study of the Chicago Child Parent Centers.[75] The estimate is likely to be an upper bound because the CPC had more highly qualified teachers than most Head Start centers.[76] Arthur Reynolds reported that the effect of participating in CPC for one year was 0.64 of a standard deviation increase in academic skills in the fall of kindergarten.[77] If Head Start boosts skills as much as CPC, then with 19 percent of black children in Head Start, black children's skills would be about 0.12 of a standard deviation lower, on average, if they did not attend Head Start or other early education programs. Since the black-white test score gap is estimated at close to 0.50 of a standard deviation, such a reduction implies that the black-white test score gap would be about 24 percent larger (at 0.62 of a standard deviation) in the absence of Head Start. The proportions of Hispanic and black children in Head Start are similar; it is therefore likely that the program also has reduced Hispanic-white test score gaps. In terms of lower bounds, we think it is likely that Head Start's effects are greater than zero and thus are fairly confident that the program has played an equalizing role.

Have other public preschool programs also affected racial and ethnic patterns of preschool enrollment or achievement gaps? Prekindergarten is more likely to be offered in schools with a large percentage of racial and ethnic minority children, which suggests that black and Hispanic children may be more likely than white children to attend publicly funded prekindergarten. However, precise national estimates of the number of black, Hispanic, and white children attending publicly funded prekindergarten programs are not available.[78]

Racial and Ethnic Differences in the Intensity and Quality of Early Childhood Care and Education

Comparing racial and ethnic enrollment trends tells only part of the story. Other important pieces of evidence are the time spent in preschool and the quality of programs attended by white, black, and Hispanic children. Unfortunately, information on racial and ethnic patterns in hours and quality of center care is hard to find.

Lacking published estimates of the number of hours a week spent in preschool and cen-

ter care by children of different racial and ethnic groups, we turn to the ECLS-K data set for estimates of the average number of hours that children were in center care (including Head Start, prekindergarten, and preschool) during the year before kindergarten. Racial and ethnic differences are evident: both black and Hispanic children spent significantly more time in center care each week (thirty-one and twenty-three hours, respectively) than did white children (twenty hours). National data sets find similar patterns for hours spent by young children in all types of nonparental care.[79]

Should one conclude that the longer time spent by black and Hispanic children in center care narrows the gap? Again, we are uncertain, because the answer should be based on precise estimates of the additional benefits derived from thirty hours of care rather than twenty hours, but none is available. Finding no evidence that minority children are spending *less* time in preschools than white children, however, we are confident that differences in the number of hours that children spend in center care are not widening achievement gaps.

As noted, the quality of child care can be measured by structural indicators, such as teacher certification and education, class size, and child-to-staff ratios, and by process measures, such as observations of interaction between caregivers and children.[80] Here, we use evidence on differences between the quality of care experienced by African American and white children from a study by Margaret Burchinal and Debby Cryer.[81] One of their data sources, the Cost, Quality, and Outcomes (CQO) study, collected information on the quality of center care received by four-year-old children in four states (and thus was not nationally representative). It included four different measures of quality of care, assessing teacher's interactions and responsiveness to children as well as the extent to which the program was child centered (rather than didactic). Across all measures, white children on average experienced higher-quality care than black children, but the differences were less pronounced for caregivers' responsiveness and sensitivity

Across all measures, white children on average experienced higher-quality care than black children, but the differences were less pronounced for caregivers' responsiveness and sensitivity than for other measures.

than for other measures. The difference on a summary measure of quality, which combined these indicators, was about 0.3 of a standard deviation.[82]

Burchinal and Cryer present results from similar analyses for three-year-olds from the NICHD Study of Early Child Care, which followed a large (but not nationally representative) sample of children born in 1991. In contrast to the CQO study, this research included children in all types of care and education settings, not only center care. Consequently, differences in the quality of care may be caused not only by variations in quality within types of care, but also by the different distribution of children across types of care. The measure used by the NICHD study, the Observational Record of the Caregiving Environment (ORCE), captures the

quality of caregiver interactions with children, including their sensitivity and responsiveness. Again, black children experienced lower-quality care than white children; the gap was even larger than in the CQO study, at more than 0.7 of a standard deviation. Taken together, these studies suggest that black children may receive lower-quality care than white children, both within centers and across other types of care.

How Much Do Differences in Early Childhood Care and Education Matter for Racial and Ethnic Gaps in Readiness?

To sum up, racial and ethnic differences exist both in enrollment in early childhood care and education and in the quality of care received. Black children are more likely than white children to be enrolled in some form of preschool, although almost 20 percent of these are Head Start programs. Black children also may attend lower-quality preschool programs than their white peers. Although Hispanic children are much less likely than white children to be in preschool, they are also more likely than white children to be in Head Start. If Head Start programs are of lower quality or less academic in focus than other types of preschools, the high rates of black and Hispanic enrollment in Head Start may mean that these programs are doing less than they might to alleviate early achievement gaps.[83]

How might early childhood care and education policies narrow racial and ethnic achievement gaps at school entry? First, funds might be targeted to promote the enrollment of racial and ethnic minority children in center care or preschool. Given the current low enrollment of Hispanic children relative to white children, such initiatives could be particularly effective in closing Hispanic-white school readiness gaps. Second, additional funds might be used to increase the quality of the preschools that black and Hispanic children attend (including Head Start programs).[84] The magnitude of effects will depend on how much quality is improved and on the number of children affected.

How much might such changes in enrollment and quality narrow racial and ethnic test score gaps? We conducted some back-of-the-envelope estimates that, although rough, allow us to place some bounds on the likely share of the school readiness gaps that could be closed by changing current patterns of preschool enrollment or quality. We assume at the outset that the role of incremental changes in early child care and education is likely to be limited, given the many other influences on the school readiness gaps (documented in the other articles in this volume). We do not attempt to identify specific policies that might increase center care enrollment or quality or to model the effects of specific policies. Rather, we demonstrate how changes in early childhood care and education might narrow racial and ethnic gaps in school readiness.

Increasing Enrollment

We begin by considering the potential effect, by race and ethnicity, of five different changes in enrollment (table 2). Each scenario involves boosting the enrollment in preschool of three- to five-year-olds who are not now in Head Start, prekindergarten, or any other form of preschool. Clearly, the size of the benefit from increases in enrollment depends on how much preschool improves children's school readiness. For each scenario, we draw on the most reliable research to give three different estimates of preschool effects on children's reading scores at school entry: 0.15, 0.25, and 0.65 of a standard deviation.[85]

In the first scenario, Hispanic children's enrollment rises from 40 percent to 60 percent to match that of white children. Depending on the size of the preschool effect, this scenario could narrow the Hispanic-white reading gap at school entry by 0.03 to 0.13 of a standard deviation. Given that the average Hispanic-white gap in reading at school entry is about 0.50 of a standard deviation, this amounts to closing between 6 percent and 26 percent of the gap.[86] (Although we use the estimate of 0.50 of a standard deviation throughout the remainder of our discussion, it is important to recognize that these figures will overstate the percentage reductions if racial and ethnic school readiness gaps are in fact larger.) In the second scenario, both Hispanic and black children's preschool enrollment rates increase to 80 percent, 20 percentage points above that of white children. Such changes would narrow the black-white gap by 0.02 to 0.10 of a standard deviation (about 4 percent to 20 percent of the gap) and the Hispanic-white gap by 0.06 to 0.26 of a standard deviation (about 12 percent to 52 percent of the gap), again depending on how much children benefit from preschool.

Although both of these scenarios reduce school readiness gaps, particularly that between Hispanic and white children, it may be difficult to implement race- or ethnicity-specific policies. For this reason, we also consider the effect of increases in preschool enrollments across all racial and ethnic groups. In the third scenario, the enrollment of all children living in poverty rises to 100 percent; in the fourth scenario, enrollment for all low-income children (under 200 percent of the poverty threshold) rises to 100 percent; and in the fifth scenario, enrollment is universal without regard to income. Initiatives that boost preschool enrollment without regard to racial or ethnic backgrounds (scenarios 3 to 5)

Table 2. Effects on Reading Scores at School Entry of Increasing Preschool Enrollment for Children Aged Three to Five Who Are Not in Head Start or Preschool

Standard deviation

Scenario	Preschool effect	Increase in population average			Decrease in gap	
		Blacks	Hispanics	Whites	Black-white	Hispanic-white
1. Boost Hispanic enrollment to the level of white enrollment (from 40% to 60%)	.15	-	.03	0	-	.03
	.25	-	.05	0	-	.05
	.65	-	.13	0	-	.13
2. Increase Hispanic and black enrollment to 80%, no change in white enrollment (60%)	.15	.02	.06	0	.02	.06
	.25	.04	.10	0	.04	.10
	.65	.10	.26	0	.10	.26
3. Preschool for all children below 100% of poverty; full enrollment	.15	.02	.03	.01	.01	.02
	.25	.04	.05	.02	.02	.03
	.65	.10	.12	.04	.06	.08
4. Preschool for all children below 200% of poverty; full enrollment	.15	.03	.06	.02	.01	.04
	.25	.06	.09	.03	.03	.06
	.65	.14	.25	.08	.06	.17
5. Preschool for all children; full enrollment	.15	.05	.10	.06	−.01	.03
	.25	.10	.14	.10	0	.04
	.65	.24	.38	.26	−.02	.12

Sources and notes: Estimates of the percentage of children in preschool are taken from National Center for Educational Statistics, *The Condition of Education 2002* (U.S. Department of Education, Office of Educational Research and Improvement, 2000). National rates of preschool attendance among all children, by race and ethnicity, are as follows: white, 59 percent; black, 63 percent; Hispanic, 40 percent. For poor children, the corresponding estimates are white, 46 percent; black, 60 percent; Hispanic 36 percent. For nonpoor children, the estimates are white, 60 percent; black, 66 percent; Hispanic, 42 percent.

Poverty rates were taken from the National Center for Children in Poverty. Estimates are based on the following poverty rates for 2002: children below 100 percent of poverty line: whites, 13 percent; blacks, 38 percent; Hispanics, 30 percent (Child Trends Database, "Children in Poverty," www.childtrendsdatabank.org/indicators/4Poverty.cfm [July 20, 2004]). Children below 200 percent of poverty line: whites, 25 percent; blacks, 58 percent; Hispanics, 62 percent (National Center for Children in Poverty, "Low-Income Children in the United States, 2004," www.nccp.org/pub_cpf04.html [July 20, 2004]).

would be less effective at closing racial and ethnic school readiness gaps than the more targeted initiatives (scenarios 1 and 2). In scenarios 3 to 5, the Hispanic-white gap would fall by between 0.02 and 0.17 of a standard deviation; but the black-white gap might either slightly increase (by up to 0.02 of a standard deviation) or slightly decrease (by up to 0.06 of a standard deviation).

Although boosting Hispanic or black preschool enrollment rates beyond that of white

children would be the most effective means of closing racial and ethnic gaps, the universal programs may offer benefits that our estimates do not capture. For example, if universal programs are of higher quality or if children benefit from attending preschools with peers of diverse socioeconomic backgrounds, then our estimates may be too low.[87]

Improving Quality

What about improving the quality of center care that black and Hispanic children re-

Table 3. Effects on Reading Scores at School Entry of Improving Quality of Head Start and Preschool Programs for Children Aged Three to Five

Standard deviation

Scenario	Quality effect	Increase in population average			Decrease in gap	
		Blacks	Hispanics	Whites	Black-white	Hispanic-white
1. Increase quality of Head Start	.1	.02	.02	0	.02	.02
	.2	.04	.03	.01	.03	.02
	.3	.06	.05	.01	.05	.04
2. Increase quality of Head Start and other preschools for children below 100% of poverty	.1	.02	.01	.01	.03	.00
	.2	.05	.02	.01	.04	.01
	.3	.07	.03	.02	.05	.01
3. Increase quality of Head Start and other preschools for children below 200% of poverty	.1	.04	.02	.01	.02	.01
	.2	.07	.05	.03	.05	.02
	.3	.11	.07	.04	.07	.03
4. Increase quality of Head Start and other preschools for all children	.1	.06	.04	.06	.0	−.02
	.2	.13	.08	.12	.01	−.04
	.3	.19	.12	.18	.01	−.06

Notes: See sources and notes for table 2. Current levels of enrollment are assumed for all scenarios. Estimates of the number of children served by Head Start for scenario 1 are taken from data published by the Head Start Bureau, but the numbers of children in Head Start and preschool are taken from the National Household Education Survey (NHES), 1995. Thus it is not possible to compare directly scenarios 1 and 2, the effect of increasing the quality of Head Start and the effect of increasing the quality of all Head Start and preschools for poor children. Although the NHES indicates that only 36 percent of poor Hispanic children are in center care, the numbers from the Head Start Bureau suggest that 18 percent of all Hispanic children are in Head Start, and if Head Start primarily serves poor children this would imply that close to 60 percent of poor Hispanic children were in Head Start.

ceive?[88] We answer this question, again, by considering the effect of several different scenarios for quality improvement (see table 3). And, again, because these estimates will be sensitive to the extent to which quality influences children's outcomes, we provide a range of estimates, reflecting the incremental effects of increased preschool quality on children's reading skills of 0.1, 0.2, or 0.3 of a standard deviation. However, we note that to bring about such large increases in children's outcomes would involve large increases in the process and structural measures of quality, in some cases over a full standard deviation increase in the quality of care.[89]

The first scenario involves raising the quality of Head Start programs. Depending on the size of the increased quality effects, this scenario would reduce the black-white school readiness gap by 0.02 to 0.05 of a standard deviation (4 percent to 10 percent of the gap) and narrow the Hispanic-white gap by 0.02 to 0.04 of a standard deviation (4 percent to 8 percent of the gap). The second scenario entails raising the quality of all preschool programs (including Head Start) for currently enrolled children. It would improve the achievement of black children somewhat more than scenario 1 because they have the highest rates of enrollment in center care. But reductions in black-white gaps would still be fairly modest, ranging from 0 to 0.07 of a standard deviation, depending on whether the quality increase were universal (scenario 4) or targeted to low-income children (sce-

Table 4. Effects on Reading Scores at School Entry of Improving the Quality of and Increasing Enrollment in Head Start and Preschool for Children Aged Three to Five

Standard deviation

Scenario	Quality effect	Increase in population average			Decrease in gap	
		Blacks	Hispanics	Whites	Black-white	Hispanic-white
1. Increase quality of Head Start and other preschools for children below 100% poverty with 100% enrollment	.1	.08	.08	.03	.05	.05
	.2	.11	.11	.04	.07	.07
	.3	.15	.14	.05	.10	.09
2. Increase quality of Head Start and other preschools for children below 200% poverty with 100% enrollment	.1	.11	.16	.05	.06	.10
	.2	.17	.22	.08	.09	.14
	.3	.23	.28	.10	.12	.18
3. Increase quality of Head Start and other preschools for all children with 100% enrollment	.1	.19	.25	.20	−.01	.05
	.2	.29	.35	.30	−.01	.05
	.3	.39	.45	.40	−.01	.05

Notes: See sources and notes for tables 2 and 3. All scenarios assume 100 percent enrollment and an effect of 0.25 before increase in quality.

narios 2 and 3). Because Hispanic children are less likely to experience center care, raising the quality of preschools without changing current enrollment patterns would do little to narrow the Hispanic-white gap and could even increase it (scenario 4).

The estimates in table 3 lead us to conclude that even large increases in the quality of center care would have only a small effect on the black-white school readiness gap and even less of an effect on the Hispanic-white gap. However, we note that raising the quality of preschools attended only by black and Hispanic children would result in slightly larger reductions in school readiness gaps.

Increasing Quality and Enrollment

The estimates thus far have shown what could result from initiatives that either increase enrollment or increase quality. How much more effective would initiatives be if they attempted to do both? In table 4, we

show estimates for three different scenarios that increase center care quality and enrollment at the same time. As in table 3, for each scenario we model the effects of a range of quality improvements, again with increases in center care and preschool effects ranging from 0.1 to 0.3 of a standard deviation.

In the first scenario, preschool enrollment of children in poverty becomes universal and the quality of programs they attend increases. We assume that before the increase in quality, preschool raised children's school readiness by 0.25 of a standard deviation (our middle-ground estimate from table 2); with the quality improvement, preschool raises school readiness by 0.35, 0.45, or 0.55 of a standard deviation.[90] Universal enrollment in higher-quality care of children in poverty would narrow the black-white school readiness gap at school entry by 0.05 to 0.10 of a standard deviation (that is, 10 percent to 20 percent of the gap) and would narrow the Hispanic-white gap by 0.05 to 0.09 of a standard deviation (10 percent to 18 percent of the gap). In the second scenario, enrollment in preschool becomes universal for children from families with household incomes below 200 percent of the poverty threshold. Such a change would narrow the black-white school readiness gap by 12 percent to 24 percent, and the Hispanic-white gap by 20 percent to 36 percent. The third scenario, universal enrollment and higher-quality care for all children regardless of family income, would do little to close racial and ethnic gaps, primarily because white children would also benefit from this change.

As table 4 shows, initiatives that substantially raise both enrollment in and the quality of center care for low-income children could narrow racial and ethnic school readiness gaps considerably, reducing black-white gaps by up to 24 percent and Hispanic-white gaps by up to 36 percent. In addition, table 2 indicates that race- or ethnicity-specific increases in enrollment—in particular, increasing the enrollment of Hispanic children but not that of white children—could also narrow school readiness gaps. Other changes would also improve black and Hispanic children's school readiness, but would not reduce racial and ethnic gaps much, because they would also improve white children's achievement. If raising black and Hispanic children's school readiness regardless of their relative levels of achievement is a goal, then these changes should be considered.

Implications for Policy

We draw two conclusions about the role of early childhood care and education in closing racial and ethnic gaps in readiness at school entry. First, public funding of early education programs is probably already reducing ethnic and racial gaps. Large shares of Hispanic and black children are attending Head Start; as an upper bound, we estimate that the black-white test score gap at school entry might be as much as 24 percent larger in the absence of Head Start. Yet questions remain about the extent to which Head Start provides lasting academic benefits for children, particularly of differing ethnic and racial backgrounds, making conclusions about Head Start's role in reducing test score gaps speculative.

Second, the effects of incremental increases in enrollment or improvements in quality will depend on the specific changes adopted. For example, boosting the enrollment of Hispanic children in center care to meet or exceed the enrollment of white children would raise their test scores at school entry and narrow the gap between their scores and those of non-Hispanic white children. The overall effect could be quite large (because the gap in enrollment between Hispanic and white children is fairly large), but would depend on the quality of the preschools. Thus, our analysis affirms the wisdom of policies that specifically boost the enrollment of Hispanic children, starting at age three, for example, by funding early education programs in Hispanic neighborhoods.

Likewise, improving the quality of center care would modestly boost children's test scores. Such improvements in quality would do more to close black-white school readiness gaps than Hispanic-white gaps, because more black children are now enrolled than Hispanic children. Yet these effects would be fairly small for both groups, because quality improvements would also benefit white children attending preschool.

What about simultaneous increases in children's preschool enrollment and quality? Universal enrollment in higher-quality center care or preschools for low-income children could close a substantial portion of school readiness gaps based on race and ethnicity, narrowing the black-white reading gap at school entry as much as 24 percent and the Hispanic-white reading gap as much as 36 percent. Such findings point to the potential for policies that raise enrollment in Head Start, prekindergarten, and other preschool programs for children in and near poverty, while substantially improving the quality of these programs.

In keeping with the focus of this issue, and given data limitations, in this article we have concentrated mainly on test scores as a measure of school readiness. But school readiness encompasses many aspects of development in addition to academic skills, including health, social skills, positive and problem be-haviors, and motivation to learn.[91] As noted, early childhood care and education programs may affect these other aspects of school readiness, positively or negatively, and such effects should also be taken into account.[92]

Finally, we need to keep in mind that the benefits even of the best early childhood programs tend to fade over time. Preschool programs may need to be followed up with interventions for school-age children, as in the successful Chicago CPC program.[93] As others have observed, it is not realistic to expect a preschool program, however effective, to "inoculate" a child for life against the risk of low academic achievement.[94] But we can and should expect such programs to help narrow racial and ethnic differentials in young children's academic skills, so that they enter school on a more even footing.

Endnotes

1. NICHD Early Child Care Research Network, "Early Child Care and Children's Development prior to School Entry: Results from NICHD Study of Early Child Care," *American Educational Research Journal* 39 (2002): 133–64.-

2. Few prior studies have explicitly considered these questions. For general discussions, see David Grissmer, Ann Flanagan, and Stephanie Williamson, "Why Did the Black-White Score Gap Narrow in the 1970s and 1980s?" in *The Black-White Test Score Gap*, edited by Christopher Jencks and Meredith Phillips (Brookings, 1998), pp. 182–226; Marcia K. Meyers and others, "Inequality in Early Childhood Education and Care: What Do We Know?" in *Social Inequality*, edited by Kathryn M. Neckerman (New York: Russell Sage Foundation, 2004).

3. Cynthia T. Garcia Coll and others, "An Integrative Model for the Study of Developmental Competencies in Minority Children," *Child Development* 67 (1996): 1891–914. The racial and ethnic categories and terms we use in this article reflect the terminology and categorizations used in the bulk of studies we review.

4. Alejandro Portes and Ruben Rumbaut, *Ethnicities: Children of Immigrants in America* (New York: Russell Sage Foundation, 2003). Unfortunately, few studies distinguish among Hispanic children based on characteristics such as immigration status or language ability, so this review is unable to make these important distinctions.

5. Garcia Coll and others, "An Integrative Model" (see note 3).

6. Child care subsidy programs reach only a small share of eligible children: in 1998, only about 15 percent of eligible low-income families.

7. Forum on Childhood Family Statistics, "America's Children in Brief: Key National Indicators of Wellbeing." Accessed from http://childstats.gov, on November 3, 2004.

8. Gina Adams and Monica Rohacek, "More than a Work Support? Issues around Integrating Child Development Goals into the Child Care Subsidy System," *Early Childhood Research Quarterly* 17 (2002): 418–40; Suzanne W. Helburn and Barbara Bergmann, *America's Child Care Problem* (New York: St. Martin's Press, 2002).

9. NICHD Early Child Care Research Network, "Child Care Structure → Process → Outcome: Direct and Indirect Effects of Child-Care Quality on Young Children's Development," *Psychological Science* 13 (2002): 199–206; NICHD Early Child Care Research Network and Greg J. Duncan, "Modeling the Impacts of Child Care Quality on Children's Preschool Cognitive Development," *Child Development* 74 (2003): 1454–75.

10. Nicholas Zill and others, *Head Start FACES: A Whole Child Perspective on Program Performance* (U.S. Department for Health and Human Services, Administration for Children and Families, 2003).

11. Helburn and Bergmann, *America's Child Care Problem* (see note 8); Eugene Smolensky and Jennifer A. Gootman, eds., *Working Families and Growing Kids: Caring for Children and Adolescents* (Washington: National Academy Press, 2003).

12. NICHD Early Child Care Research Network, "Child Care Structure → Process → Outcome" (see note 9); Elizabeth Votruba-Drzal, Rebecca L. Coley, and P. Lindsay Chase-Lansdale, "Child Care and Low-Income Children's Development: Direct and Moderated Effects," *Child Development* 75 (2004): 296–312.

13. See recent reviews in David Blau, *The Child Care Problem* (New York: Russell Sage Foundation, 2001); Helburn and Bergmann, *America's Child Care Problem* (see note 8); Smolensky and Gootman, *Working Families and Growing Kids* (see note 11).

14. Suzanne W. Helburn, ed., *Cost, Quality, and Child Outcomes in Child Care Centers: Technical Report* (University of Colorado at Denver, Department of Economics, Center for Research in Economic and Social Policy, 1995).

15. NICHD Early Child Care Research Network, "Early Child Care and Children's Development prior to School Entry" (see note 1); NICHD Early Child Care Research Network, "Child Care Structure → Process → Outcome" (see note 9).

16. In 2003, 12.5 percent of children in Head Start programs had disabilities.

17. A small number of children under the age of three are served by the Early Head Start program, which began in 1995.

18. These estimates are based on the number of funded Head Start slots and the U.S. poverty rates; see Janet Currie and Mathew Neidell, "Getting Inside the 'Black Box' of Head Start Quality: What Matters and What Doesn't," Working Paper 10091 (Cambridge, Mass.: National Bureau of Economic Research, 2003).

19. Zill and others, *Head Start FACES* (see note 10).

20. Carol H. Ripple and others, "Will Fifty Cooks Spoil the Broth?" *American Psychologist* 54 (1999): 327–43; Edward Zigler and Sally. J. Styfco, "Head Start: Criticisms in a Constructive Context," *American Psychologist* 49 (1994): 127–32.

21. Private schools also offer such programs for a fee, but to simplify our discussions we use "prekindergarten" to refer to publicly funded programs.

22. Ripple and others, "Will Fifty Cooks Spoil the Broth?" (see note 20); Karen Schulman, Helen Blank, and Danielle Ewen, *Seeds of Success: State Prekindergarten Initiatives 1998–1999* (Washington: Children's Defense Fund, 1999).

23. "Quality Counts 2002: Building Blocks for Success," *Education Week* 21, no. 17 (January 10, 2002) (www.edweek.org/sreports/qc02/templates/article.cfm?slug=17exec.h21[June 27, 2003]).

24. "Quality Counts 2002" (see note 23); Schulman, Blank, and Ewen, *Seeds of Success* (see note 22); Ripple and others, "Will Fifty Cooks Spoil the Broth?" (see note 20).

25. William Gilliam and Edward Zigler, "State Efforts to Evaluate the Effects of Prekindergarten," mimeo, Yale University, 2004; Timothy Smith and others, *Prekindergarten in U.S. Public Schools* (U.S. Department of Education, National Center for Education Statistics, 2003).

26. Ripple and others, "Will Fifty Cooks Spoil the Broth?" (see note 20).

27. Smith and others, *Prekindergarten in U.S. Public Schools* (see note 25).

28. Blau, *The Child Care Problem* (see note 13).

29. Dan Bellm and others, *Inside the Pre-K Classroom: A Study of Staffing and Stability in State-Funded Prekindergarten Programs* (Washington: Center for the Child Care Workforce, 2002).

30. Gary Henry and others, *Report of the Findings from the Early Childhood Study* (Andrew Young School of Policy Studies, Georgia State University, 2003).

31. Cynthia Esposito Lamy and others, "Inch by Inch, Row by Row, Gonna Make This Garden Grow: Classroom Quality and Language Skills in the Abott Preschool Program," Working Paper (National Institute for Early Education Research, Rutgers University, 2004).

32. W. Steven Barnett, "Long-Term Effects of Early Childhood Programs on Cognitive and School Outcomes," *The Future of Children* 5, no. 3 (1995): 25–50; Blau, *The Child Care Problem* (see note 13).

33. Barnett, "Long-Term Effects of Early Childhood Programs on Cognitive and School Outcomes" (see note 32); Janet Currie, "Early Childhood Intervention Programs: What Do We Know?" *Journal of Economic Perspectives* 15 (2001): 213–38; Lynn A. Karoly and others, *Investing in Our Children: What We Do and Don't Know about the Costs and Benefits of Early Childhood Interventions* (Santa Monica, Calif.: RAND, 1998); Jane Waldfogel, "Child Care, Women's Employment and Child Outcomes," *Journal of Population Economics* 15 (2002): 527–48.

34. Cecilia McCarton and others, "Results at Age 8 Years of Early Intervention for Low-Birth-Weight Premature Infants: The Infant Health and Development Program," *Journal of the American Medical Association* 277 (1997): 126–32.

35. Jeanne Brooks-Gunn and others, "Enhancing the Cognitive Outcomes of Low Birth Weight, Premature Infants: For Whom Is Intervention Most Effective?" *Pediatrics* 89 (992): 1209–15.

36. Frances A. Campbell and Craig T. Ramey, "Cognitive and School Outcomes for High-Risk African American Students at Middle Adolescence: Positive Effects of Early Intervention," *American Educational Research Journal* 32 (1995): 743–72; Craig T. Ramey and others, *Early Learning, Later Success: The Abecedarian Study* (Chapel Hill, N.C.: Frank Porter Graham Child Development Institute, 1999).

37. Barnett, "Long-Term Effects of Early Childhood Programs on Cognitive and School Outcomes" (see note 32); Karoly and others, *Investing in Our Children* (see note 33); Waldfogel, "Child Care, Women's Employment and Child Outcomes" (see note 33).

38. Lawrence J. Schweinhart, Helen V. Barnes, and David P. Weikart, *Significant Benefits of the High-Scope Perry Preschool Study through Age 27* (Ypsilanti, Mich.: High-Scope Press, 1993).

39. McCarton and others, "Results at Age 8 Years of Early Intervention for Low-Birth-Weight Premature Infants" (see note 34).

40. Hiro Yoshikawa, "Prevention as Cumulative Protection: Effects of Early Family Support and Education as Chronic Delinquency and Its Risk," *Psychological Bulletin* 115 (1994): 28–54.

41. Michael Foster, "Trends in Multiple and Overlapping Disadvantages among Head Start Enrollees," *Children and Youth Services Review* 24 (2002): 933–54.

42. Ron Haskins, "Beyond Metaphor: The Efficacy of Early Childhood Education," *American Psychologist* 44 (1989): 274–82; Ruth H. McKey, *The Impact of Head Start on Children* (Department of Health and Human Services: Government Printing Office, 1985).

43. Valerie Lee and others, "Are Head Start Effects Sustained? A Longitudinal Follow-Up of Disadvantaged Children Attending Head Start, No Preschool, and Other Preschool Programs," *Child Development* 61 (1990): 495–507.

44. Janet Currie and Duncan Thomas, "Does Head Start Make a Difference?" *American Economic Review* 85 (1995): 341–64; Janet Currie and Duncan Thomas, "Does Head Start Help Hispanic Children?" *Journal of Public Economics* 74 (1999): 235–62; Eliana Garces, Duncan Thomas, and Janet Currie, "Longer-Term Effects of Head Start," *American Economic Review* 92 (2002): 999–1012. For an exception, see Alison Aughinbaugh, "Does Head Start Yield Long-Term Benefits?" *Journal of Human Resources* 36 (2001): 641–65.

45. Currie and Thomas, "Does Head Start Make a Difference?" (see note 44). But see also Garces, Thomas, and Currie, "Longer-Term Effects of Head Start" (see note 44), who find some evidence that Head Start might reduce crime among black children; and Lee and others, "Are Head Start Effects Sustained?" (see note 43), who find larger effects of Head Start on academic and social outcomes for black children than white children.

46. Currie and Thomas, "Does Head Start Help Hispanic Children?" (see note 44).

47. Gilliam and Zigler, "State Efforts to Evaluate the Effects of Prekindergarten" (see note 25).

48. Arthur J. Reynolds, "Effects of a Preschool Follow-On Intervention for Children at Risk," *Developmental Psychology* 30 (1994): 787–804.

49. Arthur J. Reynolds, "One Year of Preschool or Two: Does It Matter?" *Early Childhood Research Quarterly* 10 (1995): 1–31.

50. Reynolds, "Effects of a Preschool Follow-On Intervention for Children at Risk" (see note 48); Arthur J. Reynolds and others, "Long-Term Effects of an Early Childhood Intervention on Educational Achievement and Juvenile Arrest: A Fifteen Year Follow-Up of Low-Income Children in Public Schools," *Journal of the American Medical Association* 285 (2001): 2339–46.

51. William Gormley and Ted Gayer, "Promoting School Readiness in Oklahoma: An Evaluation of Tulsa's Pre-K Program," mimeo, Georgetown University, 2003.

52. Henry and others, *Report of the Findings from the Early Childhood Study* (see note 30).

53. Katherine A. Magnuson and others, "Inequality in Preschool Education and School Readiness," *American Educational Research Journal* 41 (2004): 115–57.

54. Gilliam and Zigler, "State Efforts to Evaluate the Effects of Prekindergarten" (see note 25).

55. Katherine A. Magnuson, Christopher Ruhm, and Jane Waldfogel. "Does Prekindergarten Improve School Preparation and Performance?" Working Paper 10452 (Cambridge, Mass.: National Bureau of Economic Research, 2004).

56. Gilliam and Zigler, "State Efforts to Evaluate the Effects of Prekindergarten" (see note 25).

57. Barnett, "Long-Term Effects of Early Childhood Programs on Cognitive and School Outcomes" (see note 32); Meyers and others, "Inequality in Early Childhood Education and Care" (see note 2); Smolensky and Gootman, *Working Families and Growing Kids* (see note 11).

58. Deborah Phillips and Gina Adams, "Child Care and Our Youngest Children," *Future of Children* 11, no. 1 (2001): 35–51.

59. This study included Head Start and prekindergarten as center-based care.

60. NICHD Early Child Care Research Network and Duncan, "Modeling the Impacts of Child Care Quality on Children's Preschool Cognitive Development" (see note 9).

61. Magnuson and others, "Inequality in Preschool Education and School Readiness" (see note 53). Unfortunately, data were not available on the quality of care children received so we were unable to explore its influence on school readiness.

62. Jay Belsky, "Developmental Risks (Still) Associated with Early Child Care," Emanuel Miller Lecture, *Journal of Child Psychology and Psychiatry and Allied Disciplines* 42, no. 7 (2001): 845–59; NICHD Early Child Care Research Network, "Does Amount of Time Spent in Child Care Predict Socioemotional Adjustment during the Transition to Kindergarten?" *Child Development* 74 (2003): 976–1005.

63. NICHD Early Child Care Research Network, "Does Amount of Time Spent in Child Care Predict Socioemotional Adjustment during the Transition to Kindergarten?" (see note 62).

64. Authors' calculation of 1999 SIPP data.

65. NICHD Early Child Care Research Network, "Early Child Care and Children's Development prior to School Entry" (see note 1); Phillips and Adams, "Child Care and Our Youngest Children" (see note 58).

66. These estimates and those that follow are from our analyses of the ECLS-K. For further details, see Magnuson and others, "Inequality in Preschool Education and School Readiness" (see note 53).

67. The October CPS began collecting data in 1964, but the microdata for 1964–67 are not readily available. The 2000 data were the most current available at the time the analysis was conducted.

68. From 1968 to 1984, the survey asked: "Is [name] attending or enrolled in school?" In 1985, the question was changed to read: "Is [name] attending or enrolled in regular school?" Then, in 1994, a prompt was added after the question, so that the full question now reads: "Is [name] attending or enrolled in regular school? (Regular school includes nursery school, kindergarten, or elementary school and schooling which leads to a high school diploma)." The October CPS and the National Household Education Survey find a similar share of three- to five-year-old children enrolled in preprimary school programs (for instance, both surveys find 68 percent in 1999). In contrast, two major child care surveys, the National Survey of American Families (NSAF) and the Survey of Income and Program Participation, find a lower share of three- to five-year-olds enrolled in center- or school-based programs; this is likely because these two surveys do not ask explicitly about school programs and also because they interview some families during the summer months, when such programs would be closed.

69. These figures chart the preschool enrollment of three- and four-year-olds, using data from the October Current Population Survey. See note 68 for more details.

70. Table 1 uses SIPP data. Rates of center care enrollment are lower than in the CPS, because infants and toddlers are less likely to experience nonparental care and more likely to experience informal child care than children aged three and four. Estimates of child care arrangements from various data sources should be compared with caution, because of differences in question wording, timing of data collection, and coding categories (see also note 68).

71. Office of the Assistant Secretary for Planning and Evaluation, *Trends in the Well-Being of America's Children and Youth: 2002* (U.S. Department of Health and Human Services, 2002).

72. It is beyond the scope of this article to consider whether racial and ethnic differences in parental employment have affected differentials in test scores, above and beyond any effects that may work through early childhood care and education. Parental employment could affect child development through several pathways, such as economic resources, parenting, and the home environment. For recent reviews on the effects of parental employment on child development, and discussion of how they may vary by racial and ethnic group, see Jack P. Shonkoff and Deborah Phillips, eds., *From Neurons to Neighborhoods: The Science of Early Childhood Development* (Washington: National Academy Press, 2000); Smolensky and Gootman, *Working Families and Growing Kids* (see note 11).

73. Authors' estimation of enrollment rates, using data from the Head Start Bureau and the 2000 decennial census. The calculation is based on the number of Head Start slots available, not the number of children served, which is larger because of turnover. Consequently, our estimates likely understate the number of children who have ever participated in Head Start.

74. These estimates are derived by subtracting each group's rate of attendance in Head Start from its October CPS rates of preschool attendance. For example, because 19 percent of black four-year-olds are in Head Start and CPS data indicate that 72 percent of black four-year-olds are in preschool, without access to Head Start (and without enrollment in other programs), their enrollment rate would be 53 percent. By comparison, only 5 percent of white four-year-olds are in Head Start, so without access to Head Start (and without enrollment in other programs) their enrollment rate would fall from 67 percent to 62 percent, resulting in a black-white enrollment gap of 9 percent (compared with black children's current enrollment advantage of 5 percent).

75. Reynolds, "Effects of a Preschool Follow-On Intervention for Children at Risk" (see note 48).

76. Per pupil expenditures in CPC and Head Start were comparable (in the early 1990s), and both programs emphasize parental involvement and deliver comprehensive services. See Reynolds, "One Year of Preschool or Two" (see note 49). It is also important to keep in mind that Reynolds's estimated effect sizes are considerably larger than estimates derived from Head Start studies. For example, Lee and others, "Are Head Start Effects Sustained?" (see note 43) find Head Start effects of 0.25 on verbal skills at school entry; Currie and Thomas, "Does Head Start Make a Difference?" (see note 44) find almost no lasting effects from Head Start on the academic skills of black children.

77. Reynolds, "One Year of Preschool or Two" (see note 49).

78. Smith and others, *Prekindergarten in U.S. Public Schools* (see note 25).

79. Calculations from the 1999 National Survey of American Families by the Urban Institute found the average numbers of hours spent in nonparental care by children under age three with employed mothers were as follows: twenty-two for white non-Hispanic children, thirty-two for black children, and twenty-one for Hispanic children. See Jennifer Ehrle, Gina Adams, and Kathryn Tout, "Who's Caring for Our Youngest Children? Child Care Patterns of Infants and Toddlers," Occasional Paper 42 (Washington: Urban Institute, 2001). Data from the National Household Education Survey in 1995 found the average numbers of hours spent in center-based nonparental care by children under age six were as follows: twenty-eight for white non-Hispanic children, thirty-six for black children, and thirty-one for Hispanic children. See National Center for Educational Statistics, *Digest of Education Statistics, 2002* (Washington, 2003), table 44.

80. Smolensky and Gootman, *Working Families and Growing Kids* (see note 11).

81. Margaret R. Burchinal and Debby Cryer, "Diversity, Child Care Quality, and Developmental Outcomes," *Early Childhood Research Quarterly* 18 (2003): 401–26. Burchinal and Cryer also provide information on the quality of care received by Hispanic children, but sample sizes for this group are so small that we do not include them in our summary. In addition, they examine whether the measures of quality of care had equivalent effects across ethnic and racial groups They conclude that these measures are equally reliable across groups and that higher quality care was linked to higher levels of cognitive and social skills among all groups. For a discussion of racial and ethnic differences in measuring the quality of child care, see Deborah L. Johnson and others, "Studying the Effects of Early Child Care Experiences on the Development of Children of Color in the United States: Toward a More Inclusive Research Agenda," *Child Development* 74 (2003): 1227–44.

82. Black children in the CQO sample were much more likely than white children to be poor (30 percent versus 6 percent) or working poor (32 percent versus 11 percent). See Burchinal and Cryer, "Diversity, Child Care Quality, and Developmental Outcomes" (see note 81).

83. Zigler and Styfco, "Head Start" (see note 20).

84. Although improving the quality of informal child care might reduce racial and ethnic gaps, it is much more difficult for policies to influence the quality of informal care given by, for example, babysitters or grandparents, than to improve formal child care.

85. The estimate of 0.15 is from Magnuson and others, "Inequality in Preschool Education and School Readiness" (see note 53). The estimate of 0.25 is from NICHD and Duncan, "Modeling the Impacts of Child Care Quality on Children's Preschool Cognitive Development" (see note 9). The estimate of 0.65 is from Reynolds, "Effects of a Preschool Follow-on Intervention" (see note 48).

86. See Greg Duncan and Katherine Magnuson's article in this volume.

87. Pam Sammons and others, *Measuring the Impact of Pre-School on Children's Cognitive Progress over the Pre-School Period* (Institute of Education, University of London, 2002).

88. We do not attempt to estimate how children may benefit from improvements in informal care, because it is difficult to construct effective policies to this end.

89. Burchinal and Cryer, "Diversity, Child Care Quality, and Developmental Outcomes" (see note 81); NICHD Early Child Care Research Network, "Early Child Care and Children's Development prior to School Entry" (see note 1).

90. If we estimate the effects of preschool or Head Start to be 0.65 (and increase the quality of care by 0.2), we find that the population effects would be larger; for example, closing 0.10 of the black-white gap and 0.11 of the Hispanic-white gap (compared with 0.07 for both gaps) for children under 100 percent of the poverty line. If we assume the estimated effects of preschool or Head Start care to be 0.15 (and increase the quality of care by 0.20), we find the population effects are smaller, resulting in slightly smaller reductions in the gap; for example, the black-white gap does not decrease, whereas the Hispanic gap would decrease by 0.06 (compared with 0.07) for children below 100 percent of the poverty line.

91. Shonkoff and Phillips, *From Neurons to Neighborhoods* (see note 72).

92. Zigler and Styfco, "Head Start" (see note 20).

93. Arthur J. Reynolds and Judy A. Temple, "Extended Early Childhood Intervention and School Achievement: Age Thirteen Findings from the Chicago Longitudinal Study," *Child Development* 69 (1998): 231–46.

94. Jeanne Brooks-Gunn, "Do You Believe in Magic? What Can We Expect from Early Childhood Intervention Programs?" *SRCD Social Policy Report* 17, no. 1 (2003); Zigler and Styfco, "Head Start" (see note 20).